I0199828

ALL ABOUT STOCK MARKET STRATEGIES

OTHER TITLES IN THE "ALL ABOUT..." FINANCE SERIES

All About Stocks, 2nd edition
by Esme Faerber

All About Bonds and Bond Mutual Funds, 2nd edition
by Esme Faerber

All About Options, 2nd edition
by Thomas McCafferty

All About Futures, 2nd edition
by Russell Wasendorf

All About Commodities
by Thomas McCafferty and Russell Wasendorf

All About Real Estate Investing, 2nd edition
by William Benke and Joseph M. Fowler

All About DRIPs and DSPs
by George C. Fisher

All About Mutual Funds, 2nd edition
by Bruce Jacobs

ALL ABOUT STOCK MARKET STRATEGIES

The Easy Way to Get Started

DAVID L. BROWN
KASSANDRA BENTLEY

McGraw-Hill

New York   Chicago   San Francisco   Lisbon   Madrid
Mexico City   Milan   New Delhi   San Juan   Seoul
Singapore   Sydney   Toronto

Library of Congress Cataloging-in-Publication Data

Brown, David L.
    All about stock market strategies / David L. Brown, Kassandra Bentley.
      p.   cm.
Includes index.

    1. Stocks. 2. Speculation. I. Bentley, Kassandra. II. Title.
    HG4661 .B768 2002
    332.63'2—dc21

                                  2002003843

McGraw-Hill

*A Division of The **McGraw·Hill** Companies*

Copyright © 2002 by David L. Brown and Kassandra Bentley. All rights reserved. Printed in the United States of America. Except as permitted under the United States Copyright Act of 1976, no part of this publication may be reproduced or distributed in any form or by any means, or stored in a data base or retrieval system, without the prior written permission of the publisher.

7 8 9 0   DOC / DOC   0 9 8 7

ISBN 978-0-07-183163-5

This book was set in Palatino by The Composing Room of Michigan, Inc.

This publication is designed to provide accurate and authoritative information in regard to the subject matter covered. It is sold with the understanding that the publisher is not engaged in rendering legal, accounting, or other professional service. If legal advice or other expert assistance is required, the services of a competent professional person should be sought.

> *—From a declaration of principles jointly adopted by a committee of the*
> *American Bar Association and a committee of publishers.*

McGraw-Hill books are available at special quantity discounts to use as premiums and sales promotions, or for use in corporate training programs. For more information, please write to the Director of Special Sales, Professional Publishing, McGraw-Hill, Two Penn Plaza, New York, NY 10121-2298. Or contact your local bookstore.

This book is dedicated to Carolyn Brown

CONTENTS

Appendix A

Appendix B

Over the past several years we've written a number of books, primarily about investing tools, and we've also given speeches and seminars on the subject. Our audiences and readers have been generous in their praise for the books and the tools, but many have confessed that they don't know enough about what they're looking for to use the tools. There is not, after all, a single indicator that will tell you *this* is a good stock.

The problem of not knowing what to look for has been particularly acute since the market decline in 2000. In the raging bull market that preceded the decline, it was easy to make money. Just pick a stock, almost any stock. But the market decline badly hurt many investors and made them aware that there was more to investing than jumping on the stock-pick-of-the-day bandwagon. We began to realize that many investors do not have a strategy or a plan for investing. While they could learn to use the many and varied investing tools and use them well, without a plan for what they were trying to accomplish, they ended up floundering and being victimized by the market.

It occurred to us as we talked with successful investors who have done well over many years that each had a plan or a strategy for making investment decisions. This fact was reiterated by Jack Schwager in his Market Wizard books in which he interviewed the world's most successful traders and investors. He found, as we did, that investing tools and access to information are important, but a good strategy and the discipline to stick with it are absolutely essential to successful investing.

The key is the discipline to stick with a strategy. We came to the conclusion that if a strategy doesn't fit a person's basic personality, he or she either won't have the discipline to stick with the strategy or else won't execute it very well. For example, a person who likes to buy stocks at a bargain price but lacks the patience to wait for long-term rewards won't be very good at value investing, one of the many investing strategies described in this book.

The purpose of this book is to provide an overview of the many strategies that have been (and are being) used successfully by investors and to discuss the personality traits that are needed in order to be successful in each strategy. Unlike our previous books, we don't offer specific instructions or tools for "making money in the stock market," because our objective is to help you find a strategy or style that fits your basic personality and to outline a process for implementing that strategy. We will consider our purpose well served if, after reading this book, you have a clearer picture of the kind of investor you are at heart, are able to select an investing style or strategy that feels right for you, and are convinced that a systematic process is necessary to execute that strategy.

ACKNOWLEDGMENTS

We would like to thank Luiz Alvim, Paul Alvim, and Theodore Spradlin for their careful review of the chapters on growth, value, momentum, and technical investing. Our thanks to Carolyn Brown and Victoria Lara for reviewing the entire manuscript and for their encouragement and support during the writing of this book. We thank Mark Wilkinson for his help with graphs, Kameron Were for his surfing analogies, and Roderick Hare and John Ehlers for their continued support. We also wish to thank Pattie Amoroso for her meticulous editing, and Stephen Isaacs for his patience and perseverance in bringing this book to publication.

The stock graphs in this book were created with TIP@Wallstreet™ using data supplied by Telescan, Inc.

David L. Brown
Santa Barbara, California

Kassandra Bentley
Phoenix, Arizona

What is *your* investing strategy? How do you select stocks in which to invest? Do you take a tip from a friend or from the stock pickers on CNBC? When you find a stock you think that you like, how do you determine when to buy it? Even more importantly, how do you decide when to sell? Do you sell if it makes a quick 20 percent gain? Do you buy more if it drops 50 percent? (If you liked it at $20, you're really going to like it at $10, right?) How many securities do you hold at a time? What percentage of your portfolio do you keep in cash? When does that change?

These decisions are what makes up your investing strategy.

A strategy is simply a plan for attaining a goal. A football coach would not think of starting the next game without a strategy. A military leader develops a strategy for winning a war. And who would start a business without having several strategies at hand? At a minimum, you'd need a strategy for financing the business, a strategy for developing your products, and a strategy for marketing them.

As one of the most important actions of our lives, investing definitely requires strategy. First, we must have a strategy for selecting our investments. Second, we must have an entry strategy and an exit strategy, so we'll know when to buy and, more importantly, when to sell a stock. Finally, we must have a strategy for managing our portfolio, a strategy that tells us how much of our portfolio should be in cash and how much in securities, how many stocks or funds it should hold, and how much diversification it should have with regard to industries and sectors.

Why do we need all these strategies? Because investing is not intuitive. In fact, it is counterintuitive. For example, our intuition tells us to stay out of a bear market. But if everyone is bearish, that's the time to buy. Why? Because when the market is at an extreme low, everyone who's going to bail has already done so. Therefore, the market is most likely to rebound. But that's counterintuitive. And so is a raging bull market that's at an extreme high. When the kid who washes your car talks about day trading on the side, as we personally witnessed at the height of the dot-com craze, it's time to sell.

When everyone around you seems to be getting rich in the market, it is a natural impulse to want to get in on the action. But with everyone already in the market, there's no one left to drive it higher. The smart money got out a long time ago.

It is not easy, however, to tell when a bear market is ready to rebound or when a raging bull market is about to collapse. Because all this is counterintuitive, you can't rely on your instincts about investing. And you certainly can't rely on your emotions. In fact, emotions are the number one enemy of investing, particularly fear of loss and greed for excessive gain. Since we are all emotional critters, we are unlikely to succeed as investors without strategies to counteract our emotions and proper tools to implement the strategies.

An investing strategy pays off in increased returns. We believe and indeed have proved in other publications that if you use a systematized investing strategy—and maintain the discipline to stick to it—you can more than double your annual returns compared to simply investing at random. And doubling your return can perform some interesting "magic" on your principal. For example, if you invest a nest egg of, say, $10,000, at 5 percent, your money will double over 15 years. But if you can double that return—make 10 percent instead of 5—you'll *quadruple* your nest egg over 15 years. Even more astonishing, if you can double the 10 percent return—make 20 percent instead—your original investment will increase by *almost sixteenfold over 15 years* and *almost fortyfold over 20 years* (see Figure I–1).

As you can see, every point you can add to your return is worth a lot more than just that one point. Because those extra points are so powerful, it is worth selecting an investing style that will work for you because you will not be fighting your basic instincts with every decision you make. It's worth having an entry strategy and an exit strategy, because timing strategies can increase your returns by getting you in and out of a stock at more appropriate times. It's worth having a portfolio management strategy that will keep you in a proactive mode, which can certainly enhance your returns. Developing and using these strategies can dramatically increase your returns in the market. This is not difficult and won't require a great deal of time, but the time you do spend will be well worthwhile.

If you already have a strategy for selecting stocks that's working for you, if you capture most of the possible profit when you buy

FIGURE I–1

At 20 percent per year, a $10,000 investment will grow to $383,376 over 20 years.

How $10,000 Will Grow over 20 Years at 5, 10, and 20%

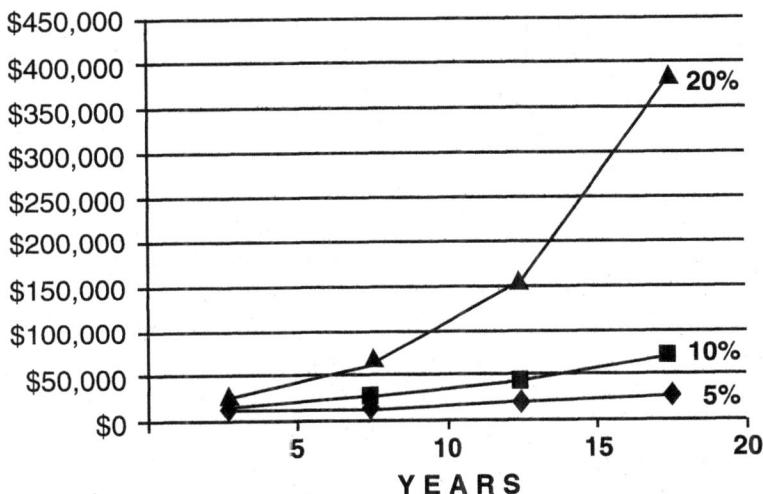

and sell, if you're happy with the returns on your portfolio—then you really don't need this book. "If it ain't broke, don't fix it." But if you select stocks at random or on whims, if you buy and sell them based more on emotion than thought, if you are not doing as well in the stock market as you would like—then perhaps you need to develop an investing strategy. The purpose of this book is to introduce you to numerous investing strategies, systems, and styles so that you can decide which ones best fit your basic personality, because your personality dictates (or should dictate) how you will approach the market.

Approaching the market is somewhat like conducting a war. Whether your approach is like Attila the Hun or Colin Powell depends on your basic personality. Based on your personality you will naturally gravitate toward a particular investing *style*—growth, value, momentum, or technical. Your investing *strategy*, which is based on your style, is your overall game plan to "win the war." This strategy is made up of multiple smaller strategies or methodologies or techniques for selecting, buying, selling, and managing your stocks—somewhat like the general's tactical warfare. And like a general, you may employ a computerized system or methodology to implement a strategy—a timing system, for example, for entering and exiting a stock. The general who wins a war—and the investor who wins in the market—are the ones who stick to their strategies regardless of popular opinion or their own conflicting emotions.

The key to finding a strategy or system that you will use consistently, regardless of what the crowd around you is doing, is to match your strategies to your investing style and your investing style to your personality. In his books about how top traders generated extraordinary returns, Jack Schwager concluded that each of the "market wizards," as he called them, used a strategy or system that was unique to him or her. But what really set these winners apart from the crowd was their ability to follow their systems religiously, adhering to them through difficult market conditions or when everything seemed to be going against them. You can only do this consistently if you're acting in accordance with your basic personality. Of course, one does need to adapt to differing market conditions, but having a system or strategy that matches your basic personality takes much of the emotion out of your decisions.

Most amateur investors find it difficult to stick with a system, but we'd be willing to bet that's because the system doesn't match their basic personality. For example, if you're impatient and like to see a lot of action, you would make a terrible value investor but would probably be happy trading momentum stocks. Why? Because value investors sometimes have to wait years to see their rewards while momentum investors buy the stocks that are moving the fastest right now and sell them as soon as their momentum starts to slow, which means they are in and out of the market a lot.

There's a lot more to these two popular investing styles, which we will explore in later chapters, but for the moment, take our word for it: Matching your investing style to your personality can save you a lot of discomfort and anguish and can go a long way toward ensuring your investing success.

Fund Managers Have Styles, Too

Determining your investing style is important even if you are a mutual fund investor because mutual funds are distinguished by their different investing styles and strategies. By understanding strategies and styles you will be better equipped to select funds that fit your particular investment goals, and you'll be able to take a more active role in switching funds when they do not meet your goals. While this book is aimed at the individual stock investor, we believe the mutual fund investor can benefit from it as well.

A TALE OF TWO STOCKS

We mentioned earlier that investing is counterintuitive. One of the most counterintuitive tenets of investing is to cut your losses but let your profits run. Most of us do just the opposite. If we make a profit on a stock, our tendency is to sell as soon as it is clear that we have made a nice profit. If we have a loss, we hate to admit it so we tend to hold on, thinking the stock will come back and we'll recoup our loss. Sometimes we even buy more of the sinking stock with an eye to lowering our average cost per share. In both of these events we're acting on intuition and emotions. This is such an important point—and so wrong—that we'd like to demonstrate with two real stocks what can actually happen if you follow your emotions or intuition.

M.S. Carriers, Inc. (MSCA) and Vignette Corporation (VIGN) were two stocks recommended by a well-known service on November 11, 2000. Both were priced at about $25. Now let's just say that we bought both of these stocks on November 11, 2000. Take a look at the chart in Figure I–2 and see what happened to the stocks.

Ten days after our purchase, MSCA had risen to $30, which gave us a quick 20 percent profit, and VIGN had fallen to about $18 for a 30 percent loss. Many investors would have been overwhelmingly tempted to take the quick profit on MSCA because 20 percent in 10 days is an excellent return. Some would have been tempted to take that money and double or triple their holdings of VIGN. After all, if Vignette was a good stock at $25 when we bought it, shouldn't it be a better buy at $18? Both these actions are based on our psy-

FIGURE I-2

A comparative chart of MSCA and VIGN shows the wide
divergence of two stocks that started out on November 11,
2000, at the same point.*

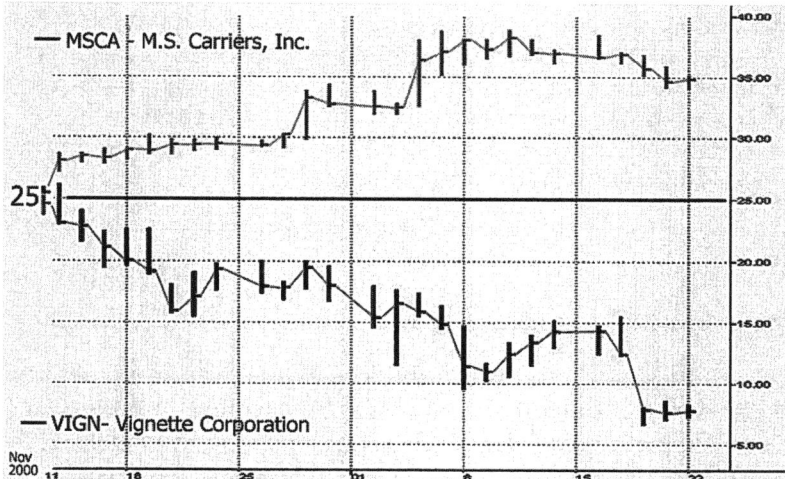

*For comparative purposes, the price of both stocks have been adjusted to begin at $25 on the chart, as well as in the text.

chological needs. It makes us feel good to take a profit, and it makes
us feel bad to admit a loss.

For another few days, we would have felt pretty smart about
selling M.S. Carriers and buying more of Vignette. VIGN was still
hovering around $18 where we had increased our position, and al-
though MSCA moved up another 10 percent, we had still pocketed
a nice profit. By December 5, however, we would have been feeling
rather foolish. VIGN had fallen to $12, so now we've lost 50 percent
on our initial investment and another 30 percent on our second investment of VIGN. And, to add insult to injury, MSCA had climbed
to $38, up 50 percent from our original purchase.

In retrospect, what we needed to do was to get out of VIGN as
quickly as possible and hang on to MSCA through the end of December. But that would be counterintuitive. Acting on emotions and
intuition, most people have an overwhelming urge to take quick
profits and keep buying more of a stock that's going down. In fact,
your strategy should be exactly the opposite. Cut your losses and

let your profits run. To do that, we need a strategy or system that takes the emotions out of our decisions.

We will show you a technical analysis strategy in Chapter 4 that would have given a buy signal for MSCA in early November and kept you in it through the end of December, allowing you to capture the bulk of the profits. That same strategy would have kept you out of VIGN, or, if you had bought it anyway, the strategy would have prevented a huge loss by taking you out quickly and not letting you get back in.

This tale of two stocks exemplifies the reasons that we need a strategy for entering and exiting stocks, a strategy that is strictly me-chanical so that it will override any emotions you might have about a stock. If you take just one thing from this book, let it be the deter-mination to develop a good strategy for entering and exiting your stocks.

HOW THIS BOOK IS STRUCTURED

In writing this book we have assumed an entry-level knowledge of the market. We assume that you know what a stock is and basical-ly how the market works. Our job, as we see it, is to introduce you to the idea of selecting an investing style to match your personality and then choosing investing strategies, systems, and methodologies to match that style.

In the first two chapters we lay a foundation on which to talk about investing strategies and styles. In Chapter 1 we talk about what makes stocks go up—in short, market perception and investor confidence—and discuss a number of events that tend to change ei-ther or both. Chapter 2 presents the three general strategies that make up the investing process—stock selection, entry and exit tim-ing, and portfolio management. Although this three-step investing process is basic to every investing style, the strategies for selecting stocks, buying and selling them, and managing your portfolio will differ, depending on your style or approach to investing.

Chapter 3 begins our discussion of investing styles. It pro-vides an overview of eight distinct styles and introduces you to our PQ chart—for psychological quotient—which rates each investing style for 10 different psychological or personality traits. Chapters 4 through 7 present the four major investing styles—growth, value, momentum, and technical investing—with a personality profile of that style, a look at the characteristics of stocks that represent that style, and strategies for implementing the style. Each of these style chapters includes a section on how to apply the style to mutual funds and exchange-traded funds and a section on how to find on-line resources for the style. Hints for success conclude each of these chapters.

Chapter 8 examines the role of market capitalization (market cap) in an investing strategy. Market cap is a way of measuring the size of a company (it is the number of shares outstanding times the stock price). Some people prefer to buy large-cap or mid-cap stocks and others prefer small-cap or micro-cap stocks. Because these preferences create critical masses within the different caps, market caps move differently in different markets, which allows them to be used as a supplemental investing strategy.

Chapter 9 examines strategies for five minor investing styles—fundamental investing, income investing, active trading, hybrid investing, and style surfing—all of which are derivations or combinations of the four major styles, and also discusses strategies such as top-down investing and insider trading which can be used to enhance any investing style. Chapter 10 introduces you to a number of advanced strategies that can be incorporated into any investing style, such as short selling, market-neutral investing, index trading, option hedging, and global investing. Appendixes A and B contain a list of online resources; the Glossary defines the terms used in this book.

As you read the book, keep our objective in mind: to help you select a style and convince you to use a strategy to select your stocks, a strategy to enter and exit them, and a strategy to manage your portfolio of stocks.

CHAPTER 1

Market Perception and Investor Confidence: The Forces That Move Stock Prices

Before we start talking about investing strategies, we need to talk about how and why stock prices move. Then the discussion about strategies will make sense.

Everyone knows that stock prices are somehow related to earnings. But the fact is that stocks go up and down based on changes in the market's *perception* of a stock's future earnings and the *confidence* investors have that those earnings will be achieved. If stock prices reacted solely based on a company's meeting or not meeting its earnings goals, then a company that missed its goals or estimates for earnings per share (EPS) by, say, just one penny, should see its stock price go down by roughly the same percent. For example, if Company A were expected to make 12 cents in the second quarter—the consensus estimates—but made only 11 cents, it missed the estimates by about 8 percent. Consequently, it would be reasonable to expect the company's stock price to drop by about the same percentage. But what actually happens is often dramatically different.

A company that misses its estimates by a penny can see its stock price drop by 30, 40, or even 50 percent or more. Why? Because of the *fear* that this quarter's lower earnings may be a harbinger of bad things to come—that the company's targeted earnings growth may not be achievable. In other words, investors may fear that what the company anticipated as a 20 percent growth rate for the next few years may turn out to be only 10 or 15 percent. This perception, however irrational, lowers investors' confidence in the company's future earnings potential, and that lowered confidence is often reflected in dramatic drops in the stock price.

You may still think that a 30, 40, or 50 percent drop in the stock price is an unfair penalty for a company to pay for missing earnings by one penny in one quarter. But the size of the drop relates to the change in expectations of future growth. If you will recall Figure I–1 in the Introduction, we showed how a $10,000 nest egg will grow based on different rates of return. Your investment will grow sixteenfold over 15 years with a 20 percent per year return, compared with only a quadrupling at a 10 percent return. The percentages work whether you're talking about interest rates or the growth rate of earnings per share. If the fear is that a company's growth rate is slowing from 20 percent to 10 percent—in effect, halving—then it is not unreasonable to expect a drop of 50 percent or even more in the company's stock price.

As you can see, current earnings are only the most visible piece of the market's valuation of a stock. The retaining walls of that fragile structure are the market's *perception* of future earnings and investors' *confidence* that those earnings will be achieved.

Market perception is influenced by many factors. A favorable research report with high projected earnings can make the market sit up and take notice of a company. So can the release of a new product or the advent of a new and aggressive management team. All would be perceived as fueling future earnings, and the perception would be reflected in the company's price-to-earnings (P/E) ratio. P/E is the company's stock price divided by its most recent earnings—in actuality, the P/E is what the market has agreed to pay for the company's *future* earnings, which is based on *the market's perception of what those earnings will be*. (See "The Role of an Expanding P/E" on page 14.) These factors help to explain why we see such a tremendous disparity of P/E ratios among stocks.

Advent Software (ADVS) and Morgan Stanley (MWD) are instructive examples. Advent had estimated earnings of $0.90 for fiscal year 2001. For the same year Morgan Stanley had estimated earnings of $3.88.[1] In August 2001, when we wrote this chapter, Advent had a P/E of 51, based on its projected earnings and a stock price

---

[1]All figures as of August 18, 2001.

around $46; Morgan Stanley had a P/E of 13 based on its projected earnings and a stock price around $50. That means the market was paying 51 times earnings for Advent but only 13 times earnings for Morgan Stanley. Why? Why would investors pay almost as much for a stock with earnings of only 90 cents as they would for a stock with earnings of almost $4? *Perception of future earnings!*

The market perceived that Advent's future earnings were going to grow at a rate that was well above average. In fact, Advent's projected earnings growth rate for 2002 was approximately 40 percent, and about 33 percent per year for at least 5 years into the future. Expectations for Morgan Stanley, on the other hand, were considerably lower. Its historical 5-year EPS growth rate had been about 14 percent, but it was projected to grow at only 5 percent a year for the next 2 years. In fact, the 2001 forecast was a reduction in earnings from the previous year of about 20 percent.

Perceptions can change, however. In fact, the market's perception of a company's potential can change quickly, resulting in a dramatic effect on the stock price. The Advent/Morgan Stanley example was written in August 2001. By the time our manuscript was turned over to the publisher in November 2001, Advent had announced its third-quarter earnings of $.14—although the projections had been $.21. As you can see in Figure 1–1, the market's reaction preceded the third-quarter earnings announcement, most likely as a result of rumors circulating on Wall Street about the cessation of rapid earnings growth. Even though the company placed the blame on the events of September 11, the stock had been in a steady decline since mid-July and took a sharp drop the first week of September. After September 11, the stock's value fell even further.

This real-life example demonstrates the high P/E levels that can be generated from high estimated growth rates, and it also illustrates the double-edged sword of high P/Es: When a company fails to meet the market's expectations, the drop in stock price can be swift and painful.

Although market perception can change dramatically and quickly, the change in stock price often takes place over time as a *wave of knowledge* sweeps through the market. At first, such knowledge or concern is limited to a few people. For example, say an analyst who follows a stock decides to raise his or her estimates of future earnings. Initially, that information will be limited to the favored in-

F I G U R E   1–1

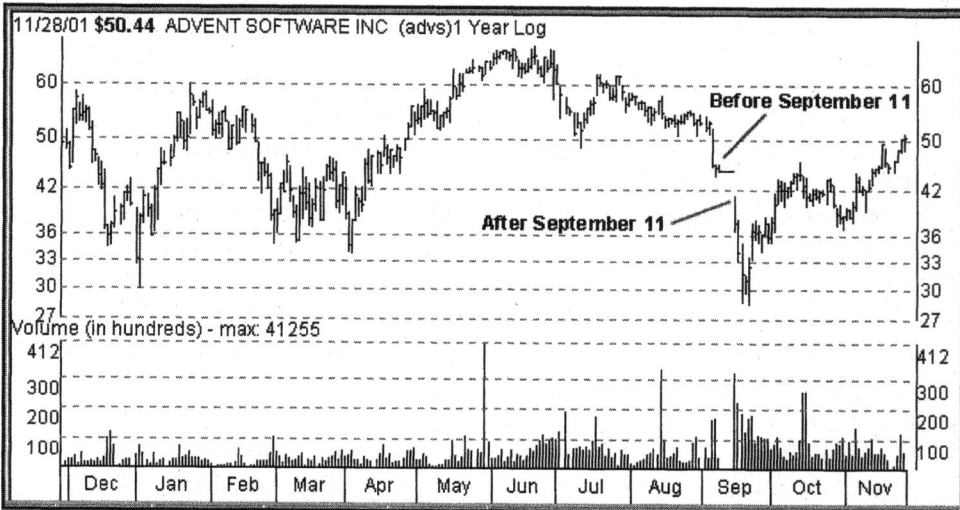

Advent Software (ADVS) dropped more than 20 percent after its September earnings release.

vestors of the firm for which the analyst works—it is not supposed to work that way but that is the reality much of the time. The wave of knowledge then spreads as the information becomes more public. Eventually, brokers will inform their less favored clients, and then the revised estimates will hit the media, at which time the general public becomes aware of the "new" information.

The first sign that this wave of information has become public may be a sharp drop in price. In fact, the stock might gap up or down, opening 10 or 20 percent higher or lower than it closed the day before. But it may take several weeks or months for the full effect of the change in market perception to be reflected in the stock price. One reason for this delay is that institutional investors take a long time to build (or sell off) a position in a stock because of the size of their holdings. So even though the wave of knowledge began with the first kernel of information, the change in market perception won't be complete until the institutions have built or relieved themselves of their positions.

Earnings Growth

Historical earnings and projected earnings are readily available on-line (see Appendix A). Historical earnings are usually stated as annual growth rates over the past 1, 3, and 5 years. A longer history is more reassuring than a short one, and a growth rate that is accelerating increases investor confidence. Earnings estimates are given for the upcoming quarter and for the current and next fiscal years. A very important estimate is the projected EPS growth rate, which is usually given for the next 1 to 5 years. (The projected EPS growth rate is one of the factors that you compare the P/E to when you are trying to determine whether or not the P/E is acceptable.) Be sure to note the number of analysts giving estimates. Five analysts inspire more confidence than one, and you can have more of a sense of confidence if all five are projecting similar earnings, rather than if the analysts' estimates are spread out all over the map. By the way, the mean of all the analysts' estimates is what is taken as the consensus or "official" estimate that the company needs to meet or beat.

Investor confidence is the other retaining wall in the structure of stock valuation. To maintain a stock's valuation, confidence that future earnings will actually materialize is just as critical as the market's perception that the EPS growth rate will be high. Think about it. Wouldn't you be willing to pay more for a stock that you're fairly certain is going to grow at 30 percent a year than for one that you're not quite so sure about? Obviously, the more confident you are that a certain earnings figure or growth rate will be reached, the more you will be willing to "bet" on that event taking place.

Confidence is based on the company's past performance. Once the company has a history of meeting or exceeding its earnings projections quarter after quarter, investors become confident that it will continue to do so. If a company has grown at 20 percent per year for many years, it is easy to believe that it will continue to grow at 20 percent if that is what the analysts are projecting. A strong earnings history gives us confidence in the projected future earnings. This confidence in the company's future earning ability is reflected in a higher P/E—a higher stock price compared with current earnings. That is why investors were willing to pay over 50 times current earnings for Advent Software stock in the summer of 2001; they were apparently very confident that Advent would meet or exceed its earnings goals.

Confidence doesn't usually come and go quickly. Just as there is a wave of knowledge that changes the market's perception of a company, there is a wave of investor confidence that changes with time. An excellent example was the Enron accounting debacle in the fall of 2001. In its wake, a wave of declining confidence swept through the market, causing a reduction in the prices of virtually all companies with complex accounting issues.

This combination of market perception and investor confidence in the future earnings growth of a company is what drives stock prices and thus P/E ratios. Changes in either or both create a change in stock price, either up or down. We will be talking about these two factors throughout this book.

EVENTS THAT CHANGE PERCEPTION OR CONFIDENCE

Sometimes earnings history and earnings projections are the only solid data on which you can base your decision about a stock. That may be enough, but you must constantly monitor your stocks for events that can change either market perception or investor confidence, because these two factors go hand in hand. If one stubs its toe, the other one stumbles.

Let's look at some events that can change the perception of a stock's future earnings and the confidence level about those earnings. The different strategies you may use in implementing a given investment style will closely follow these factors. The following 10 events are listed (in our opinion) in the order of those that have the most impact on market perception and/or investor confidence.

1. Earnings Announcements: You Beat the Street or the Street Beats You

A company's quarterly earnings are the number one factor in changing market perception and investor confidence—although the direction of the change may not always be what you'd expect. We've already talked about what can happen when a company misses its projections by a mere penny, but how many times have you heard a company announce record earnings and watched its stock go down instead of up? This counterintuitive movement is once again owing to market perception of the company's future earnings. The just-announced earnings might be record setting, but the market apparently expected an even bigger number, one based on "whisper numbers." Consequently, what looks like positive news is perceived as negative, and the stock sells off, to the amazement of novice investors. A company's failure to meet its whisper numbers is often viewed as an early warning that future earnings and the attendant growth rate may not be met.

Whisper Numbers

Whisper numbers are those unofficial earnings estimates that are bandied about by brokers and analysts in phone calls, over lunch, at cocktail parties, a week or two before a company's earnings announcement. Whisper numbers were once the privileged information of Wall Street professionals. Now they are published on the Internet (see Appendix A). Whisper numbers may be based on rumors of a significant event or unofficial discussions with corporate insiders. Whatever their source, they are the market's "real" expectations of a company's earnings, and if a company fails to meet its whisper numbers, the stock can take as big a hit as if the company had failed to meet the published estimates.

The text of the earnings announcement itself may trigger a negative change in perception or confidence. The announcement may include an overt negative statement, such as a warning that future quarters will challenge the company. Sometimes it is the mere omission of positive statements from the company that will cause a stock to sell off. As you will see later in our discussion of investing styles, there is a danger in buying the stocks of companies that have very high expectations and whose price is based on extraordinary earnings projections far in the future. Even a minor change in the market's perception or in investors' confidence level might cause dramatic changes in the price of such a stock.

The good news is, if a company announces earnings that meet or exceed the market's expectations—and especially, if it has a history of doing so—the perception of a rosy (or rosier) future and investor confidence that it can be achieved can propel a stock to new heights.

2. Revising Estimates: The Impact of a Change of Mind

It has been proven in a number of publications (including our own books) that one of the most accurate predictors of positive or negative moves in stock price is the one-month change in analysts' estimates. The first research report written by an analyst is usually positive. Frequently, the analyst is doing his duty to his firm and looking for good things to say. A revision of those estimates, however, is very meaningful because it takes a separate initiative by the analyst to say, "I've changed my mind," or "I was wrong." For example, if an analyst says, "Last month I was saying the company will make $1.00, and now I think it will make $1.10," that is a very positive act for two reasons. First, the analyst has taken the initiative to raise the estimates, and, second, the announcement generally reflects some new event or improvement in the industry or in the company. It is not surprising then that an upward revision in earnings estimates should result in a positive change in the price of a stock.

A downward revision in an analyst's estimates has an even more dramatic effect on the stock price than does an upward revision; in fact, it can be downright devastating. It takes a great deal of courage for an analyst to lower an estimate, because in many cases he or she is saying something negative about a client of the firm.

Once again, the number of analysts who make a revision is significant. Several analysts raising or lowering an estimate will have much more impact on the stock than just one analyst issuing a revision.

3. Company Warnings: "We Regret to Inform You . . ."

When the company itself warns stockholders that it won't meet its next earnings estimates, look out. In 2001 it became extremely common for companies to issue warnings that things would not go as well in the future as expected. This is one of the reasons we found ourselves knuckle-deep in a bear market by the third quarter. Each earnings season that year, company after company stepped up to the plate to lower expectations about its future performance. This kind of pronouncement causes such a penalty to the company's stock price that you can be pretty sure that when a company makes such a statement, it is speaking the truth. Company disclosures are one of the best ways of knowing what is likely to happen to future earnings.

There are exceptions, however. Some companies, such as Microsoft, have been known to sandbag analysts, influencing them to make projections that were lower than what the company knew it could achieve. As a result, the company could meet or beat the Street consistently. Generally speaking, though, when a company says it is not going to do as well as expected, you should believe them.

Earnings Conference Calls

The Internet has bridged the gap between a company's management team and individual investors. Now you can get earnings announcements direct from the horse's mouth, so to speak, by listening to earnings conference calls. These quarterly tête-à-têtes between the chief executive officer (CEO) and chief financial officer (CFO) and the analysts are now, for the most part, open to the public via the Internet. A listing of Web sites that broadcast earnings conference calls can be found in Appendix A, along with sites that post calendars of upcoming earnings announcements.

---

4. Interest Rate Changes:
When Greenspan Speaks . . .

The lowering of interest rates has two potential impacts on stocks, both generally thought to be positive. The prevailing school of thought is that lower interest rates give consumers more money to spend, which translates into higher profits for businesses, which makes companies more willing to spend money on inventory, research, new products, and expansion—all of which stimulate the economy. Higher profits are expected to lead to increased earnings, so investors become more confident about the future earnings potential of companies in general. In this way, lower interest rates produce positive ripples throughout the economy. That's why the Federal Reserve lowered interest rates throughout 2001, hoping to stem the nation's slide into recession.

The second positive impact of lowering interest rates has nothing to do with market perception of future earnings or investor confidence. Lower interest rates simply make investors less likely to buy debt instruments and more likely to buy equities, thereby driving up stock prices across the board.

An increase in interest rates has exactly the opposite effect. Higher rates curtail consumer spending, squeeze business profits, act as a restraint on company spending, all of which represent a negative stimulus on the economy. And higher interest rates pull money out of the equity markets and direct it toward debt instruments. There are, of course, companies and business sectors that benefit from higher rates, such as the banking industry, and these companies and sectors may react quite differently to interest rate changes.

5. Insider Trading: They Must Know Something We Don't

If company insiders take their hard-earned (some might argue not-so-hard-earned) money and buy stock in the open market, that is a pretty good sign that they believe their company's future earnings are going to be better than the market expects. At minimum, it indicates that they feel the company's stock price is too low at that time. After all, who knows more about a company's prospects than the top executives of that company? Of course, insiders are not always right. Sometimes the future does not turn out the way they expected. Even if it does, the market sometimes never attains the confidence level of the insiders, and so the stock price may languish. Nevertheless, insider buying is one of the two best predictors of future positive stock movement (the other, as we have discussed, is the change in analysts' estimates).

On the other hand, insider selling, while not a good sign, is not necessarily as bad as it may seem. Many companies base executive compensation programs on stock, which leaves insiders with no practical way to buy new homes or send kids to college other than by selling stock. Furthermore, insiders often have just a few weeks each quarter in which they can execute such sales. There are no hard-and-fast rules, but most public companies generally allow their insiders to trade company stock only from the point that last quarter's earnings are public and next quarter's earnings are yet unknown even to insiders. The point is to prevent insiders from trading on information that has not been disseminated to the public. Nevertheless, insider selling does not imply confidence in a company's future—and if insiders are selling in large quantities, that sends a very poor signal indeed.

6. The Ripple Effect of Industry News

Industry group performance can also boost investor confidence and market perception. If most stocks in an industry are doing well, this trend reflects favorably on all stocks in that industry. Thus, news that affects an entire industry can boost or damage market perception and investor confidence for all the stocks in the industry.

Consider the oil industry in late 2000 and early 2001. One after another, oil companies reported significantly improved earnings for the simple reason that energy prices had moved up. Indeed, this was a good forecast of the future revenues for virtually all companies in the oil industry. If companies in an industry are doing well because of a common event, the assumption is that the "good news" will probably extend to everybody in the industry.

Bad news has a similar ripple effect. Cost reductions, for example, might be good news for consumers, but they are bad news for company profits. The slashing of PC prices in 2001 lowered expectations and investor confidence in the whole PC industry. And recurring price wars in the airline industry affect all airline stocks negatively.

7. Changes in Margins: Good News or Bad?

When a company's revenues expand, its margins frequently expand as well. In general, this means that the company's volume is increasing to the point that the company can afford to buy raw materials in larger quantities at cheaper prices, or that fixed costs can be spread over a larger base. It could also mean that the company is doing so well it can raise its prices. Improvements in margins can only come from improved sales prices or lowered costs. Either is a good sign, and either will raise expectations for improved results in the future.

On the other hand, margin squeezes are typically caused by decreased sales, which result in aggressive pricing, or they are caused by increases in the costs of raw materials. Although a company rarely makes a public announcement about changes in its margins, news of price slashing may hit the media. Price wars or price slashing implies that margins are going to come down, and odds are good that market perception about the future growth of the companies involved will change as well. Confirmation of lowered margins can be found by consulting the company's 10Q and 10K or by using stock filters that are available on the Internet.

8. Changes in Inventories: A Sign to Dig Deeper

A change in a company's inventory can affect future earnings, and thus market perception and investor confidence. Expanding inventories are almost a sure sign that sales are slowing down, and slowing sales do not bode well for future earnings.

The effect of shrinking inventories on future earnings is not as clear-cut. In general, smaller inventories are good, but inventories can also shrink owing to troubles in the manufacturing process. If you see a change in inventories in a company's 10Q or 10K, you might want to dig a little deeper to figure out what is really going on.

9. Technology and Products: New Is Good

A technological breakthrough obviously raises expectations for future earnings in the companies that are involved. So does a new product. If a pharmaceutical company receives approval from the Federal Drug Administration (FDA) for its new drug or if a chip maker starts shipping a new chip, confidence increases that future earnings will materialize. You have to be aware, however, of the time frame for bringing a breakthrough or new product to market. There are generally three stages to the process.

The first stage is the company's initial announcement that it is going to develop a new product based on the technological breakthrough. The product announcement is generally positive and raises expectations for future revenues.

The second stage comes when the product is finished or approval is granted by the FDA, if required. At this time, investor confidence increases because it begins to look as if the earnings will actually materialize.

The third stage comes when the product is available for sale and profit margins are known. Assuming the sales and margins are good, confidence levels again go up, resulting in a positive impact on the company's earnings.

10. Product Failure: Is It Fatally or Temporarily Flawed?

Product failure has a more dramatic impact on market perception and investor confidence than does product success. For example, if FDA approval is required to get a product to market, the withholding of that approval can send a company's stock price tumbling. If a product fails for any reason and does not get to market as planned, there can be no doubt that the company's future earnings won't materialize, and the stock price suffers immediately.

Except of course when it doesn't.

There is always the exception to the rule that surprises many investors. Sometimes the announcement that a product line is going to be discontinued or a division will be shut down has a positive effect on market perception and investor confidence. This usually happens if there have been rumors that the company was troubled by that division or if the discontinued product had lowered investor confidence and shaken market perception of future earnings. In such cases, the realization that the losses are going to stop can increase investor confidence and is therefore considered a positive event.

The foregoing is only a partial review of factors that can affect the market perception of future earnings or investors' confidence that earnings will be met. The important point is that regardless of strategy or style, you need to be aware that it is the future earnings and/or the confidence in those future earnings that affects future stock prices. The investing strategies that you adopt must take these factors into account.

The Role of an Expanding P/E

It might be worth illustrating once again the effect of an expanding P/E ratio, as compared with the contracting P/E described at the beginning of this chapter. In that example we looked at a company that made 11 cents one quarter when it was expected to make 12 cents, and the stock price dropped dramatically. Now let's look at a company that exceeds its projected earnings estimate. Clearly, this is an overly simplistic example, but it is to be hoped that it will illustrate the concept.

Let's say that ABC Company has a current P/E of 10, and a stock price of $44, and is projected to make $1.10 this quarter (and $4.40 cents for the year). Last year ABC made $1.00 for the same quarter, which gives it a current growth rate of 10 percent. But instead of making $1.10, the company makes $1.20 this quarter, which bumps its growth rate up to 20 percent (compared with the $1.00 for the same quarter last year). Now something interesting can happen if the market responds to this event by beginning to believe that the company can continue to grow at this higher rate. With a 20 percent growth rate, investors should be willing to pay at least 20 times current earnings for ABC Company. A 20 percent growth rate would result in earnings of $4.80 this year (instead of $4.40), so if people are confident enough to pay up to 20 times current earnings, giving the stock a 20 P/E, the price would rise to about $96 per share!

Just by beating estimates by 10 cents in one quarter and demonstrating an ability to increase earnings, a $44 stock becomes a $96 stock—so you've earned a return of 2.5 times on your original investment. All of this is because of a change in perception and confidence.

The stock in this example more than doubled because of the expanding P/E, but some stocks do even better. Five-baggers and ten-baggers—those stocks that grow to five or 10 times their original price—happen in exactly the same way, with a combination of earnings growth and P/E expansion. To illustrate, let's take that same ABC stock, which the market perceived would have a growth rate of 20 percent, assuming, in other words, that earnings will grow to $4.80 this year. Let's say ABC makes $1.30 for the next quarter, which could give rise to the belief that the company could grow at 30 percent a year rather than 20 percent. So we now have a company that was supposed to make $1.10 a couple quarters ago, and two quarters later it's making $1.30.

If the market now believes that this stock, which had been projected to grow at 10 percent a few quarters ago, is in actuality going to grow at 30 percent—and if it furthermore believes that a 30 percent rate is sustainable—investors in all likelihood will be willing to pay 30 times earnings or more, which will expand the P/E to 30 or more and the stock price will rise to nearly $160. The stock is now a four-bagger, the kind we'd all love to own.

An expanding P/E is caused by the market's willingness to pay more for a stock's current earnings than it is currently paying—and that willingness is based on a foundation of market perception and investor confidence concerning future earnings. The higher the P/E, however, the more unstable that foundation becomes, and any bad news that signals a lowering of perception or confidence can send the P/E tumbling. We must keep this in mind as we formulate our investing strategies.

Keep in mind that P/Es must be judged in relation to market P/E, which is the average P/E of all stocks. Historically, market P/Es have ranged between 15 and 25. So, assuming market P/Es are near the high end of this range, it would not be unreasonable to have a P/E of 30+ or even 50+ for a rapidly growing company. Nonetheless, the market will demand that such companies continue to grow at well above average growth rates and will penalize them dearly if they fail to do so.

CHAPTER 2

The Investing Process

Underlying every investing style is the investing process. Whatever your style, whether it is based on momentum, growth, value, or your preference for technical stocks—even if you have no discernible style—you must still select the stocks you wish to buy, enter and exit each stock so as to maximize your profits, and manage your portfolio. Your strategies may differ, depending on your investing style, but every investor goes through the investing process in one form or another. If you are a value investor, you will look for quite different characteristics in a stock than a momentum investor would, but each type of investor needs a systematic way to select stocks. You need a timing system to enter and exit your stocks, but your system should be consistent with your investing style if you are to have real success as an investor. And, regardless of your style, you must manage your portfolio, deciding such things as asset allocation, diversification, and other portfolio issues.

These three strategies—stock selection, timing of the entry and exit, and portfolio management—make up the investing process. They constitute the framework, the bare bones, of any investing style. Before we move on to specific investing styles, let's take a closer look at the three steps of the investing process. Then, when we talk about styles, we will provide specific strategies for each step.

STEP 1: SELECT A STOCK

It should go without saying that the whole investing process begins with stock selection. Deciding which stocks to buy is clearly the first and most important step. As we write this, there are more than 10,000 stocks listed on the New York Stock Exchange (NYSE), the American Stock Exchange (AMEX), and Nasdaq (NASD), and grouped generally into 100 to 200 industries. The stocks range in market capitalization from a few million dollars to hundreds of billions of dollars. The companies vary widely in stock price, earnings growth, revenues, sales, and other important factors. With such a vast range of choices, how should you go about finding those stocks that fit *your* specific needs and goals and provide the returns you want?

Too often, people choose stocks randomly, acting on tips or recommendations by friends or neighbors or on a story they read in the newspaper or learned about on television. This is obviously not a good way to select stocks. The investing public is usually among the last to know what is really going on, and by the time a rumor or story about a stock becomes public knowledge, that first wave of knowledge that we talked about in Chapter 1 has already been circulating on Wall Street. It is a safe bet that any impact from the story has already been factored into the stock price. So any time you're tempted to act on such story, ask yourself if the current price is reasonable, regardless of the story. (See "The Price According to GARP" in Chapter 4 for guidelines.) Even if the price is reasonable, acting on a random tip is not a very effective way to select a stock. Instead, why not buy the best possible stock for your investment goals, rather than just an "okay" stock?

That is the purpose of this book: to help you select stocks that are among the best you can find to match your investing goals. When you start using the stock selection strategies that we recommend, you may be surprised to find that there are *dozens* of stocks that meet the goals of your style. What you'll need to do is to refine your selection strategy so that only the best of the best rise to the top.

Stock selection is best accomplished with an online search engine that allows you to create a screen with criteria that reflects your investing goals. All stocks in the database are then filtered through that screen and only those that match your requirements are allowed through. It is similar to using a matchmaking service to search for an ideal date. A matchmaking profile might specify that the person must live within a 10-mile radius of your home in order to eliminate geographically undesirable candidates. Similarly, a stock search screen might specify a maximum P/E ratio of 30 to eliminate potentially overvalued stocks. The more sophisticated search engines go a step further, however, and let you also specify whether you want high or low values for your criteria. You could then, for example, search for stocks with the lowest P/E's *and* a maximum P/E of 20—or for a date that lives the closest to your house *within* a 10-mile radius. This kind of search engine uses both "absolute filters" and "fuzzy logic."

Absolute Filters versus Fuzzy Logic

There are two types of stock search engines on the Internet that use screens or filters created by the user. One uses "absolute filters," the other uses "fuzzy logic." With an absolute filter, a screen is created to eliminate all stocks above a maximum number and/or below a minimum number. For example, you can create a filter that will eliminate stocks that have less than a 20 percent earnings-per-share growth rate or a higher than 25 P/E ratio. A search engine that uses fuzzy logic "scores" each of the stocks for the criterion in question and returns a list of stocks with the highest or lowest scores. (These are also called "relevance" search engines.) For example, you can request stocks with the highest earnings growth rates, and the stocks will be listed in order of highest score first, second-highest score second, and so on. The more sophisticated search engines use a combination of absolute filters and fuzzy logic, which lets you screen for the highest or lowest scores within absolute ranges. Some search engines also let you weight each criteria for its importance in your overall search. Several Web-based stock search engines are described in Appendix A.

Creating a search filter is not particularly difficult, even when you have hundreds of criteria to choose from. All you need to do is formulate your investment goals in a question or set of questions. For example, a growth investor might ask, Which stocks have the highest possible expected future earnings growth with the best earnings history? A value investor might ask, Which high growth stocks are currently selling at an all-time low P/E? A momentum investor might ask, Which stocks have had the greatest momentum over the past 3 weeks? A top-down investor starts with the question: Which are the top performing industry groups right now? And then, What are the best stocks in that industry? Any investor might ask, Which stocks have the highest insider buying?

All searches can be reduced to these sorts of general questions. Then all you have to do is select the screening criteria that will deliver the stocks that are best for your requirements. We will discuss specific search strategies in each of the style chapters, but if you are formulating a search strategy of your own, it is helpful to outline your goals in a few simple questions.

Evaluating a Short List of Stocks

Once you perform a search, you will likely end up with a short list of 20 to 25 stocks. Obviously, you can't buy them all. You will need to narrow the list to an even shorter list of the four or five most likely candidates. You could, if you wish, buy the top four or five stocks on the list or even do an "eenie meenie miney mo." If you had used a good search filter, you would probably end up with some decent stocks. But if you take a little time to eliminate those stocks that have less desirable characteristics, you can greatly increase your odds of picking winners.

To evaluate a stock, you will need to look at stock charts on each of the stocks, as well as company profiles, earnings estimates, and other reports (all readily available on the Internet). The questions you will seek to answer may include some or all of the following:

- Does the stock show signs of upward momentum?
- What is the stock's current price in relation to its long-term trend?
- Does the stock have huge drops and steep rises, or does it move in a relatively smooth manner?

- Which stocks on the list have the highest 5-year earnings growth rate?
- Have there been recent positive or negative revisions of earnings estimates by the analysts?
- Have there been any positive or negative earnings surprises lately?
- How does the P/E ratio compare with the industry average and the S&P 500?
- How many buy recommendations does the stock have? How many hold or sell recommendations?
- How many analysts have made projections?
- Has there been any recent news on the company, good or bad?
- Have insiders been buying or selling the stock?
- How is the stock's industry group doing?

Once you eliminate the stocks with the most negative answers, you'll have a short list of candidates that best match your investing style and that will cause you the least amount of concern.

But not every stock on your short list will be a winner.

No matter how much time you spend or how carefully you select and evaluate the stocks on your list, you will make mistakes. Even the best investors make mistakes. Sometimes a stock's lack of performance is due to industry issues or changes in the company's fortunes. Sometimes you simply misjudge the evidence. Sometimes you can be misled by the company, as in the case of Enron. Whatever the cause, mistakes are made in the selection and evaluation process, which is why we need the second step in the investing process.

STEP 2: TIME YOUR ENTRY AND EXIT

Entry and exit strategies are important for successful investing. The goal of an entry strategy is to buy a stock when it is about to enter an uptrend and to avoid those stocks that are in a downtrend or a long basing pattern. The goal of an exit strategy is to sell a stock at the time when it appears that the uptrend is over or at least before a downtrend has progressed very far.

Basing Patterns

A stock is in a basing pattern when it trades within a narrow price range for an extended period of time. For example, in Figure 2–1, AmeriCredit (ACF) based between $34 and $36 from mid-January through late February. Basing patterns are caused by an equilibrium of supply (sellers) and demand (buyers). The stock will break out of the basing pattern only when buyers outnumber sellers (a positive basing pattern breakout) or when sellers outnumber buyers (a negative basing pattern breakout). Basing patterns themselves are frustrating for investors, but positive basing pattern breakouts are often a good buy signal, depending on volume and other factors.

Pinpointing the *exact* beginning and end of a trend isn't possible, of course, so we must be content merely to capture as much of the profits as possible, as quickly as possible. How quickly that is depends on whether you are a short-term or long-term investor. As a short-term investor, we use short-term strategies to improve the odds that we will buy near a short-term low point, that the stock will move positively in the short run, and that we will sell it when the short-term run is over. Long-term strategies would ignore all the short-term trends and signal a sell only when the long-term uptrend appears to be over.

Why do we sell on these trend reversals? Because we don't know that a new downtrend will be short. Perhaps the stock will drop over an extended period and give up 50 percent or more of its price. We have no way of knowing how long or how severe the downtrend will be. For that reason we prefer to exit with either short-term or long-term indicators to avoid major meltdowns. Studies have shown that avoiding major meltdowns is the single best reason to use exit indicators.

Figure 2–1 clearly shows three short-term uptrends for Ameri-Credit within a long-term uptrend. As you can see from this chart, when we talk about using entry and exit signals, we're not talking about buying and selling stocks every day or every week or even every month. A long-term investor would have bought AmeriCredit somewhere in the low $20s in November or December 2000 and held it until late July or August 2001, getting out between $50 and

FIGURE 2-1

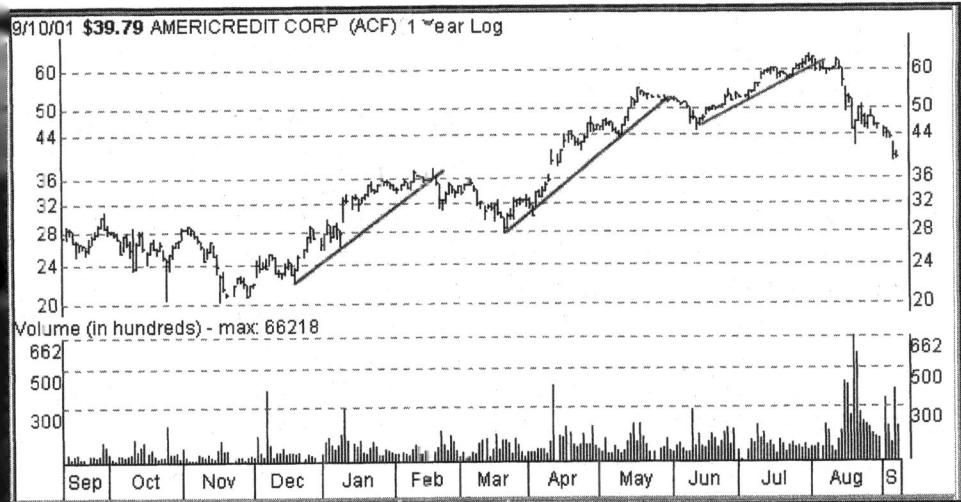

9/10/01 $39.79 AMERICREDIT CORP (ACF) 1 Year Log

AmeriCredit (ACF) had a long-term uptrend that began in late November and lasted through early August, taking the stock from about $21 to $61. During that time there were three distinct short-term trends, marked with trendlines, that could have provided excellent opportunities for the short-term investor.

$60. A short-term investor would have bought and sold the stock three times, trying to capture as much as possible of the three short-term trends shown on the chart

Trendlines like the ones in Figure 2–1 were drawn after the fact, although very similar trendlines could have been drawn as the moves materialized. Some technicians use breaks of these trendlines to signal entries and exits. Others use indicators to signal that a trend has likely changed. There are dozens if not hundreds of such indicators that have been designed to provide a signal that a particular uptrend or downtrend has likely ended. Some are better for short-term moves, others for long-term moves. Some indicators signal best during bullish runs, others during bearish times. Some can even provide early warnings that a trend is "stalling." It is beyond the scope of this book to delve deeply into these indicators. Suffice it to say that the primary goal of such indicators is to take our emotions out of the process.

Timing our exits is particularly important. Not only can timing protect us to some extent when we have made a bad stock selection decision (by helping us cut our losses) but it also helps us keep our profits when we have selected a winner. Even though we may sometimes get out a bit too soon, it is always better to take some profit than to end up getting no profit at all or, worse, incurring a loss. The prime objective, of course, is to avoid the inevitable meltdown when a stock may fall 70, 80, 90 percent or more, and there were plenty of those in 2000 and 2001 and not only among dot-coms. Stalwarts such as Cisco, Nortel, and Enron melted down right along with Internet biggies Amazon.com and Yahoo!

It is always hard to admit to oneself (or to one's spouse) that we have made a mistake. So we often hang on, praying that the stock will reverse. Even worse, if we let our emotions rule, we may buy more of the stock as it drifts downward. It is equally hard to let our profits run. We buy a stock at $10, sell it at $12 or $15 simply to get our quick profits, and then watch it soar on for another 20 points. Even more dismaying is when we hold stock too long, watching it go from, say, $10 to $20 and then watch it retrace all the way back to $10 or worse. There was a point when we should have gotten out, and we can only know that point with an appropriate technical timing system.

The points at which we need to cut our losses or take our profits are not as elusive as you might think. Stocks rise and fall, rebound and retreat, zig and zag their way up the chart for a good reason. Stocks rise because more people want to buy them than sell them, and they fall because more people want to sell them than buy them. That's a simple way of looking at it, but it's true. The point at which a declining stock rebounds is when sufficient pain has been caused to finally dry up the selling of the stock. Everyone who wanted to get out of the stock has done so, and with no more sellers, even a small amount of buying will cause the stock to rebound.

Similarly, the point at which a rising stock halts and retreats is when the enthusiasm for the stock finally reaches a saturation point. There is no one left with sufficient optimism to buy the stock at the current price and the buying dries up. With no more buyers, the stock loses its momentum and begins to retreat from its high. As we said, this is overly simplistic, but the points at which the stock rises and falls back are based on logical reasons.

Technical indicators of all shapes and sizes are designed to signal these points, although no indicator or trading system can pinpoint the absolute top or the absolute bottom of a trend. Many are based on moving average crossovers. Simplistically stated, if a stock is moving up, a buy signal is given when the stock crosses its 30-, 50-, or 200-day moving average. If a stock is moving down, a buy signal is given when it crosses below the moving average. Such a simple system would likely give too many buy and sell signals (called *whipsaws*), and no wise investor would use such a system by itself. Nevertheless, complex multi-indicator systems are built from such simple indicators. The best ones have been built by very smart, experienced people and tested over thousands of stocks and dozens of years.

Even so, there is no perfect trading system. No matter how much we are willing to pay for one, trading systems rarely get us in at the exact bottom and out at the exact top. Nonetheless, some that have stood the test of time can be valuable in helping us enter stocks that are more likely than not to be in an uptrend and exit them when they are more likely than not to trend downward. If you will recall our "Tale of Two Stocks" in the Introduction, we needed a timing system to let our profits run on MSCA and to cut our losses on VIGN, because our emotions would have impelled us to do just the opposite. In Chapter 4 we'll show you the system we used.

It is beyond the scope of this book to delve deeply into any one system, but we will address specific timing methods and strategies for each of the major investing styles. (Some of the more complex timing systems are listed in Appendix A for those who wish to study them further.) Whatever your style, technical timing can play a valuable role in the investing process.

STEP 3: MANAGE YOUR PORTFOLIO

The third step in the investing process is portfolio management. Once we have found some stocks to buy with our stock selection strategy and have selected an appropriate timing indicator for getting in and getting out of the stock, several questions still remain to be answered.

+ How many stocks should we hold at a given time?
+ How many different industry groups should they represent?

- Should we buy international stocks?
- Should we be fully invested or should we keep some of our investment funds in cash? If so, how much?
- Should we invest in bonds? If so, what percentage of our portfolio should be in bonds?

All of these decisions depend on your portfolio management strategy.

- *Determine the size of your portfolio.* Most portfolio management experts recommend holding between 5 and 20 stocks at any given time. We think 10 to 15 is about right, but the number depends, among other things, on your investing style, how much money you have to invest, and how much time you have to manage your portfolio. In any case, it is better to own more than a couple of stocks. Let's say you're as good a stock picker as the experts—who are wrong 15 to 30 percent of the time. If you own only two stocks you will have one loser about 50 percent of the time and two losers about 10 percent of the time, based on simple probability theory. Think how discouraging it would be to have every stock in your portfolio down. It is imprudent and unnecessary to put yourself through this much stress. Spread the risk.

- *Diversify among industries and countries.* Diversifying among industry groups is always prudent. Industries can fall out of favor rather quickly due to unsettling events. Witness the dot-com crash of early 2000. Lest you think that was unusual and specific, we would remind you that there have been similar crashes (perhaps not as severe), but similar isolated bear markets in bank stocks, real estate stocks, biotechs, chip makers, and the movie industry. It simply makes good sense to diversify among two or three or more industry groups. The more stocks you own, the more you can diversify among industry groups.

  You can also diversify your portfolio by buying international stocks. While we do not feel it is imperative to do so, diversification across country borders may be of benefit. If U.S. markets are doing poorly and other economies are

doing well, it makes sense to invest in those economies, assuming you do so in an informed manner and adhere to
your investing style and strategies. As we discuss in Chapter 10, an easy way to get into global investing is to buy
baskets of stocks related to foreign economies through exchange-traded funds (ETFs) or closed-end country funds.

♦ *Allocate your resources* Aside from diversification, two of
the toughest questions an investor must answer are, How
should I allocate my investment capital? Should I be fully
invested or should I keep part of my portfolio in cash?
Much has been written about the desirability of staying fully invested at all times, but we believe it makes sense to
have some cash on the table during periods in which the
market has reached high or extreme valuations. First, it will
protect you against the inevitable decline, and second, it
will give you cash to go shopping in the aftermath. Those
investors who started moving to a larger cash position in
early 2000, when the Nasdaq was extremely extended (see

F I G U R E   2–2

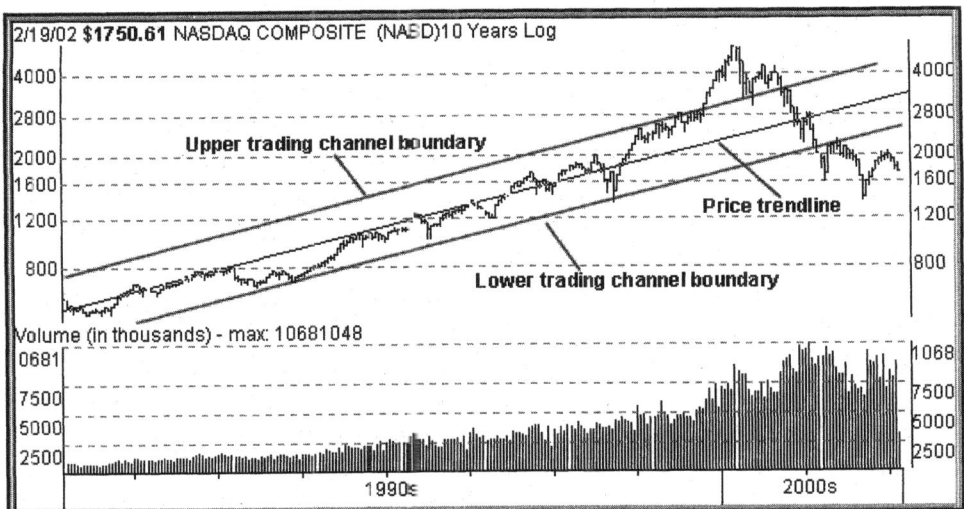

The Nasdaq Composite Index (NASD) with trading channels. Note the
extreme overextended period in early 2000.

Fig. 2–2), avoided some or all of the pain of the subsequent crash and they also had cash on hand to pick up the pieces—all those greatly devalued stocks—after the crash.

How you allocate your resources between stocks and cash will depend in part on your investing style. A long-term growth investor will be less concerned about keeping cash reserves than a momentum investor and will tend to have a much lower cash position than a momentum investor. We will discuss this topic in each of the investing styles chapters.

The Case Against Bonds

Most asset allocation programs recommend that a certain percentage of your investment funds should be allocated to bonds or fixed income securities. This is a matter you should address with your financial planner or other experts in the field based on your own goals, your age, and your risk tolerance. But unless you have the foresight to move in and out of bonds at exactly the right times, you might want to rethink this advice. Studies have shown very few periods since 1920 in which it turned out better to hold a significant percentage in fixed income than to hold equities. We are talking of course about long-term government bonds with maturities of 10 to 30 years. Short-term, fixed-income vehicles, such as certificates of deposit (CDs), are a different matter.

Frequently, the very time when you're tempted to go into a long-term fixed income security is exactly the wrong time. For example, in early 1994 the stock market was worrisome and bonds had a relatively low yield, between 5 and 6 percent. For the remainder of 1994, the Fed raised interest rates several times. As you probably know, when interest rates rise, the current value of long-term bonds fall, as investors would rather buy new bonds at the higher rates. To be sure, if you hold bonds for 30 years, you won't lose money, but in 1994 it was possible to lose over 30 percent of the *principal* value of long-term 30-year bonds. Had you wanted to sell your bonds to invest in the strengthening equity market in 1995, you would have had to sell at a substantial loss.

In this book we focus primarily on equity investing so we will not be dealing further with fixed-income vehicles or bonds. Our objective is to help you find your investing style and then arm you with sufficient strategies and systems for selecting stocks, timing your entry and exit points, and managing your portfolio. We will begin in earnest in the next chapter with an overview of investing styles.

CHAPTER 3

An Overview
of Investing Styles

The word *style* can be applied to virtually anything: art, architecture, fashion, furniture, literature, music, a way of life. The word can also be applied to investing. When we talk about *investing styles*, we're referring to the different investment goals and distinctive or characteristic ways of selecting stocks that distinguish one group of investors from another. For example, Investor A buys only those stocks with the highest possible earnings growth rates, and she doesn't mind paying the prices such stocks command. Investor B might like to have the growth potential of such stocks, but he will buy only those stocks that are a bargain or are currently out of favor with the market (undervalued, in other words). Because of a bias toward certain kinds of stocks—and other characteristics we'll talk about later—Investor A would be considered a growth investor and Investor B, a value investor.

Having an investing style can make you a better investor than having no style at all. Why? Because styles work. Hundreds of thousands of investors, if not millions, follow each of the major styles described in the following chapters, and their critical mass can cause a stock to move up or down. If you have no style at all—if you pick stocks at random or by using an esoteric, self-developed technique—the stock you pick may never move unless a sufficient number of people also discover it, using the same or similar techniques. Of course, investing styles also work because the major styles are fundamentally sound.

Investing styles are grounded in different psychological or personality traits, and people generally gravitate naturally toward one style—or automatically eliminate other styles—because of their basic personality. For example, if you break out in hives at the thought of a 30 or 40 percent drop in one of your stocks, you would not want to be a growth or momentum investor. Growth and momentum stocks are prone to sudden and dramatic reversals, so these styles carry a higher degree of inherent risk than do more conservative styles. Those investors who abhor risk would be much more comfortable as a value or fundamental investor. On the other hand, if you like a lot of action and lack the patience to wait several months or a year or more for your reward, you should steer clear of value or fundamental investing and consider momentum or growth investing instead. There are other things to consider when you select an investing style—such as the strength of your self-discipline, the amount of time you have to manage a portfolio, and the level of your investing expertise—but we can't stress enough how important it is to choose a style that reflects your basic personality. Otherwise, investing will be like trying to walk 5 miles in ill-fitting shoes—you'll wince at every step.

This chapter provides a brief overview of the investing styles that are discussed at length in later chapters. You may be able to tell from this brief glance which styles will most likely fit your personality.

MAJOR INVESTING STYLES: THE BIG FOUR

Let's start with the four major styles of investing: growth, value, momentum, and technical. We consider these to be major styles of investing because enough investors are attracted to each style to form a critical mass, which makes that style effective in the marketplace. There are other less distinctive styles, some of which we'll cover later in this chapter, but these four are far and away the most prevalent.

Growth Investing: High Risk/High Reward

Growth investing is one of the most popular investing styles. Growth investors look for companies that have exceptional projected growth of earnings along with a solid history of earnings growth. These investors are willing to pay whatever it takes to get on a high-growth train—and to stay on board as long as necessary to reap the rewards of long-term growth. The personal time commitment required of the growth investor is moderate, but most of your time will be spent in the stock selection phase. Once you've selected your stocks you could check in on them as seldom as once a quarter or so to make sure the earnings are still on track, although we recommend that you take a more active management role for all stocks.

Growth investors need to have a high tolerance for risk. Because growth stocks command much higher than normal P/E ratios, they are susceptible to dramatic reversals if a stock is affected by any of the events described in Chapter 1 that change market perception or investor confidence. A case in point is Cisco Systems (CSCO), which has been a leader in what was considered in the 1990s the most dynamic industry in the world—the equipment required to run the Internet.

During the early 1990s, when its earnings growth rate was 50 to 100 percent per year, Cisco's P/E approximated 30, which made it a favorably priced growth stock. The company performed like a champion during that time, generating nearly 5 years of consecutive, quarter-over-quarter returns in excess of 50 percent. In the late 1990s Cisco's growth rate slowed to about 30 percent, but this was during the dot-com craze, so instead of the P/E decreasing along with the growth rate, Cisco's P/E expanded, ranging anywhere from 60 to 100. In essence, before its slowdown, Cisco had a P/E of about one-half its growth rate, and after the slowdown the P/E expanded to more than double the growth rate, chiefly owing to investors' unwillingness to face the lowered growth prospects. The Internet bubble had to burst before investors would look at dot-com stocks with a clear eye, but all it took to send Cisco (and other Internet stocks) into a steady and serious decline was just a hint that the hyper growth of the Internet was slowing down.

This example is not meant to scare you away from growth investing. Some of the biggest gains that investors make are in high-growth stocks. But because these stocks carry high P/Es, as a growth investor you have to be willing to accept moderate risk and learn how to avoid the long, painful price meltdowns by having and using an effective exit strategy.

Value Investing: Hunting for Bargains

Value investors are essentially bargain hunters. They don't like risk, and they don't like the idea of paying full price for anything. Generally speaking, the value investor buys stocks that are currently out of favor with the market, generally owing to an erosion of confidence in a specific company or sector. Eroding confidence can be caused by any of the events discussed in Chapter 1: a series of earnings disappointments that signal a slowdown in growth, trouble within a company or industry, or even a perception that the stock or the industry is just not as exciting or as dynamic as it formerly was. Investors often lose confidence in a company's ability to grow, and when they do, the stock price takes a beating, the P/E ratio drops, and what was previously a growth stock becomes a value stock. Value investors may believe the stock is *unjustly* undervalued—assuming its earnings growth rate is higher than its P/E—and consider it a bargain. They are willing to accept the lower confidence in earnings growth for the relatively lower risk, and they're willing to bet that not only will the earnings grow but that investor confidence will return and the P/E ratio will expand dramatically. (Recall our discussion in Chapter 1 of the role of an expanding P/E.)

In short, the value investor wants the same reward that the growth investor wants, but without as much risk. Who wouldn't?, you might think. Well, the fly in the ointment is patience. Not everyone has the patience to wait for investor confidence to rally and for the undervalued stock to become fully valued or more fully valued. There is a way around this long wait. As we will talk about later in Chapter 5, the astute value investor can use an entry strategy whereby he or she purchases the value stock at the point where the turnaround seems to be at hand and investor confidence has begun to grow.

Momentum Investing: Where the Action Is

Momentum investors like a lot of action. They try to own the fastest-rising stocks in the fastest-moving sectors in the market, and when the stock or sector slows down, they move on to the next "best" thing. In a sense, they're like surfers who jump on the biggest wave they can find, ride it for as long as they can, then jump off before it slams them onto the rocks.

Momentum stocks are those in which the market is demonstrating great confidence. They are high and going higher on a daily basis. If you're right about a momentum stock, it will provide the fastest move in the shortest time. If you're wrong, the penalty can be swift and often painful. That risk is the downside of momentum investing, which carries probably the highest risk of the four major investing styles. With investor confidence driving the momentum, guess what happens if something shakes investor confidence or if the perception of future earnings turns even slightly negative? The stock price can drop like a rock.

For example, if a company comes out with an earnings warning or if an analyst announces a downward revision, it is not uncommon for a momentum stock to drop 30 or 40 percent on the next day's open. No technical indicator or system we know of can save you from this kind of gap. Such risks simply go with the territory. So if you can't stomach sudden and dramatic price drops, you might want to reconsider your decision to become a momentum investor.

If you can stomach the risk, you should also consider the time involved in managing a momentum portfolio. Because of the need to stay alert to daily changes in your stocks and sectors and because of the need for quick and decisive action, momentum investing involves the most serious commitment of time. It would be extremely imprudent to take on a style so fraught with risk without committing the time to manage it well. If you learn to do it well and if the style fits your personality, momentum investing can be the most "fun" and perhaps the most profitable of the four major styles.

Technical Investing: A Chart Is Worth a Thousand Words

Any investing style may make use of technical analysis—in fact, most entry and exit strategies are built on a form of technical analysis—but the pure technician uses technical analysis to decide which stocks to buy, as well as when to buy and sell stocks. Technicians, or chartists as they are sometimes called, interpret stock charts as a way to find and buy the stocks with the best patterns. These investors aren't concerned about the stock's projected earnings or its P/E ratio or the level of investor confidence or, quite frankly, about any aspect of the company itself. The technical investing style is rooted in the assumption that all the information you need to know about a company is already reflected in the current stock price. When buying stocks, technicians put their money on the chart patterns that they believe are predictive of a new upswing in the stock price. When selling stocks, they rely on the chart pattern to tell them when investor confidence begins to wane, at which point they get out quickly.

There are dozens of ways to approach technical investing, some of which we'll cover in Chapter 7. Many people think momentum investing and technical investing are very similar, and, in fact, technicians frequently end up buying momentum stocks because those stocks often have the best-looking chart patterns. But there is a major difference between technical investors and momentum investors. Momentum investors usually look for stocks with good underlying fundamentals, especially recent strong earnings growth, and they simply buy those stocks with the greatest momentum. Pure technicians have little if any interest in a company's future earnings potential, because they believe that everything known about the stock is already factored into the stock price. Nevertheless, technicians and momentum investors buy many of the same stocks, so one could argue that the risk for technicians is about the same as for momentum investors. Most pure technicians would disagree. They would argue that they know which chart patterns denote risk and would obviously avoid risky stock patterns.

Given their primary emphasis on chart patterns, technical investors have one major requirement and that is to learn how to read the chart patterns of the technical indicators of their choice.

MINOR STYLES: VARIATIONS ON A THEME

There are many minor investing styles that are derivations or combinations of the four major styles. In Chapter 9 we will examine five: fundamental investing, income investing, active trading, hybrid investing, and style surfing. Here are brief previews.

Fundamental Investing

Fundamental investing is so named because investors are primarily concerned with a company's financial statements and fundamental soundness. Fundamental investors resemble value investors in that they are both looking for undervalued stocks, but they judge the undervaluation differently. Value investors look for undervalued earnings while fundamental investors look for undervalued assets. The tricky part is that at some point the undervalued assets must be discovered and more fully valued by some critical mass of investors; otherwise the stock price will never move. The only alternative is to buy the entire company and turn it around, which is what Warren Buffett, whom we consider the quintessential fundamental investor, often does. For the average individual investor, however, fundamental investing simply connotes choosing to invest in companies with a low price-to-book ratio, a strong balance sheet, plenty of cash, and little or no debt.

Income Investing

The primary objective of income investing is income, rather than stock price appreciation. The income investor—the equity income investor—looks for companies that pay dividends, the higher the better, as long as the dividends are safe. Usually, this means buying blue chip stocks or at least the larger, more stable, more established companies. Income investing is a long-term, low-risk style that also involves relatively low rewards. A related style that is slightly more aggressive is the growth-and-income style, where an investor looks for stocks that pay dividends, have a decent earnings growth rate, and hence a growing dividend.

Active Trading

Active trading is a style defined by the frequency with which investors make trades; it includes day trading, swing trading, and position trading. *Day traders* make numerous trades every day, week, or month, seeking relatively small profits on each trade. They typically hold a position for less than one day (often for just minutes or hours), hence the name. *Swing traders* trade less frequently, usually making several trades a week, and they hold positions for 2 to 5 days. *Position traders* seem to be half active trader and half momentum or technical investor: They tend to make several trades a month and hold their positions for 5 to 10 days or longer. These are very loose, arbitrary definitions. Within each "style" are hundreds of strategies that distinguish one trader from another.

In general, active traders are looking for the short-term upswing, which, for the true day trader, can occur several times a day in the same stock. The key word here is *trader*, rather than investor. Active traders must be highly disciplined, risk-tolerant, and very knowledgeable of the market and their particular trading strategies.

Hybrid Investing

In investing, it is common to graft the best part of one investing style onto another. The result is what we call a *hybrid investor*. For example, a growth investor with little patience for the long haul might make short-term momentum plays on high-growth stocks. A value investor might wait to buy an undervalued stock until it shows signs of upward momentum. A technician might concentrate on a top-performing sector or industry and consider himself a top-down investor. A risk-averse day trader might lessen her risk by trading only a handful of blue chip stocks.

A hybrid investor can create a unique style that fits like a custom-made suit. The trick is to define the style precisely and stick to your customized rules.

Style Surfing

Investing styles wax and wane in popularity and effectiveness, particularly momentum, value, and growth investing. During 1999 value investing was out and momentum investing was in. The Nasdaq was on a tear, rising some 2000 points over a 5-month period in late 1999/early 2000, and momentum players enjoyed the ride of their lives. After the bubble burst in the spring of 2000, momentum stocks fell and didn't recover, so value investing stepped into the spotlight. During this period, an investor who could easily switch styles would have been a momentum player throughout the dot-com craze and then would have switched to value investing when the markets turned south. When growth investing comes back into vogue, as it surely will, this nimble-footed investor will jump on the growth train.

We call this *style surfing* because this kind of investor moves from style to style, depending on which style is working best at the moment. Riding the style that is currently in favor has the potential for bringing higher and faster rewards, but style surfing is demanding. It requires that you be knowledgeable about all three styles and comfortable using them. This is not as easy as it may sound. As you will see in the following chapters, the qualities needed by a value investor are often diametrically opposed to those needed by the momentum or growth investor. Momentum and growth investing, as we have said, involve much more risk than does value investing, so if you're a value investor at heart, you might have a hard time being a style surfer.

Style surfing requires a large time commitment to learn all the investing styles, a flexible mind to switch back and forth, and enormous investing confidence. It is obviously not for someone who is new to the market.

AND THE WINNING STYLE IS . . .

Any investing style can be a winner, because there is no *best* style; there is only the best style for *you*. Any style can produce excellent returns and, in fact, different styles can produce great results on the same stock. As you might have guessed by now, a single stock can be a growth stock, a value stock, a momentum stock, or a technical stock at different times, and often at the very same time. Take a look at the chart in Figure 3–1.

During 2001, AmeriCredit (ACF) showed up as a value stock pick, a growth stock pick, and a technical charts pick according to an investment research service to which we subscribe. In November/December 2000 ACF had excellent value characteristics, with a historical earnings growth rate of about 38 percent, which was about 5 times its P/E ratio, and it kept its value standing throughout the following year. In April 2001, ACF appeared on the growth radar screen as a high-growth stock with a 1-year projected earnings growth rate of 64 percent and a 5-year projected earnings growth rate of 27 percent. In fact, it retained its high-growth stock definition until it began a downturn in early August 2001.

Although ACF was not an official momentum stock pick (according to our investment research service), you can see from the chart that the stock had three good short-term momentum runs. It

FIGURE   3—1

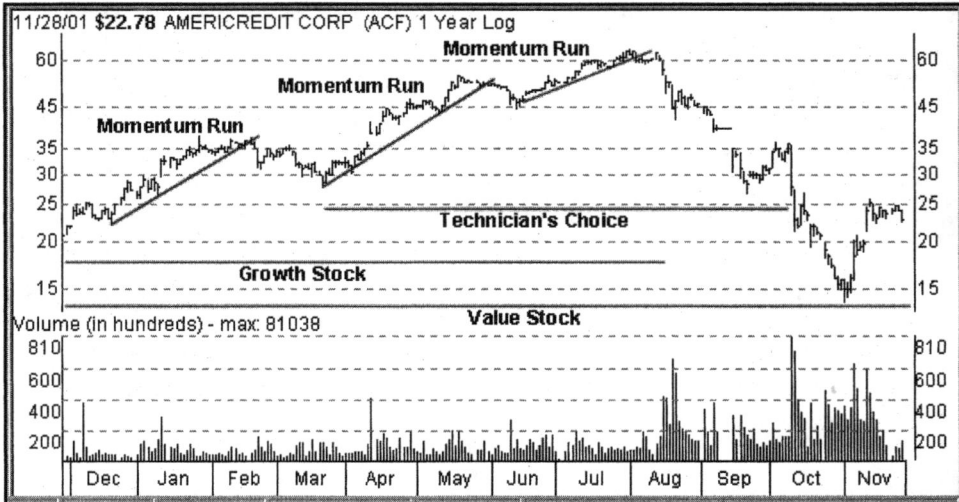

11/28/01 $22.78 AMERICREDIT CORP (ACF) 1 Year Log

AmeriCredit (ACF) has been a value stock, a growth stock, a momentum stock, and a technical stock during the past year.

was also a technical favorite. More than 30 times between April and September it was chosen as one of the top five best chart patterns of the day. It was originally chosen in April because of chart patterns that showed, among other things, that the stock had closed at a new all-time high and traded 1½ times its usual daily (30-day average) volume, that it closed 92 percent above the low of its daily range, that its price-volume relationship remained very bullish, that its relative strength was very positive, and that there was no further resistance above its present price. In September the stock reversed and fell through two support levels (at $36 and $28) but still had appeal as a technical candidate until its large drop at least $35.

Growth, value, momentum, and technical investors could have all done well with this particular stock. So there is no best style. Nevertheless some styles are favored by investors during different market conditions and thus present better, more immediate opportunities. At one time or another, the market has favored growth stocks, momentum stocks, and value stocks, while technicians seem to thrive in any market. In the bear market of late 2001, value stocks were ripe for the picking, but that changed as market conditions changed. So the question should *not* be Which is the best investing style? but Which is the best style for you? Which style will you be able to adhere to with the most discipline? Which will be most comfortable? Comfort is easier to come by and discipline easier to maintain if you select a style that fits your personality. Keep this in mind as we move through the rest of the book.

STRATEGIES WITHIN STYLES

There are a number of investing strategies that are not sufficiently complex to be considered styles but can be very effective when used along with different styles.

Top-down investing, for example, means looking first at the general market to determine its direction, then at the sectors and industries to find the best-performing ones, before selecting a stock in a top-performing industry. Top-down investing can be used with virtually any style of investing, as can an insider trading strategy. By tracking insider trading as reported to the Securities and Exchange Commission, any investor can buy a stock when the insiders buy in large quantities and sell when they sell.

To alleviate some of the risk in a high-risk style of investing, you can incorporate a market-neutral strategy by buying stocks that are expected to go up and shorting stocks that are expected to go down. (Shorting means selling a stock you don't own with the intention of buying it back later at a lower price.) Other strategies that can be used with almost any investing style include pure short-selling, global investing, and using options to hedge your portfolio. We will examine each of these in later chapters.

MARKET CAPITALIZATION: STYLE OR STRATEGY?

While not exactly a strategy, market capitalization (market cap) plays a role in the stock selection strategies of many investors. Investors seeking security, for example, frequently invest only in very large companies, while growth investors may have an affinity for small-cap stocks. Market caps can play an even bigger role if you follow the rotation of the caps.

Market Cap

Market cap refers to the size of a company as measured by its market capitalization, which is the stock price multiplied by the number of outstanding shares. There are large-cap, mid-cap, small-cap, and micro-cap stocks, each defined by the market capitalization ranges in Table 8–1.

Like investing styles, market caps rotate into and out of favor with investors, depending on market conditions. If you invest in the favored caps, you can enhance the immediacy of your returns. For example, in the 1960s, large-cap stocks went through a long period of the doldrums (the Dow, which is made up of 30 large-cap companies, flirted with the 1000 level for 10 years before breaking through that "barrier"!). During the same period, small-cap stocks rose more than 15 percent annually. The investor who was willing to switch to small caps would have done better, more quickly than the large-cap investor would have. Similarly, small caps languished in the late 1990s, while large caps, driven by index mania, boomed, presenting opportunities for immediate gains.

If you don't have an allegiance to a particular market cap, switching to whichever cap is in favor adds one more force in *your* favor. Whether or not you have a favorite cap, in Chapter 8 we'll show you how to use market caps in your investing strategy.

THE PSYCHOLOGICAL QUOTIENT (PQ) CHART

To make it easier to grasp the essence of each investing style, we've created a psychological quotient (PQ) chart that rates each style of investing based on 10 psychological or personality traits and other qualities, including discipline, patience, risk tolerance, reward expectation, volatility tolerance, time horizon, time commitment, quantitative skill, charting skill, and investing confidence. The higher the rating for a particular trait or quality, the more important it is to the investing style. An example of the PQ chart for a momentum investor appears in Figure 3–2. These PQ ratings, by the way, are not "official" ratings; they simply reflect our personal assessment of the traits needed for each investing style.

FIGURE 3-2

PQ Chart for a Momentum Investor

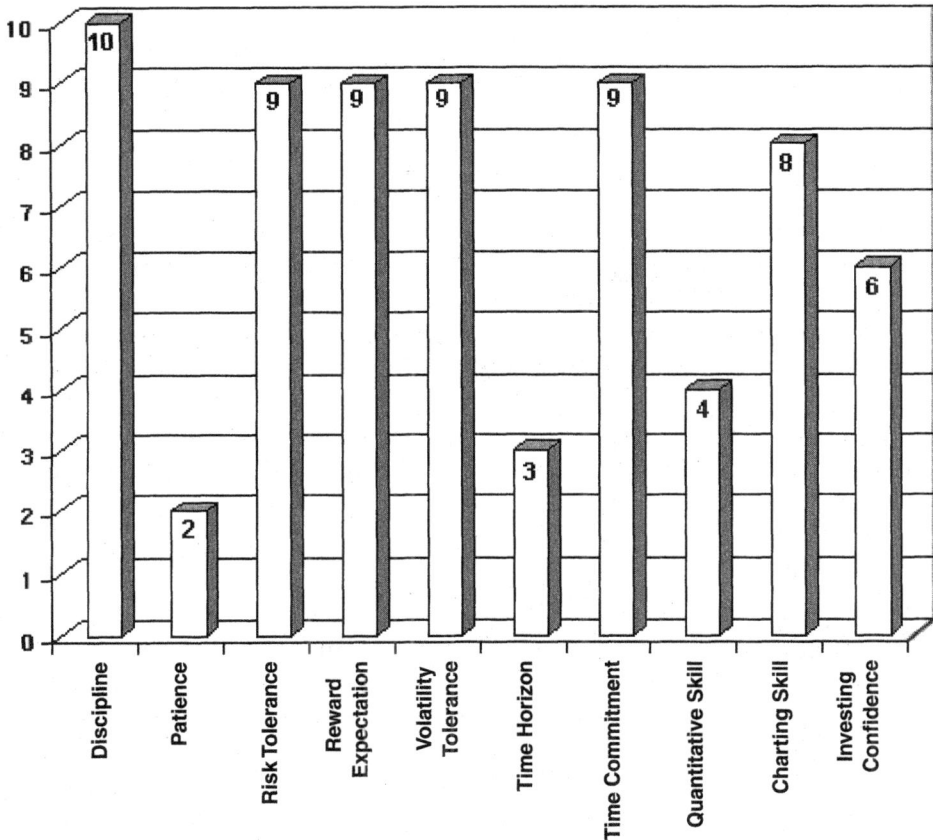

Discipline

Discipline refers to the ability to follow rules, particularly self-imposed rules. All successful investors need the discipline to stick to their rules of investing, whatever those rules might be. In fact, discipline is the number one trait needed by investors, according to market wizard Jack Schwager, who interviewed dozens of the most successful investors for his books. But some rules require more discipline than others. Some styles, such as momentum investing, require very close attention to the rules of entry and exit so that the investor can minimize risk and maximize reward. Fundamental investing, on the other hand, requires a great deal of work to uncover a stock with hidden assets or at least a better than average balance sheet, but little discipline is required to make the actual trade. Therefore, on a PQ chart, momentum investing would rate a 10 for discipline while income investing might get a 2.

Patience

Patience refers to how long you are willing to wait to reap the rewards of your investment. Do you want immediate gratification, or are you willing to wait for the fruit to ripen? The undervalued stocks sought by value investors may take several years to become fully valued and generate the expected returns, so a value investor needs to be very patient. Day trading, on the other hand, requires virtually no patience because returns are generated in days, hours, or even minutes. Value investing would get a 9 on the PQ chart for patience; day trading, a 1.

Risk Tolerance

Risk refers to the amount your investments are likely to move against you before they recover, if at all. If you have a high risk tolerance, you wouldn't be devastated with a 20 to 30 percent drop in stock price as long as the stock still met your basic investing goals. But someone with a low risk tolerance would be very uncomfortable with such large losses. Growth and momentum investors are much more likely to see sharp price reversals in their stocks than are value investors owing to the fact that growth and momentum stocks carry very high prices on a per earnings basis. As we've said, high P/E stocks are vulnerable to even the slightest negative news. On the PQ chart, momentum investing would rate a 9 or so for risk tolerance; value investing, which concentrates on stocks that are out of favor, would rate about a 3.

Reward Expectation

What kind of reward—that is, what rate of return—do you want from your investment? As much as you can get, obviously. But reward is closely aligned with risk, and investors always have a minimum goal based on the amount of risk they are willing to tolerate. This risk/reward ratio may dictate certain styles of investing over others. An investor seeking annual returns above 25 percent will have to adopt some of the more aggressive (that is, riskier) styles, such as momentum or technical investing. Value investing would be an unlikely choice for someone seeking extraordinary returns, because the average annual return for the value investor rarely exceeds 25 percent.

Twenty percent per year, by the way, has long been considered a truly exceptional return for equity investments. The goal for most investors was—and still is for many—to simply beat the market. Over the past 20 years, the market has averaged 10 to 12 percent per year for New York Stock Exchange stocks and 12 to 14 percent per year for Nasdaq stocks. The PQ charts show that the investing styles that offer the highest potential rewards, such as momentum investing, also require the highest risk tolerance. Frankly, that's life!

Volatility Tolerance

Volatility has to do with the frequency and degree of a stock's ups and downs. It is related to, but not the same as, risk. The types of investors who are holding a stock can affect its volatility. Day traders, for example, can greatly increase a stock's volatility as they move into and out of the stock. So can institutional holders. Because of the size of their trades, professionals that manage pension funds and mutual funds can increase a stock's volatility as they move into and out of their positions. Message board postings can also affect the volatility of a stock that is thinly traded (a daily volume of less than, say, 20,000 to 50,000 shares). And, as we have said repeatedly, growth and momentum stocks with high P/Es are susceptible to even minor fluctuations in investor confidence and can exhibit a great deal of volatility.

Volatility is not necessarily bad if the stock you have chosen meets the criteria of your investing style. Some investors such as day traders and momentum investors actually look for stocks with high volatility (they both rate a 9 for volatility on the PQ chart). But if the thought of frequent drops of 10 to 20 percent in value makes you sick to your stomach, we suggest that you try a style with low volatility, such as value, fundamental, or income investing.

Time Horizon

A time horizon has to do with how long your money is tied up in an investment before profits are likely to be realized. Your time horizon might be a function of patience or of need. In other words, you may be a short-term investor because you're impatient and want immediate gratification, or you may be a short-term investor because of your impending retirement and a desire to invest in a retirement property.

Generally speaking, momentum and technical investors are short-term investors, holding stocks for less than 3 months (they rate a 3 for time horizon on the PQ chart). Growth investors would be considered medium-term investors, with a time horizon of 3 to 12 months (a 7 on the PQ chart). And value investors, who usually hold stocks for a year or longer, would be considered long-term investors and would get a 9 on the PQ chart.

Time Commitment

How much time do you have to spend selecting and maintaining a portfolio of stocks? That's what we mean by time commitment on the PQ charts. In this area, investing styles are like relationships: Some are high-maintenance; some are low-maintenance. Momentum investing is high-maintenance because it requires daily care and attention, particularly with regard to monitoring your exit points. Charting is high-maintenance because it requires extensive analysis of charts and graphs, when you are both entering and exiting a stock. Growth and value investing are both lower-maintenance styles (a 3 and a 5, respectively, on their PQ charts) because once the selection process is done (which does take some time), you can check in on your portfolio every month or even every quarter and still be comfortable. The greatest time commitment is required of fundamental investors, day traders, and style surfers.

Quantitative Skill

Quantitative skills constitute the ability to understand numbers and make mathematical comparisons. If you can't balance a checkbook or have trouble understanding the concept of ratios, forget about fundamental investing, because you'll need near-CPA-level skills to pore over balance sheets and income statements and ferret out stocks that have solid fundamentals. Any style that requires a facility with numbers will be rated high for quantitative skills. Two of the more demanding styles in this area are value investing and fundamental investing.

Technical or Charting Skill

Charting is a visual skill. Basically, all you're doing (after you learn the rules of your particular technical indicator) is comparing chart patterns. Obviously, the technician is the embodiment of charting skills. Technical investors spend all their time reviewing and analyzing technical charts, so that style would rank the highest in the charting category (a 10 on the PQ chart). Momentum players also need good charting skills, as do some types of day traders. Although we know of successful growth, value, and fundamental investors who rarely look at a stock chart, we strongly recommend that you learn how to use some simple technical tools to time your entries and exits, regardless of your investing style.

Technical analysis is a skill that can be learned, and you need not eliminate styles that rank high in this area if you want to make the effort to learn the necessary charting skills.

Investing Confidence

How confident are you of your ability to select and manage a portfolio of stocks successfully? Confidence is important when you have to use your judgment about why stock A is better than stock B. For example, the whole objective of value investing is to seek out stocks that are undervalued, so you have to be able to learn about criteria that are signs of undervaluation, and you have to have the confidence to apply these criteria in the face of market skepticism. There is no label that proclaims a stock as "Undervalued" in big red letters, so value investing requires a fair amount of quantitative judgment and the confidence to carry through with decisions. Technical investing, on the other hand, is fairly cut and dried. Once you have assimilated a set of rules, you need little confidence, as a technical investor, in your own qualitative judgment. All you have to do is follow your own rules.

Investing confidence comes with knowledge and success. Beginning investors don't have much of either, so if you're just starting out, you will probably want to avoid an investing style that requires a great deal of investing confidence, such as fundamental investing and style surfing.

Again, the PQ charts in the following chapters reflect our personal assessment of the traits needed for each investing style. They offer a quick visual reference for comparing the styles.

If selecting an investing style sounds a bit overwhelming, take heart. If you are an investor, you already have an investing style, however rudimentary. The next few chapters can help you figure out whether or not that style fits you and your needs. If you're just beginning as an investor, keep in mind that there is no right or precise style for trading stocks. Your style may end up being a little bit of this, a little bit of that. Play with the different styles until you find one that feels comfortable, or combine the styles in any way that makes sense. Just remember, having an investing style—*any* investing style—is better than having no style at all.

CHAPTER 4

Strategies for Growth Investing

Growth investors want to own the fastest-growing companies in the market and they're generally willing to pay whatever it takes to own them. High-growth companies are measured by gains in earnings per share (EPS), and growth investors seek a minimum annual growth rate of 15 to 20 percent, generally much higher. Growth investors expect that by buying and holding such stocks over a long period the price of the stocks—and thus the growth portfolio—will also grow more than 15 or 20 percent a year.

All of which is good. But high-growth stocks are also high-risk stocks. Because of investors' willingness to pay premium prices for high-growth stocks, these stocks frequently sell at generous price-to-earnings (P/E) ratios. Implicit in this willingness to pay premium prices is the assumption that such stocks deserve higher-than-average multiples because of their growth potential. It is further assumed that these high P/Es should stay relatively stable as the company continues to roll off its high earnings growth rate over the next 3 to 10 years. But high P/Es are very vulnerable to changes in the perception of that future growth or to a lessening of investor confidence in that growth. Such changes in perception or confidence can cause rather dramatic drops in the P/E ratio of growth stocks.

We're not trying to discourage you from being a growth investor, as there are ways to protect yourself from the worst risks, but you should be aware of what can happen. A good example of the vulnerability of high P/Es is the Cisco story.

In the 1990s Cisco Systems (CSCO) was the quintessential growth stock, growing at a rate of 30 to 50 percent per year for almost a decade. A provider of communications equipment and solutions for the Internet, Cisco totally dominated its industry. But in late 2000 Cisco warned that it was not going to be able to grow indefinitely at such a rate, due to the technology glut, the dot-com meltdown, and problems within the domestic and international economies. Cisco was still a strong growth franchise and still dominated its industry, but, after the announcement, investor confidence in super growth began to wane rapidly. Investors who had been willing to pay upward of 100 times earnings suddenly balked. They took Cisco at its word that the 30 to 50 percent growth rate could not be sustained and refused to pay the high P/E. Despite the fact that nothing terrible actually happened to the company—other than a slowing of earnings—the stock fell more than 75 percent over a *4-month period* (Figure 4–1). The result was very painful to those who saw their holdings drop from over $50 a share to about $13, and for those who had been holding Cisco since 1999, the drop from $80 to $13 was even more painful.

F I G U R E   4–1

Cisco Systems fell more than 75 percent from December 11, 2000, to April 6, 2001.

Vulnerability to high P/Es is a common risk with high-growth stocks and one that the growth investor must be willing to accept. This is one of the reasons that we believe an exit signal is important to help mitigate this risk, even for long-term growth investors. Keep in mind that risk varies among industries. In an industry like the Internet where valuations were extraordinarily high, the risk is also extraordinarily high. If you are somewhat risk-averse but still want to be a growth investor, you might want to concentrate on industries that aren't quite as volatile as the Internet.

THE PQ CHART OF A GROWTH INVESTOR

As you can see from the PQ Chart in Figure 4–2, it takes an interesting combination of traits to be a successful growth investor. You need relatively high levels of patience and risk tolerance because you must be able to endure possible dramatic market fluctuations due to the vulnerability of high P/Es.

Because of its long-term nature, growth investing doesn't require a lot of portfolio management, so you don't need to spend as much time on this task as you do with certain other styles. Just be sure to set up the appropriate e-mail alerts for your stops and also for news on your stocks so that you can be aware of setbacks for your holdings or the beginning of any erosion of confidence in the company or industry. Certainly the most important time to scrutinize your holdings is during earnings season because quarterly earnings are the barometer of whether or not the growth is still there *and* at the level you assumed when you originally bought the stock.

A typical growth investor can do well with modest quantitative skills and minimal technical skills. The need for discipline is also modest because of the buy-and-hold nature of growth investing. The most urgent need for discipline is to keep your fingers off the sell button when the stock goes through a minor fluctuation.

ANATOMY OF A GROWTH STOCK

Growth stocks can be found in virtually any sector or industry group. They may be small companies that have the ability to grow extraordinarily fast, mid-sized companies moving into dominance in an old or a new industry, or large industry leaders that can sus-

F I G U R E   4–2

PQ Chart of a Growth Investor

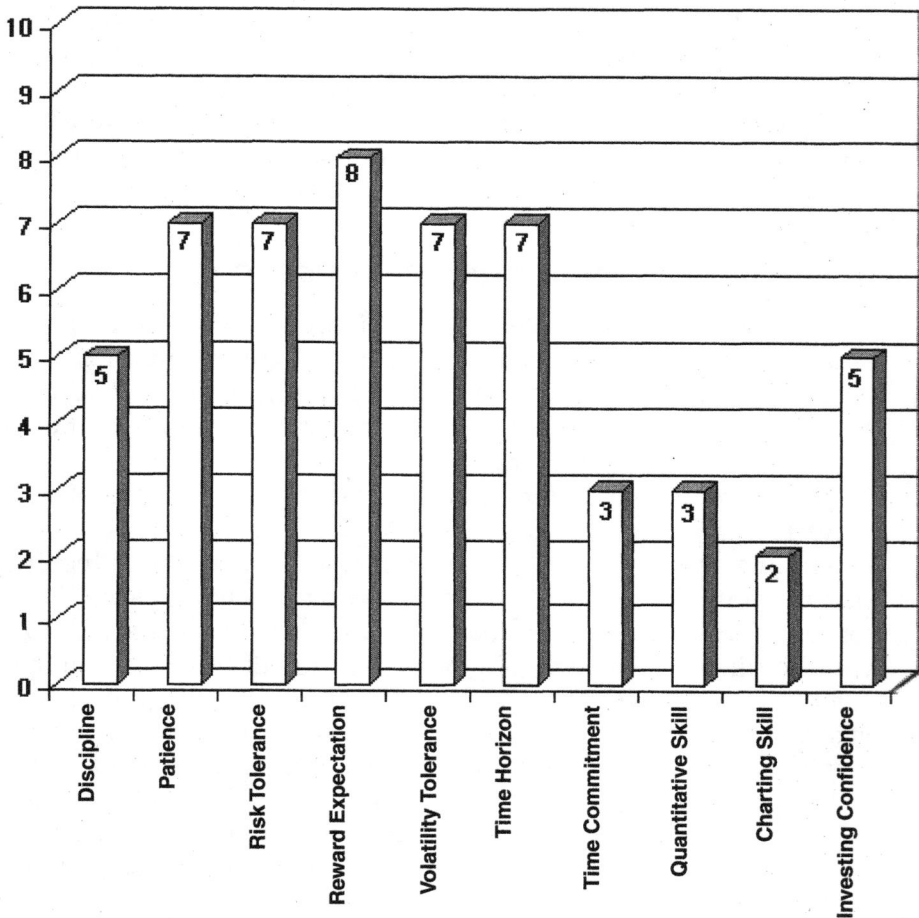

tain their earnings growth rates far into the future. There are also emerging growth companies with new technologies that have not yet had tremendous earnings growth but are poised to take off. The typical growth stock, however, is usually in a growth industry— a sector of the economy in which revenues are expanding very rap- idly.

In late 2001 two of the best growth industries were telecommunications and genetic engineering, both high-tech industries that were growing much faster than the rest of the economy. But we shouldn't write off the more traditional industries just because they've been around for a while. Certain industries always seem to spawn exceptional growth stocks. Pharmaceuticals, for example, may be past its aggressive growth phase, but it is likely to continue as a growth industry as aging Baby Boomers begin to fill up their medicine cabinets. The entertainment industry, especially the gaming group, is booming now because of the proliferation of casinos and the public's changing attitude about gambling. And the restaurant industry continually serves up a few high-growth stocks. In fact, you can always find a growth company within a nongrowth industry if the company has a technological advantage, an aggressive management style, or a strong brand name. These are the primary attributes of a good growth company, whatever its industry.

Technology, Management, and Brands: The Forces that Create Growth Stocks

A new or superior technology is always a hotbed for growth stocks. That's why many growth investors look for stocks in the sexy high-tech sector. In a high-tech industry such as telecommunications or the Internet, the leading growth stocks are easily recognized by their superior brand names (think AOL and Yahoo!) or aggressive management styles (think Intel and Microsoft). But there is a disadvantage in concentrating on high-tech growth stocks. In most cases, revenue growth outpaces earnings, which can lead to inflated price-to-earnings ratios, and inflated P/Es create higher than normal risk. If investor confidence falls or the earnings themselves are revised downward, then the P/E must come into line. You saw what happened to Cisco—and hundreds of other Internet-related stocks—in 2001.

Those who believe that growth companies must be technologically based will probably be "trapped" into buying high-multiple, high-risk stocks. But high-growth stocks do exist in the mundane Old Economy industries. What could be less exciting than a funeral home? Well, take a look at Service Corp. International (SRV), which owns more than 4000 of them.

SRV has been around since 1974 and is the largest funeral ser-

FIGURE 4-3

11/29/01 $5.90 SERVICE CORP INTL (SRV)10 Years Log

30 30
20 20
12 12
8 8

4 4

Volume (in hundreds) - max: 429740
4297 4297
3500 3500
2500 2500
1500 1500

1990s   2000s

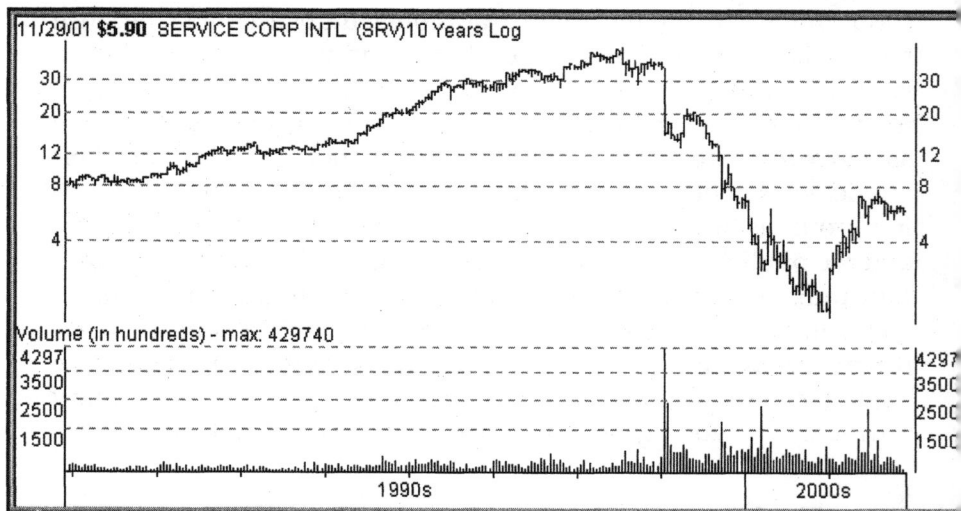

Service Corporation International was a respectable growth stock
through the 1990s—before the bottom fell out in 1999.

vices company in the world. As you can see in Figure 4–3, it took a
nasty drop in 1999–2000, but over a 10-year period from 1988 to 1998
SRV averaged more than 15 percent per year in earnings growth.
This placed SRV in the upper echelon of growth stocks during that
period, and they did it not through superior technology but through
superior aggressive management.

Superior management can turn an ordinary company into a
growth stock, as it did with SRV, and it can turn an unknown company into a superior brand, as an upstart retailer did in the 1970s.
Sam Walton began with an unprecedented concept to build large
discount stores in smaller cities, and his aggressive management
team turned Wal-Mart (WMT) into a perennial growth stock and
one of the enduring name brands of America. After almost 30 years,
you'd think Wal-Mart would have peaked as a growth stock, but
take a look at Figure 4–4. During the 1990s its earnings grew nearly 25 percent per year, its stock price grew more than 1000 percent,
and today Wal-Mart is the number one retailer in the United States.

Aggressive management or superior technology (or both) is

FIGURE 4-4

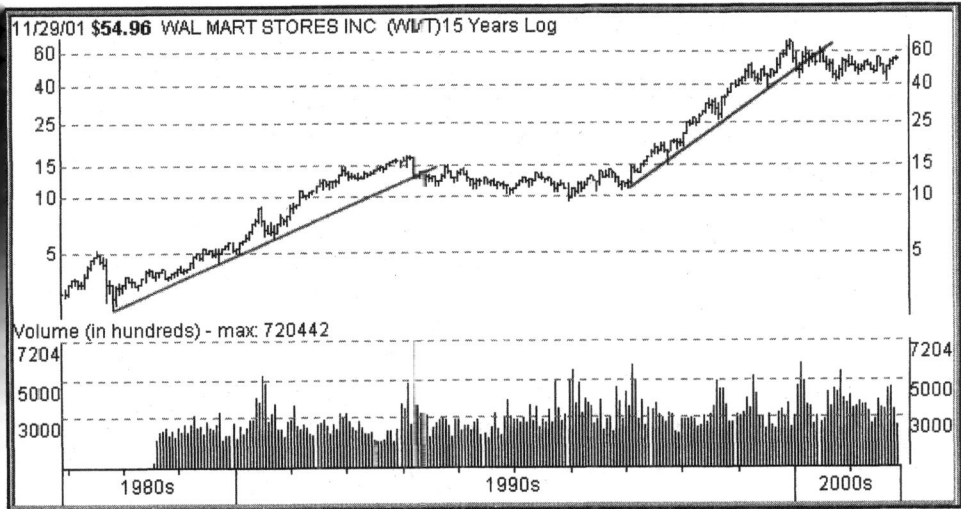

11/29/01 $54.96 WAL MART STORES INC (WMT)15 Years Log

Wal-Mart (WMT) had a growth surge in the late 1980s and early 1990s,
and then participated in the bull market of the late 1990s.

what creates superior brands. In a new industry like the Internet, superior brands are sometimes made just by getting there first. Witness companies like Yahoo! (YHOO) and Amazon.com (AMZN),
which dominated the Internet early on. But it will take superior
management to stay in front of the pack and remain tomorrow's
leaders.

Coca-Cola (KO) was one of those who got there first in the soft
drink industry, and it had the superior management to turn Coke
into one of the best-known brands in the world and keep it growing
steadily over the decades. Between 1990 and 1998 Coke enjoyed a
renewed burst of energy, with nearly a 30 percent per year price
growth rate (Figure 4–5). The latest growth spurt was due in part
because management launched an aggressive expansion into over-
seas markets.

Procter & Gamble (PG) is another big brand name that had a
long run as a growth stock (Figure 4–6). In the early 1990s, Procter
& Gamble was growing at a rate in the low teens with an average
P/E of about 17, but its valuation got ahead of itself in the euphoria

FIGURE 4–5

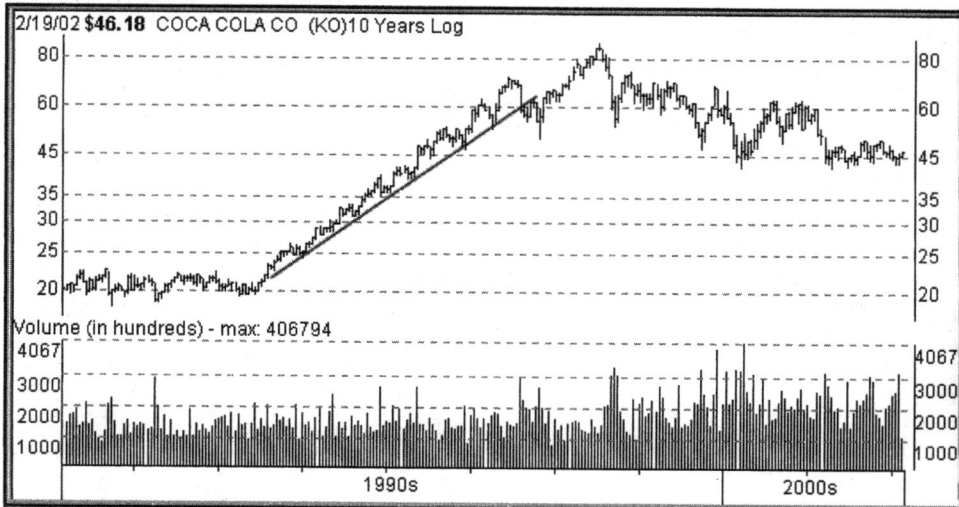

2/19/02 **$46.18** COCA COLA CO (KO)10 Years Log

Coca-Cola (KO) saw a new surge of growth in the mid-1990s. The stock suffered a setback even before the spring 2000 sell-off.

of the 1990s bull market. By the spring of 2000, PG's earnings growth had slowed to nearly 10 percent while its P/E had grown to well over 30, and when it fell, it fell hard.

As you can see, good growth stocks can be found in all sectors of the market. Not all have superior technology, a superior brand, *and* superior management, but a company that exhibits any—or any combination—of these three attributes is worth a second look. You just have to be aware of inappropriately high P/Es.

When Is a Growth Stock Not a Growth Stock?

A growth stock is not a growth stock when it stops growing. Obviously. But it's not quite that simple.

The barometer of growth is earnings, and a slowdown in earnings growth is an obvious clue that a growth stock may no longer be a growth stock. We just talked about the slowing earnings that stopped Procter & Gamble in its tracks. Like many other stocks in the booming economy of the late 1990s, PG's stock price had risen

FIGURE 4–6

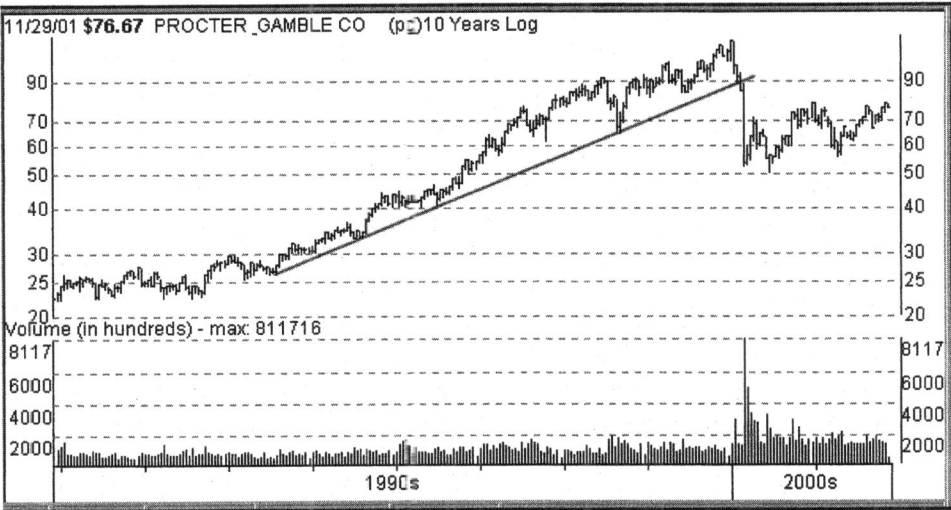

11/29/01 $76.67 PROCTER _GAMBLE CO (p)10 Years Log

Procter & Gamble (PG) had a steady uptrend through the last half of the 1990s.

far beyond the growth of its business and its earnings. So had Wal-Mart and Service Corp. International, as you can see from their charts in the previous section. (Figures 4–3 and 4–4). Wal-Mart started out the decade with an earnings growth rate percentage in the low 20s with an average P/E of about 30, but by the spring of 2000, its growth rate had slowed to 15 percent while its P/E expanded to 35. Like other overvalued stocks, Wal-Mart's price dropped as the P/E corrected. But Wal-Mart's price drop wasn't as dramatic as Service Corp. International's. SRV was growing more than 15 percent per year in the early 1990s with an average P/E of 17, but then slowed to somewhat less than 15 percent while its P/E expanded to 25. Severe earnings difficulties surfaced in 1999 and 2000, which caused SRV's plunge to the bottom of the chart (Figure 4–3).

Bloated P/Es and slowing earnings were the order of the day in the late 1990s, even for the large, conservative companies, and that is why these stocks fell so dramatically in 2000 and 2001. You simply cannot pay more for growth than the underlying earnings can sustain. If you will recall the hypothetical example in Chapter 1, we demonstrated how a drop from 20 to 10 percent in the underlying growth rate of earnings can, for good reason, drop the stock price anywhere from 50 to 75 percent.

The first sign of a slowdown in earnings is a reduction in the analysts' forecasts or an earnings warning by the company. If the lower earnings do indeed come to pass, you will need to take a hard look at the company and decide whether or not the reduced earnings are a sign of a permanent slowdown in the EPS growth rate or a temporary aberration. How can you tell? Look at the reasons the company gives for its projected performance.

For example, if a manufacturer with a 20 percent earnings growth rate suddenly warned that it might grow only 10 percent this quarter because it couldn't get parts, the stock price would no doubt take a hit. But if the company says the parts supplier has solved its problems and it expects earnings to resume soon, the blip in the stock performance might be temporary. You have to decide whether or not to believe the explanation, but if analysts are backing up the company's statement, there's probably no reason to be concerned. In industries like biotechnology or the Internet, such hiccups are frequent.

Remember, though, that high P/Es of growth stocks create a nervous environment. Worried that the P/E might fall, perhaps dramatically, investors sometimes act on unfounded rumors or fears. It's not that suddenly they have no confidence; it's just that a misplaced rumor about a problem agitates this nervous environment, and reactionary selling sets in. A plummeting P/E becomes a self-fulfilling prophecy.

Another clue that a growth stock is no longer a growth stock is declining margins. Declining margins are frequently a precursor of changes in long-term earnings—clearly not good news for a growth stock. Declining margins can be caused by price competition, by price instability in raw materials, or by rising labor costs, but whatever the cause, if you see signs of declining margins, you need to take a good hard look at the stock.

The point at which a growth stock ceases to be a growth stock boils down to this: If the reasons why you bought the stock in the first place change, the stock may no longer be for you. If you bought a stock based on an aggressive CEO and he or she is fired, retired, or takes off for places unknown, the growth may be in for a slowdown. (It might be prudent, however, to evaluate the new CEO before you make a decision.) If you bought a growth stock based on proprietary technology and the company's patents begin expiring (which frequently happens in the pharmaceutical industry), the stock's future prospects could change abruptly. A new, competitive technology can also cast a pall over the future of a growth stock. We all remember how the advent of the personal computer in the early 1980s sent a shock wave through established computer giants like IBM.

But don't let a temporary aberration throw you off course. As a growth investor, you're in for the long haul. As long as a superior management team is still in place, as long as earnings or revenues are on track, as long as the company remains a leader in its field and continues to grab market share, hang on and enjoy the ride. That's what growth investing is all about.

The Price According to GARP

In the late 1990s it was not uncommon for stocks to be selling at 3 and 4 times their growth rate. For example, companies with 20 percent earnings growth rates frequently had P/Es of 60 or 80. The astute investor knows that, mathematically, 3 or 4 times earnings growth rates simply can't work in the long run. It's the greater fool syndrome: If I buy at 4 times earnings growth, I have to hope there is a bigger fool out there who will come along and buy the stock at 5 times earnings growth, or more. (Recall our discussion of P/Es in Chapter 1.)

In the spring of 2000, every stock related to the Internet took a hit. The aftermath of the sell-off appeared to present a good buying opportunity for stocks like Cisco and Yahoo!, which had the strength of their brand names and aggressive management styles to pull them through. But could you have judged the bottom? By October 2000 Cisco had lost more than 50 percent of its value, and Yahoo! had shrunk by two-thirds. They might have looked like bargains at the time, but both stocks had much farther to fall. Cisco and Yahoo! have recovered to their pre-September 11 values, but remain at 80 percent and 90 percent, respectively, from their all-time highs of 1999.

After the dot-com crash, GARP—growth at a reasonable price— became the buzzword on Wall Street. But what, exactly, is growth at a reasonable price?

> For years, growth gurus like Peter Lynch have said growth investors should pay no more than 1 times the EPS growth rate. (By EPS growth rate we mean the annual growth rate of earnings per share over the last 3 to 5 years and projected over the next 3 to 5 years, not simply quarter-over-quarter earnings.) That would mean, for a stock growing at 20 percent per year, you would pay no more than 20 times earnings, or a P/E of 20. Peter Lynch didn't use the word GARP, but he was talking about growth at a reasonable price.
>
> But GARP is inversely affected by the general level of interest rates. In the low interest rate environment of 2000–2001, most experts would concede that up to 1.5 times the growth rate would be reasonable. That translates to a P/E of 20 to 30 for a growth stock with an EPS growth rate of 20 percent a year. The reason that investors will pay higher multiples when fixed income investments fall is that bondholders seek out better returns from equities, thereby bidding up the P/E ratios of stocks. In addition, when future receipts are discounted at a lower interest rate, the result is higher prices than we can afford to pay today. But even a 1 percent interest rate would not justify P/Es of 3 and 4 times the growth rate.

THE INVESTING PROCESS FOR GROWTH INVESTORS

The investing process that we outlined in Chapter 2—selecting stocks, timing entries and exits, and managing a portfolio—is the foundation of any style. In growth investing, however, the major emphasis should be on stock selection since timing is less of a factor in the overall scheme of growth investing.

Stock Selection Strategies: Finding Good Growth Stocks

Stock selection is critical for the growth investor, so your first question should be, How can I find the best growth stocks? You might do as Peter Lynch, the world's most famous growth investor, suggests, and observe your environment. If you look at all those people walking around with cell phones and pagers, you might conclude that telecommunications, especially the wireless group, is the place to be. That's how many investors discovered great growth stocks like Starbucks and Krispy Kreme, by noticing the stores that are pro-viding a great service in their neighborhoods.

The Peter Lynch way is fine, if you're interested in retail stocks and if the stock is reasonably priced. A more precise way to find growth stocks is to use one of the many screening programs or search filters on the Internet, some of which are described in Appendix A. The trick is to build a search filter that will sort through all 10,000 listed stocks and come up with the ones with the best growth at a reasonable price.

In building a search filter for growth stocks you have to decide whether you are going to focus on projected earnings growth or historical earnings growth. (We recommend a balance of both.) You must decide whether to look for large dominant companies or small emerging companies. You need to consider the limits on how much you will pay for growth, as we discussed in the section about GARP.

Here are the screening criteria we recommend for a search filter:

- *Highest projected growth of earnings per share for the next 1 to 5 years.* This is the definition of a growth stock. Future earn-ings are what we're buying.

- *Highest 1-year, 3-year, and 5-year historical growth of earnings per share.* Strong historical earnings growth proves that the company can produce earnings. This earnings growth gives us confidence that the company can live up to its projected EPS growth rate. Otherwise, we're just speculating.

- *Expanding profit margins.* Expanding margins mean that things are going very well for the company and that every dollar of sales will produce more profits, that is, more earn-ings per share.

- *High quarter-over-quarter EPS growth rates, both historical and current.* These criteria provide evidence that the growth is consistent and continuous.

- *Consistency of positive earnings surprises.* If a company ex-ceeds its estimates on a regular basis, it is a sign of good management. If the company misses estimates on a regular basis, it is a sign that management is not controlling costs or revenues or both. A one-time negative surprise may not

be management's fault—it could be caused by the economy or overly optimistic analysts—but negative surprises
hurt, whatever the cause.

+ *High insider buying.* If insiders put their own money in their
company's stock, they obviously believe in the company's
growth prospects—which gives us confidence to believe in
it too.

+ *Recent increases in the estimated growth of near-term earnings.*
A positive change in analysts' estimates is one of the best
predictors of an increase in stock price. As we've said, it
takes a separate initiative for analysts to issue a change,
once original estimates are made, so raising the estimates
sends a very positive signal to the market. It gives us confidence that they really do believe in the company's future.

+ *High revenue growth rates.* Revenue growth is especially per-
tinent in fledgling industries such as the Internet or a re-
search-heavy industry such as biotechnology. In these en-
vironments, we reward companies that exhibit revenue
growth, even when they have little or no earnings growth.
Rapidly increasing revenues is one way to recognize a
young high-tech growth stock.

+ *Reasonable P/E ratio compared to historical and projected earnings growth.* This ensures that the growth we're buying is at
a reasonable price—the GARP rule.

A search using these criteria—or as many of them as your
search program offers—will give you a short list of 25 or so high-
growth stocks. What you need to do now is to narrow the list down
to the four or five best candidates for purchase.

Evaluating a Short List of Growth Stocks

A good way to find the best growth stocks in a list of stocks that are
all considered high-growth stocks is to eliminate the ones with weak-
nesses in various areas. The list of questions in Table 4–1 can help
you upgrade or downgrade the stocks on your list. Then you can
consider those with the most upgrades as potential buy candidates.

This evaluation process can winnow out the weakest stocks,
but keep in mind that one or two negatives do not necessarily elim-

TABLE 4–1

Evaluating a Growth Stock

Evaluation Question	Upgrade	Downgrade
Does the stock show signs of upward momentum?	Yes	No
Does the stock show huge drops and steep rises, or does it move in a relatively smooth fashion?	Relatively smooth line	Too many ups and downs
Compared with other stocks on your list, does the stock have among the highest 5-year earnings growth rate?	Yes	No
Have analysts been revising earnings estimates higher or lower?	Higher	Lower
How many analysts offer EPS projections?	More than 5	Less than 5
Have there been any earnings surprises, good or bad?	Surprises are positive	Surprises are negative
How many buy, hold, or sell recommendations does the stock have?	Mostly buys	More holds and sells than buys
How does the P/E ratio to growth rate compare with the industry average and the S&P 500?	Same or below	Higher
Has there been any recent bad news on the company, good or bad?	Good news	Bad news
Has there been recent insider buying or selling?	Buyers outnumber sellers	Sellers outnumber buyers
How is the stock's industry group doing?	Above average	Below average

inate a stock. What you're looking for is a "preponderance of evidence," in the words of well-known economist Martin Pring, that points to the winning stocks.

Entry/Exit Strategies: How Not to Get Caught in a Meltdown

There are those who say growth investors don't need technical signals for entering and exiting stocks. They believe growth stocks should be bought and held and that growth investors should be willing to stomach any price reversal as long as things are going well in the company. While we do agree that timing methods for growth investors are not as important as in other styles, because of the long holding periods for growth stocks, we think it is essential to have a timing indicator that will keep you out of a meltdown. As we've said, it is not uncommon for a high P/E growth stock that has an earnings hiccup to decline 50 to 75 percent. If you are caught in this kind of a meltdown, it can destroy several years of good performance in your portfolio.

Moreover, when a growth stock's price weakens, especially if the weakening is significant (more than 20 percent), you as a stockholder have no way of knowing for certain that it is not the beginning of a secular decline, that the times have simply changed. Look at some of the dot-com meltdowns in 2000 and 2001, where declines of 70 to 95 percent were rampant. Such steep declines were caused predominantly by the gradual realization that Internet ad rates were falling far short of expectations. Even those companies that had successfully marketed their ads, such as Amazon.com, still faced very steep declines in advertising revenue, which was a critical revenue stream. It now appears that Internet stocks were in a secular decline. Whether the decline is short-term or long-term, it is too soon to tell.

Lest you think that the Internet is an isolated example, secular declines have also occurred in the biotech industry. In the early 1970s investors in biotechs went into a period of euphoria when everyone thought they were going to get rich on biotech stocks. Then investors began to realize that the technical challenge was greater than originally thought and the process of obtaining FDA approval turned out to be much longer and much more difficult than imagined. Reality set in and the whole industry went into a decline, falling nearly 60 percent in the late 1980s. The sector then recovered and expanded about tenfold during the 1990s, then fell back in the dot-com crash. The same euphoria-reality cycle has hit other sectors including real estate investment trusts (REITs) and franchise stocks. No one is smart enough to foresee all that can happen, so why not use a technical indicator to protect against serious erosion if you make a mistake in a new purchase. We also recommend setting loose, trailing stops to protect your profits.

Protecting Your Profits

To protect your profits, we suggest you set a "loose" stop for every stock, by which we mean a reminder to yourself to reevaluate the stock if it should fall to a certain price level, such as a support level. E-mail alerts, which are available in many online portfolios, can be used for loose stops. Just enter the stop price as the alert price. As the stock moves up, be sure to move up the stop as well, so that it is always within, say, 10 percent of the current stock price (this is called a trailing stop). When you get an e-mail alert that a stop has been reached, you can reevaluate the stock for a possible sell. A hard stop—the kind that triggers an automatic sell—is not recommended since it can take you out of a stock that you might not want to sell.

Technical exits can be accomplished with an appropriate timing indicator, such as a moving average crossover or a weekly MACD. If you use a moving average crossover, you might reevaluate your stock when it dips below its 50-day moving average as Cisco did in April 2000 (Figure 4–7). If you use the MACD, you would reevaluate the stock when it goes into negative territory on a weekly MACD, as Cisco did at about the same time as it crossed below its 50-day moving average (the lower graph in Figure 4–7).

In the "Tale of Two Stocks" in the Introduction, we told you about two stocks—M.S. Carriers (MSCA) and Vignette Corporation (VIGN)—which came to our attention as top candidates on November 11, 2000. The stock graph in Figure I–1 shows that MSCA proceeded to go up while VIGN proceeded to go down. This is where a timing signal, such as a weekly MACD, would have saved you from VIGN's decline and let you ride your profits with MSCA. As you can see in Figure 4–8, the weekly MACD for VIGN went negative around November 16, which would have taken you out of the stock shortly after you bought it (if you bought it on November 11), and would have kept you from getting back in because the weekly MACD stayed in negative territory through December, even though the daily MACD (shown in the same Figure 4–8) went positive in early December. M.S. Carriers was acquired by Swift Transportation (SWFT) in June 2001 and its stock graph, unfortunately, is no longer

FIGURE 4–7

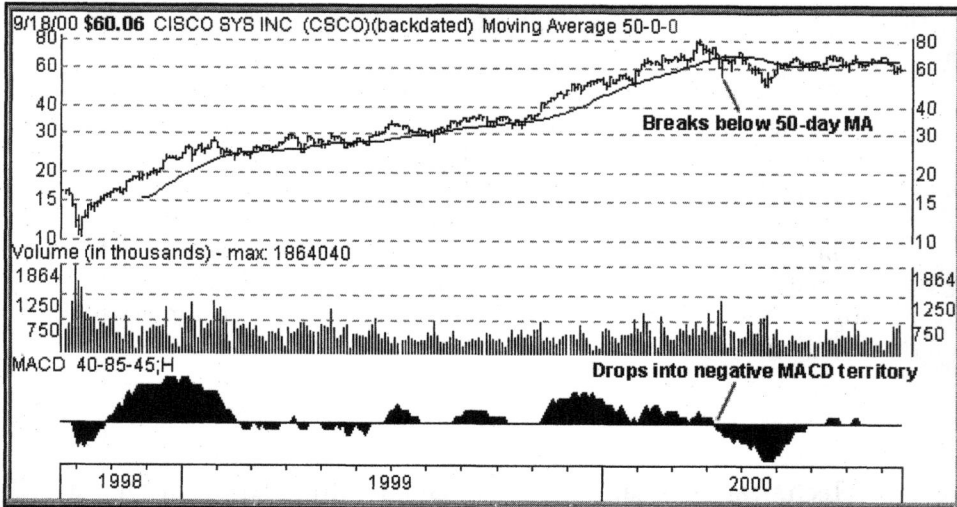

A sell signal was given in late April 2000 when Cisco dropped below its 50-day moving average. That was the beginning of its year-long slide in which it lost more than 75 percent of its value (see Figure 4–1). In late April 2000 Cisco also dropped into negative MACD territory, which would have taken you out of the stock before it began its descent.

available, but based on our research at the time, MSCA's weekly MACD never did go negative, so you would have ridden your profits all the way to the top.

There are many mechanical trading systems that can be used for timing your exit; some are listed in Appendix A.

Timing your *entry* into a growth stock is not critical, but we would suggest using the same indicator to enter a position that you use to prevent a loss. In other words, if you're going to sell a stock on a negative weekly MACD, it doesn't make a great deal of sense to enter a stock that has given or is close to giving a negative signal. Just wait until it turns positive. Similarly, if you're using a 200-day moving average as an exit signal, don't enter the position with the

FIGURE 4-8

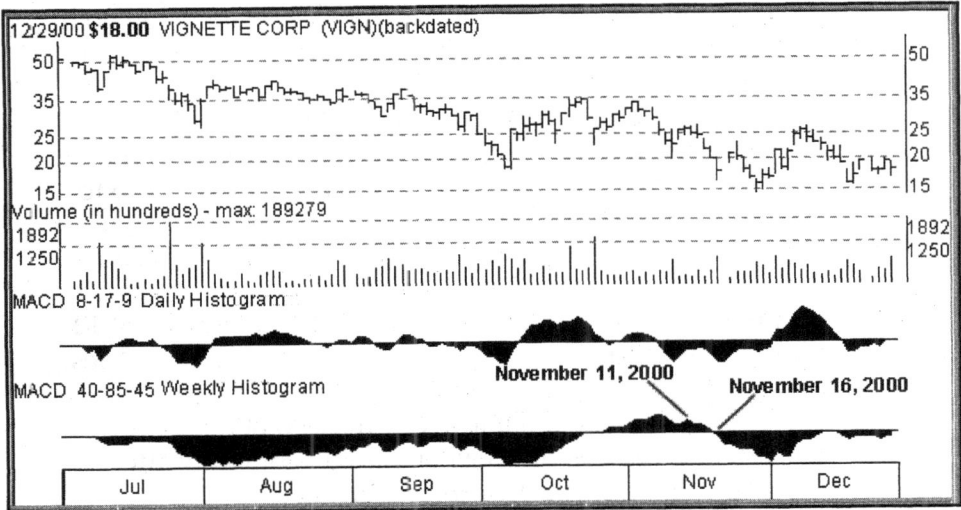

12/29/00 **$18.00** VIGNETTE CORP (VIGN)(backdated)

Volume (in hundreds) - max: 189279

MACD 8-17-9 Daily Histogram

MACD 40-85-45 Weekly Histogram

November 11, 2000   November 16, 2000

Jul | Aug | Sep | Oct | Nov | Dec

The daily 8/17/9 MACD shows VIGN in oversold territory in November 2000, and there was not a positive MACD signal until early December. But the negative weekly MACD (lower graph) would have taken you out of VIGN in mid-November and kept you out all the way through December.

stock below the average. Wait until it crosses back above the average.

Growth Portfolio Strategies

Growth portfolios are relatively low maintenance. While a lot of time and care are required to build a growth portfolio, once you're fully invested it doesn't need day-to-day attention. With appropriate e-mail alerts to notify you of unusual price moves or breaking news, you can check your stock charts once a week and pay special attention to the news during earnings season.

Here are some portfolio management strategies to keep in mind in building and managing your portfolio.

- *Diversify stocks and industries.* Because of the high risk factor of growth stocks—recall the vulnerability of high P/Es—diversification is very important. You can diversify by holding more rather than fewer stocks and by buying stocks in several different industries.

  The prudent growth investor will likely hold eight or more stocks, although if you can commit sufficient time to monitoring them we would recommend as many as 15 to spread the risk. With 15 stocks, even a 50 percent drop in one of them will decrease your entire portfolio only about 3 percent. It is not difficult to find 200 or 300 strong growth companies at any given time, so building a portfolio of 12 to 15 stocks over time, spread over three to five industries, would shelter you from a sudden decline in one of the stocks. And that would allow you to sleep better during uncertain economic times when growth company after growth company issue earnings warnings.

- *Monitor your portfolio regularly.* Even medium-term and long-term growth investors should monitor their stocks at least weekly to keep an eye out for events that might negatively affect market perception or investor confidence. With their high P/Es, growth stocks are particularly susceptible to changes in perception and confidence. (You might want to review the list of events in Chapter 1 that can change market perception and investor confidence.)

  During earnings season, pay particular attention to your portfolio in the week or two preceding the earnings announcements. Be particularly sensitive to the whisper numbers. These are frequently as important as the published estimates, particularly for stocks that regularly surprise to the upside. Once you find out that earnings are on track, you can (somewhat) relax your vigil for another quarter.

- *Monitor your cash position.* When the market is overextended (at an extreme high), increasing your cash position is another way to protect yourself. It makes sense when stocks reach historically high valuations, as the Nasdaq did in late 2000 (see Chapter 2), for you to put aside 10 to 30 percent of your portfolio in cash. This can be accomplished in most cases by simply not replacing stocks that are stopped out due to weakness.

CASE STUDY: METRO ONE COMMUNICATIONS

The objective of this case study was to identify a high-growth small-cap company for investment in order to demonstrate the selection process for growth stocks.

MTON: A Small-cap Growth Stock

On October 25, 2001, Metro One Telecommunications (MTON) appeared as one of the top stocks for high-growth companies within the small-cap universe. It had a market cap of $689.3 million and a P/E ratio of 23.70 based on FY 2001 EPS estimates. MTON scored exceptionally well for the basic characteristics of a growth stock:

- Most recent year (FY 2000) historical earnings growth rate: 365 percent
- 5-year historical earnings growth rate: 87 percent
- 1-year projected earnings growth rate (FY 2001): 106 percent
- 5-year projected earnings growth rate: 27 percent

Who Is MTON?

The first step in our evaluation process was to find out a little bit about the company. (Web sites that provide company profiles and related information are listed in Appendix A.) Metro One provides "enhanced directory assistance" (EDA) for the wireless telecommunications industry through more than 25 call centers in major cities throughout the United States. The service of a live operator is one of the features of MTON's value-added products. Others include call completion, category searches, local turn-by-turn driving directions, restaurant reservations, local events, attractions, and movie listings. MTON's customers include some of the biggest wireless carriers, such as AT&T Wireless, Sprint PCS, Nextel, and Pacific Bell

Wireless, and the company has expanded into land-line telecommunications as a service provider to GST Communications.

A Look at the Chart

As you can see from the chart in Figure 4–9, MTON had climbed from a low of $6 in 2000 to a high of $44 in mid-2001. It gave back part of those gains after July 2001, but in late October it was still well above its 2000 low. Over a 3-year period MTON's stock price increased by a factor of 10, and part of that exceptional growth was in the second half of 2000 and first half of 2001 when other stocks were doing poorly. The rebound from its September 25 low of $22 to $31 in late October was very encouraging.

The Growth Stock Evaluation Checklist

MTON grew its earnings some 365 percent in FY 2000 and at an 87 percent annual rate over the previous 5 years. Revenues and cash flow also skyrocketed during this period. Since peaking in July 2001,

FIGURE 4–9

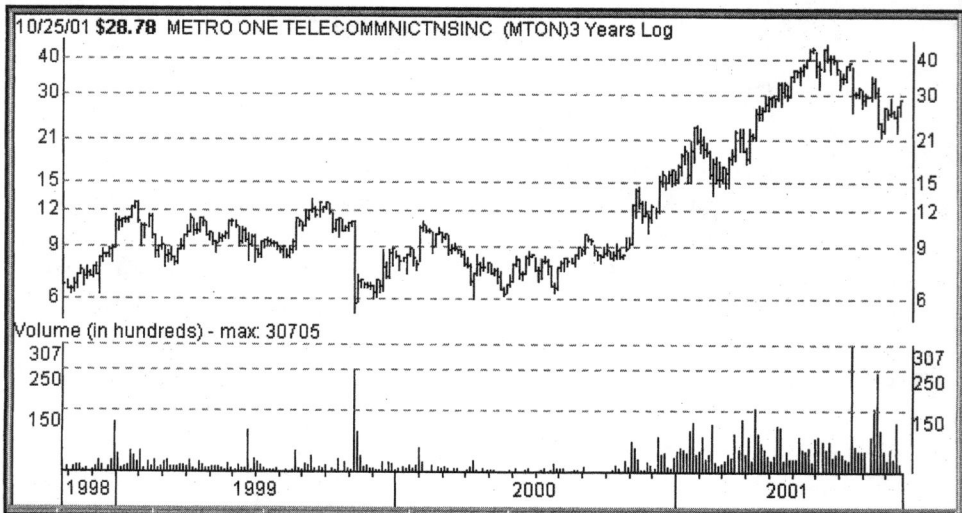

This chart shows the price growth of MTON over the past 3 years.

MTON had lost about 50 percent of its value by late October due to profit taking and the sell-off after the terrorist attacks, but then rebounded to $31. The price drop did nothing but enhance MTON's valuation. At the time of this study, MTON was still one of the high-ranking stocks on growth characteristics and passed the Growth Stock Evaluation Checklist with minor exceptions:

+ *Historical growth rate.* With a 5-year earnings growth rate of 87 percent and a 1-year earnings growth rate of 365 percent, MTON ranked in the 99th percentile of all stocks in short-term growth and 97th percentile in long-term growth.

+ *Analyst revisions.* Analysts made upward revisions of 0.9 percent for FY 2001. This was especially noteworthy because in October 2001 the high preponderance of revisions was downward, not upward.

+ *Earnings surprises.* MTON had positive earnings surprises in four out of the previous four quarters. This was outstanding in a period in which the country was headed for a recession.

+ *Number of analysts.* Six analysts were covering MTON, which is good coverage for a small-cap stock.

+ *Buy/hold/sell recommendations.* There were five buys (one strong and four moderate) and one hold; there were no sell recommendations.

+ *Comparison to industry and S&P 500.* MTON's P/E ratio and earnings growth compared well with the S&P 500 and the industry group:

	EPS Growth Rate for 2001	P/E on 2001 EPS
MTON	108.9%	23.9
S&P 500	−14.1%	22.3
Telecom Equipment/Services Group	−1.1%	N/A

+ *Recent news:* On October 16, 2001, MTON was ranked 6th in Forbes' annual list of the 200 Best Small Companies in America.

- *Insider trading:* There had been no insider buying at the time of the study. Insider selling had been modest over the past year, considering that the sales represented a relatively small percentage of the holdings of the selling shareholders and many of the sellers were exercising options. Technology companies often use stock as part of an incentive package, which generally makes insider selling less significant. Additionally, insider selling has not been particularly predictive of stock price changes in the past for most stocks.
- *Volatility:* The stock had exhibited a great deal of volatility since July, more than likely due to profit-taking in a difficult market—a slight negative.
- *Upward momentum:* Although it had been on a downtrend (with brief rallies) since mid-July, the stock was exhibiting signs of upward momentum in late October.
- *Industry group performance:* The Telecommunications/Equipment-Services industry group had been in the doldrums for the previous 9 months, although in mid-October it appeared to be on a slight upswing. It is worth noting that while MTON was 33 percent off its highs at the time of the study, its industry group was nearly 70 percent off its highs, so the stock had performed well with respect to its industry group. Nevertheless, the poor industry group performance was a negative.

Conclusion: MTON—An Exceptional Growth Candidate

With surging revenues behind its earnings momentum, strong cash flow growth rates, and recent upward revision in short-term earnings estimates, MTON was very attractive at the prices in October 2001. The stock had rebounded after appearing to find support at $22 and seemed to be resuming its previous price momentum, especially in the short term. Although analysts had raised earnings estimates for FY 2001, additional growth for 2002 was not expected, due apparently to the faltering economy in late 2001. Even so, the 5-year forecasted EPS growth of 27 percent made MTON an exceptional growth candidate, especially since it had demonstrated exceptional growth in the past.

FUNDS FOR THE GROWTH INVESTOR

If you like the philosophy of growth investing but don't want to do it yourself, check out the myriad growth funds. There are small-cap, mid-cap, and large-cap growth funds, as well as international equities growth funds. In most cases, a growth fund will have the word *growth* in its name, but not always. American Century, for example, has aggressive growth funds in the areas of life sciences and technology that are labeled "Specialty Funds." A partial list of fund families appears in Appendix A.

An alternative to traditional mutual funds would be the recent phenomenon called exchange-traded funds (ETFs). (See "The Rise of ETFs.") There are several ETFs that are designed as growth vehicles, including the following from iShares and streetTRACKS:

iShares S&P 500/BARRA Growth Index (IVW)

iShares S&P MidCap 400/BARRA Growth (IJK)

iShares S&P SmallCap 600/BARRA Growth (IJT)

iShares Russell 1000 Growth Index (IWF)

iShares Russell 2000 Growth Index (IWO)

iShares Russell 3000 Growth Index (IWZ)

streetTRACKS DJ US Large Cap Growth (ELG)

streetTRACKS DJ US Small Cap Growth (DSG)

In addition, there are growth-oriented ETFs that are built around growth industries such as biotech, telecommunications, semiconductors, and the Internet. And let's not forget the QQQ, which is a tracking stock for the Nasdaq 100, the largest 100 stocks in the Nasdaq Composite Index.

The Rise of ETFs

Exchange-traded funds (ETFs) are a new breed of investment that has been gaining in popularity over the past 2 years. They are flexible, easy to trade, cost-efficient, and diversified, and they offer certain tax advantages over mutual funds. Called a "hybrid between a stock and a fund" by Barclays (one of the main sponsors of ETFs), exchange-traded funds are index-linked baskets of stocks that trade on a stock exchange like a stock. Two of the original ETFs were the SPDR (pronounced spider), which is based on the S&P 500 index, and DIA-

MONDs, which is based on the Dow Jones Industrial Average. Then came the MidCap SPDR, based on the S&P MidCap 400; WEBS, index funds from Morgan Stanley and Barclays; and QQQ, based on the Nasdaq 100.

Once the concept was proven, ETFs began to proliferate during 1999 and 2000. Barclay's Bank came out with iShares, based on S&P, Russell, and Dow Jones indexes (iShares track investing styles and market caps, as we discuss in Chapter 9). Merrill Lynch sponsors a group of ETFs called HOLDRs, which represent more than a dozen sectors and industry groups. State Street Global Advisors offers a variety of ETFs called streetTRACKS, which are based on indexes of Dow Jones, Wilshire, Morgan Stanley, and *Fortune* magazine. (See Appendix A for Web sites on ETFs.)

At present there are well over 80 ETFs that let you slice the market almost any way you please. No doubt this figure will continue to grow in the coming months and years.

Tips for Selecting a Growth Fund

Following are key questions to ask yourself when evaluating growth funds. Most of the information can be found in the fund profile or prospectus.

- *What is the fund's stated objective?* Look for funds that seek capital growth. Some specify "aggressive growth" while others say "growth and income." The latter would be suitable for the less aggressive growth investor.

- *What is the investment strategy?* Funds usually state their investment strategy in their prospectus and often in an online synopsis. Look for funds that concentrate on high-growth sectors and be sure to note the market cap, if that is important to you.

- *What are the risk factors?* The risk factors of a growth fund will likely be stated as "aggressive risk" or "moderate risk." The fund's profile may also specify other risk factors, such as volatility or sector risk.

- *What is the past performance?* Note how the fund has done over the past 1, 3, and 5 years. Past performance is no guarantee of future performance, of course, but it can certainly provide some clues.

♦ *Who is the portfolio manager?* Note the years of experience and the track record.

♦ *Does the fund have a Morningstar rating?* Morningstar rates funds with one to five stars, which reflect the fund's historical risk-adjusted performance. Four to five stars are considered excellent, but remember that Morningstar's star ranking system is based on the past and is not necessarily indicative of the future. And, not all funds are rated. (Morningstar ratings can be found at www.morningstar.com.)

♦ *What are the top 10 holdings?* Most funds list their top 5 or 10 holdings, although these can change without notice. Some funds also list the major sectors in which they are invested.

♦ *Does the fund represent diversity?* If all your investment capital is allocated to funds, make sure you diversify by seeking out funds in different sectors (and even different fund families). You might also wish to mix domestic funds with global funds to diversify among different economies.

♦ *Have you considered an ETF?* If you want to invest in a particular sector or industry, you might consider an exchange-traded fund (ETF), rather than buying stocks in that industry.

Fund Search Engines

Perhaps the best way to find a fund to match your objectives is to use one of the several free search engines on the Web. Below is a brief overview of Fidelity.com; other mutual fund search engines are described in Appendix A.

Searching for Funds

Fidelity.com (www100.fidelity.com) has more than just profiles of Fidelity funds. It has a search engine that searches across all fund families to find those that match specific keywords. We ran a search using just the keyword *growth* and found 614 possible matches. These were categorized by fund family, investment objective (growth, aggressive growth, growth and income), market cap (large, mid, and small), and by the actual fund names. Click on a fund name to see a profile that provides the objective of the fund, performance figures, Morningstar ratings, management bios, and other facts.

The only thing not provided is the online address for the fund or fund family, which is why we've included a partial list in Appendix A.

Online Resources for Growth Stocks

A list of Web sites that specialize in growth stocks or offer sections on growth stocks appears in Appendix A. Such lists quickly become outdated, however, as new Web sites come online and current sites merge or disappear. To find Web sites relating to growth investing, whenever you might be reading this book, use some of these keywords with any of the major search engines:

GROWTH INVESTING KEYWORDS

aggressive growth funds	growth stock picks
aggressive growth stocks	growth stocks
dominant companies	growth stocks portfolio
emerging growth stocks	high earnings growth
expanding revenues	high-growth stocks
growth funds	highest projected earnings growth
growth industries	hyper-growth stocks
growth sectors	Peter Lynch
growth stock gurus	revenue growth
growth stock newsletter	

HINTS FOR SUCCESSFUL GROWTH INVESTING

Growth investing can be very rewarding, but with great rewards goes great risk. Here are a few hints on how to succeed as a growth investor.

1. *Keep your emotions out of the process.* This is the number one rule for any investor.
2. *Go for the triple play.* Look for a stock that exhibits all three characteristics of a good growth stock: superior brand, superior management, and, if appropriate, superior technology.

3. *Give your stocks the GARP test.* Be sure you're buying growth at a reasonable price—no more than 1.5 times earnings growth rate. Anything higher will make you vulnerable to the fate of high P/Es.

4. *Time your entry.* We've emphasized the importance of exit signals, but in addition, we recommend that you use the same technical indicator to time your entry as you do to time your exit. If you sell when a stock crosses below its 50-day moving average, don't buy a stock that is below its 50-day moving average. Wait until it crosses above the average. If you sell on a negative weekly MACD, don't buy a stock that is in negative MACD territory. Wait until it turns positive.

5. *Watch the industry trend.* If other companies in one of your industries start turning down, it could signal trouble for the whole industry, and that could mean the end of high growth for all related stocks. But you still have to evaluate your particular stock. Some companies are strong enough to withstand a turndown in a cycle. For example, when other retailers were falling right and left during various downturns in the retail industry, Wal-Mart continued very strong. What saw Wal-Mart through the storms were its exceptional vision, its unique business model, and the strength of its brand.

6. *Keep an eye on surprises.* Earnings surprises are a good sign of a growth stock, because good growth companies generally do better than the Street expects. They regularly beat their earnings estimates, which creates quarter after quarter of positive earnings surprises.

7. *Set protective stops.* It is important to set loose stops to protect your profits and to guard against a precipitous decline. Enter the stops in a portfolio e-mail alert program, and when the price falls to your stop price, reevaluate the stock.

8. *Watch for expanding margins.* One of the best signs of impending growth of earnings is expanding profit margins. If your growth stock's margins continue to expand quarter after quarter, you'll know you're on the right track. (And you're on the wrong track if you find the margins are con-

tracting margins.) You'll find this information in the 10K or 10Q.

9. *Use dollar-cost averaging.* If you have limited funds, set up a plan where you invest in growth stocks on a regular schedule. This way, you'll invest at various prices, which will even out the highs and lows. (See Appendix A for online resources that offer monthly direct purchase plans.)

10. *Think long term.* Growth investors buy and hold companies because they expect the stocks will continue to do extraordinarily well regardless of the market climate. But every stock is going to have reversals, especially growth stocks with their high P/Es. If you buy at the high end of the P/E range, you may have some short-term disappointments as the stock goes through its normal ups and downs. When it does fluctuate, take a hard look at it. If the same factors that caused you to buy the stock in the first place are still there, you will probably want to hold on. The whole premise in growth investing is that the long-term growth rate will more than make up for changing fads and fancies in the marketplace.

11. *Know when to fold 'em.* Should you ever sell a growth stock? Of course—when it is no longer a growth stock. This means you need to review your stocks on a regular basis. See if the brand you bought, the management you bought, or the technology you bought continues to have dominance. If you wouldn't buy it again today, based on what you know today, it may be time to sell.

12. *Know when to trade 'em.* Sometimes you should sell a growth stock when it is still a growth stock. If you find a stock that has better growth characteristics than the weakest stock in your portfolio, it might be time to trade in the weak one.

CHAPTER 5

Strategies for Value Investing

Value investors are essentially bargain hunters. They are like the shoppers who haunt sales and discount stores and refuse to buy anything at full price. If stocks were sold at garage sales, value investors would be the first ones there. It is the philosophic bent of those who become value investors to seek out stocks at attractive prices, but that doesn't mean just low-priced stocks. What value investors are seeking are stocks priced low in comparison to their historical earnings growth and earnings growth prospects. Theoretically, value investing has less downside risk potential than do other styles of investing. In fact, value investing carries among the lowest risk of any investing style.

There is a reason for this. If you recall from Chapter 1, market perception and investor confidence are what drive stock prices. If a stock price is already discounted (that is, undervalued), that valuation reflects at least some negative attitude by the market toward the company's future, so there's not as much chance that a negative reaction to some event will push the value down further, assuming, of course, that the company is not in a tailspin or fundamentally flawed. So if you can buy a stock when it is undervalued relative to its earnings history and prospects and then sell it when it is fully valued, you have the opportunity to reap a substantial reward at reduced risk.

We need to be clear about the terms *undervalued* and *overvalued*. During normal economic conditions and a period of historically average interest rates, a stock is undervalued if its P/E ratio is *less* than the expected future growth rate of its EPS. A stock is overvalued if its P/E is *greater* than the future growth rate of its EPS. To illustrate, take a company whose earnings are growing at 20 percent per year. If its P/E is 15, the stock is likely undervalued; if the P/E is 25, the stock is likely overvalued. Clearly, this example is overly simplistic, but it illustrates the point. During abnormal economic conditions or periods of high interest rates, the P/E ranges for undervalued and overvalued stocks would change.

Which Is the More Important Growth Rate: Past or Future?

Clearly, both are important, but we judge the future by how a stock has performed in the past. Let's say two stocks are projected to grow at 25 percent per year. For the past 5 years, Stock A has grown its earnings at 30 percent and Stock B at 10 percent. Which stock do you think has the better chance of meeting the 25 percent future growth rate? Naturally, the one with the superior historical growth rate. Quarter-over-quarter earnings are also important for discerning the most recent trend, and the most recent quarter is particularly significant. But the most important thing to consider is the future earnings growth rate in light of the past. There is no perfect number when it comes to earnings growth; it will always be a judgment call. That said, keep in mind that a company with an undervalued stock probably has a checkered past with some up and some down quarters. Such companies likely have had difficulties, either internally or as the result of economic conditions. In the end, you're trying to buy the most growth potential for the least investment, and the quantitative filters that we'll talk about will help you find where the value is right now.

Luckily for the value investor, stocks tend to go through cycles of over- and undervaluation. Overvaluation can be created by what Alan Greenspan called the "irrational exuberance" of the market. Undervaluation is the result of the pessimism that follows, which Warren Buffett, the world's most famous value investor, described like this:

The most common cause of low prices is pessimism . . . somewhat pervasive, sometimes specific to a company or industry. We want to do business in such an environment, not because we like pessimism but because we like the prices it produces. It's optimism that is the enemy of the rational buyer.

A textbook example of irrational exuberance occurred in the Internet sector in 1998–1999; this cycle was followed by pessimism that took the form of the crash of that sector in 2000. Irrational exuberance drove dot-com stocks up to the point where they became wildly overvalued by historical standards—and irrational despondency pulled them down to the point where many have become undervalued.

There are other, more mundane reasons why a stock may become undervalued. It could be simply the cyclical nature of its industry or the normal ebb and flow of the market. Or the decrease in the price of a stock could have a specific cause such as a temporary product failure, a setback caused by unfounded rumors or fears, or the emergence of a bigger, brighter competitor. Sometimes the economy itself drags the whole market down, as the recession did in the fall of 2001. Whatever the reason, there are usually a plethora of undervalued stocks for the value investor to choose from. The key is to find companies that are undervalued and likely to be become *less* undervalued, as we will show you later in this chapter.

The most compelling reason to be a value investor is to get the benefit of an expanding P/E, once the undervalued stock is "discovered." (See the discussion on "The Role of an Expanding P/E" in Chapter 1.) But there's another advantage. If you make sure the undervalued stocks you buy also have good earnings prospects, you can get the benefit of the earnings growth even if the company's relative valuation (that is, P/E) doesn't change, because theoretically the stock price growth should at least keep pace with the earnings growth. For example, if you buy a stock with a P/E of 12 and an earnings growth rate of 20 percent, the price of the stock should expand by the 20 percent increase in earnings each year—even if the P/E does not expand. All things being equal, as long as the stock produces earnings, it should produce an equivalent return in price growth.

THE PQ CHART OF THE VALUE INVESTOR

A love for a bargain and a disposition toward avoiding risk may bring an investor into the value camp, but he or she will need other qualities to be successful there. Take a look at the PQ chart in Figure 5–1. As you can see, in value investing, patience, time horizon, and investor confidence all have high scores. The value investor is the quintessential long-term investor because it often takes a great deal

FIGURE   5–1

PQ Chart of a Value Investor

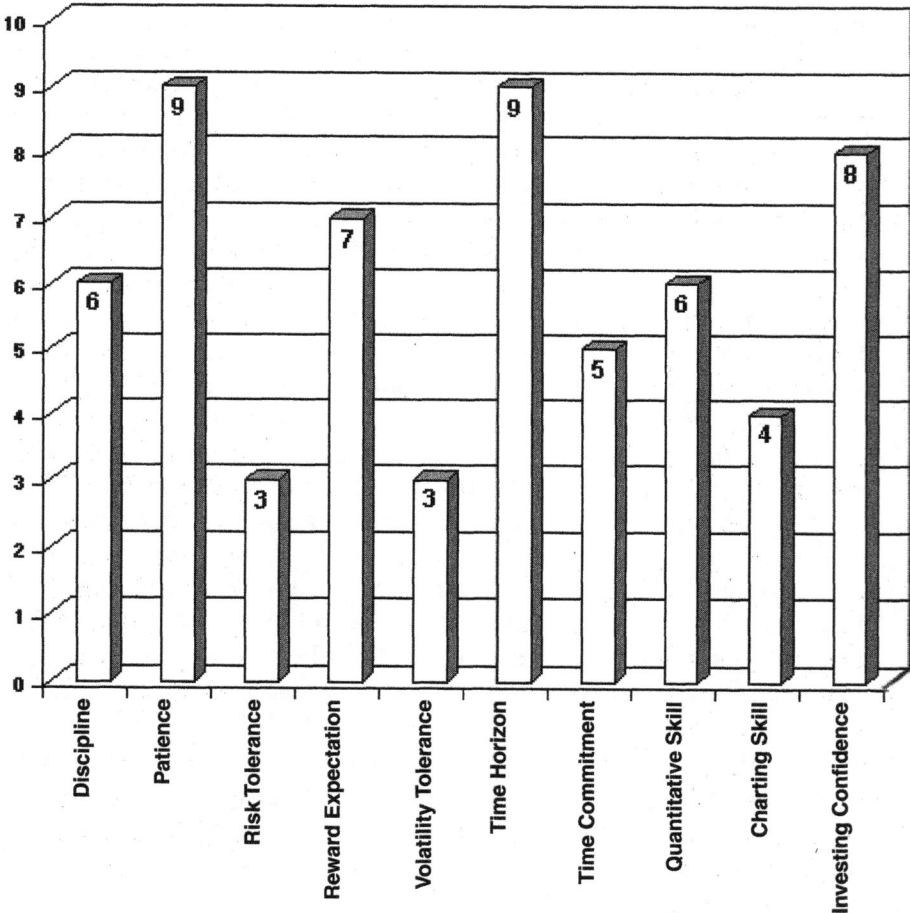

of time for the market to rediscover an undervalued stock and bid up the price until it is fully valued—that is, until the P/E ratio is approximately equal to the projected earnings growth—so as a value investor you have to have the patience to wait for your rewards. But remember, value investors are looking for increased earnings *and* increased valuation, so if the company shows increased earnings, the stock price should reflect at least that, even if the valuation multiple remains unchanged.

Investing confidence is needed because value investors go against the trend, buying stocks *they* believe in but the rest of the world doesn't think are so great (otherwise those stocks wouldn't be undervalued). As a value investor, you'll typically develop a formula or set of criteria for finding bargain stocks, and you'll put that formula—and your confidence in it—on the line every time you enter a position. Fortunately, as we will discuss later in the chapter, there are plenty of search engines that can ferret out stocks with good apparent value characteristics.

It takes a considerable amount of time to build a value portfolio because of the time and effort required to uncover and evaluate undervalued stocks. Once the portfolio is in place, however, the time required to manage it is fairly small. Considering both these factors, we rated time commitment a 5 of the PQ chart.

Evaluating undervalued stocks requires working with numbers, so a value investor needs above average quantitative skills. In effect, you're buying the ratio of P/E to growth, so you have to compare numerous ratios to determine whether the stock is a good value at the price. Again, there are tools on the Web to assist you. Moderate charting skills are needed. You don't need to be a serious technician, but you will spend some time looking at charts, as we will show later.

The two areas of value investing that get the lowest scores on the PQ chart are risk tolerance and volatility tolerance. Value investing has among the lowest risk of all styles, as we have already mentioned, and undervalued stocks are rarely volatile since they do not get as much attention from the market.

Finally, we gave discipline a middle-of-the-road score on the PQ chart, even though we think that all investors need discipline to stick with the rules for their styles of investing. But unlike the fast pace of momentum or technical investing, where you have to be constantly on the lookout for buy and sell signals, value investing does not require frequent trades because the time horizon is so much longer. That said, you still must have the discipline to stick to your rules.

ANATOMY OF A VALUE STOCK

By definition, a value stock has a P/E ratio that is lower than the stock's earnings growth rate. If the stock has an earnings growth rate of 20 percent, for example, its P/E should be below 20 to be considered a value stock. It is also nice if the current P/E is below average compared with the stock's historical P/E range (this is called *relative P/E*) and compared with the P/Es of its peers (the stocks in its industry group). But the most important factor is that the current P/E is lower than the earnings growth rate.

A value stock is not always obvious at first glance. Let's say that Stock A has a P/E ratio of 15, which is the highest P/E it has ever had. But the stock has an earnings growth rate of 20 percent, so it is a value stock even though its *relative P/E* is high. Stock B, on the other hand, also has a P/E of 15, which is the lowest P/E it has ever had, but with an earnings growth rate of 10 percent, Stock B definitely is not a value stock, because the current P/E is higher than the projected growth rate. Cisco (CSCO) is a good real-life example of a Stock B. In the fall of 2001, Cisco hit a P/E of about 45, which was very low when you consider that the stock's P/E had hit 100 in recent years. But Cisco's projected earnings growth rate was just 30 percent, so although it might have been a good growth stock, Cisco was *not* a good value stock at that time.

In short, value stocks epitomize the GARP stock—growth at a reasonable price—although a true value stock is more GABP—growth at a *bargain* price. Keep in mind that a low P/E means nothing unless the stock also has favorable earnings prospects. That's the whole ball game.

Comparing Dean Foods (DF) and Dollar Tree Stores (DLTR) stocks might be instructive. In September 2001 Dean Foods (Figure 5–2) and Dollar Tree Stores (Figure 5–3) both had P/Es around 20, which was slightly below market average. But Dean Foods' historical 5-year growth rate was less than 10 percent, and its projected 5-year growth rate was about 9 percent. Dollar Tree's historical 5-year

FIGURE 5-2

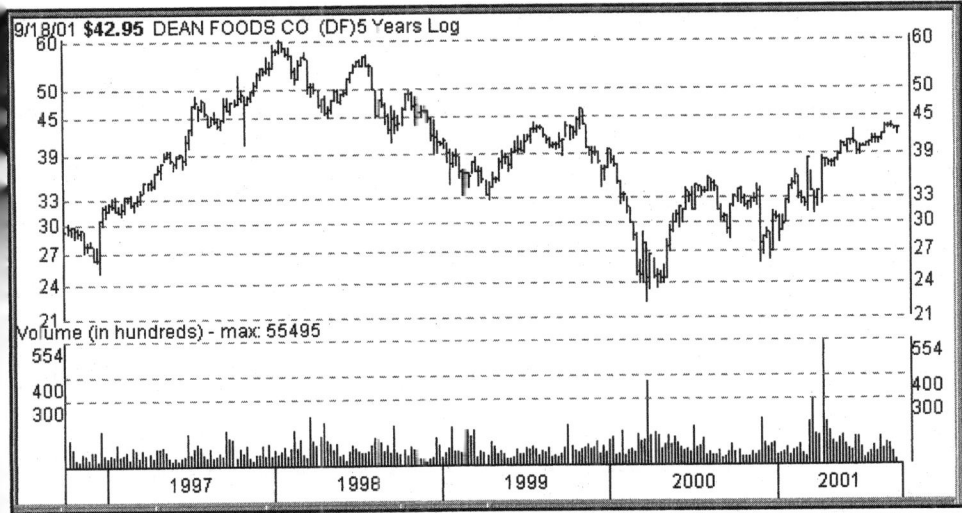

9/18/01 $42.95 DEAN FOODS CO (DF)5 Years Log

Owing to its tendency toward rather high P/Es, Dean Foods (DF) had a series of positive moves and retracements over the past 5 years.

growth rate was about 30 percent, and its projected 5-year growth rate was about 25 percent. From a value viewpoint, you're paying twice as much for Dean's earnings growth as you are for Dollar Tree's earnings growth. Clearly, in this scenario, the value investor would much prefer the Dollar Tree stock.

While earnings growth rates for value stocks are not likely to match those of growth stocks, for all the reasons we've discussed, the value investor might get close to the same total return as a growth investor by seeing the P/Es of the value stocks expand. If a stock that has historically grown at 15 percent per year has a 25 percent increase in earnings within a year, you might well see a 40 percent or larger increase in the price of the stock. Normally, a 25 percent increase in earnings would cause an approximate 25 percent increase in the stock price, but when an increase in earnings is so much more than what was expected, the market might perceive the stock as having an even higher future growth rate based on earnings. The explanation goes back to our discussion of market perception and investor confidence. If the market assumes the sharp in-

FIGURE   5–3

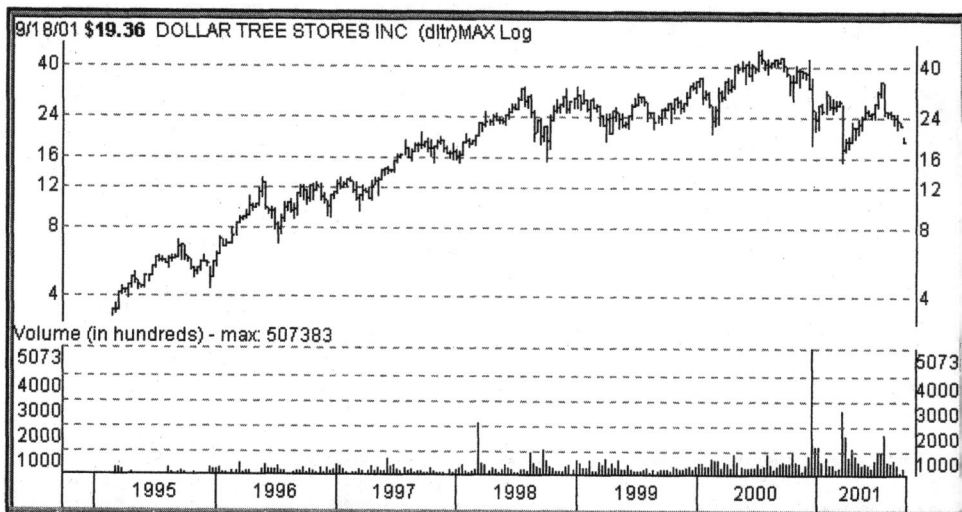

With a relative low P/E, Dollar Tree (DLTR) climbed steadily through mid-2000 as its earnings grew.

crease in earnings is not a one-time event, the stock price will reflect the greater expectations. As the wave of confidence builds, investors could bid up the price, expanding the P/E. (See "The Role of an Expanding P/E" in Chapter 1.) Even with an expanded P/E, the stock might still be modestly valued (at least for a while), although it will no longer be quite the bargain it was when you bought it.

You can't count on the fact that all undervalued stocks will be "discovered," however. A stock can stay undervalued for years. Sometimes there may be some lingering concern about the company (or a lack of investor confidence), or maybe the stock is just not sexy enough to be a favored player. Nevertheless, our objective, as value investors, is to buy stocks that are *both* undervalued and hold good prospects for earnings growth. If you make sure the earnings growth rate is greater than the P/E, you should at least get the benefit of the earnings growth even if the stock stays undervalued.

So in general, when we talk about value, we're talking about value versus earnings. In Chapter 9 we'll talk about stocks that have value in strong balance sheets (which are sought after by the fundamental investor), but strong balance sheets are not the chief focus of a value investor. The main characteristic of a value stock is an undervalued price when compared to the stock's historical and projected growth rate of earnings per share.

When Is a Value Stock Not a Value Stock?

A value stock ceases to be a value stock when its P/E becomes high compared with its earnings growth rate, and, secondarily, when its P/E becomes high compared with its historical P/E range and the P/Es of its peers. That is what you want to have happen, of course, as the company's potential is realized in its stock price. Ideally, you buy the stock at a good price, the stock responds, the public begins to see its value, and the price begins to go up. As the stock moves toward a more fully valued price, the value investor will likely sell it and buy another stock that has strong value characteristics.

The simplest way to tell when a value stock is not a value stock, however, is when it no longer has the characteristics it did when you bought it. You bought it because it had a low P/E compared with the stock's earnings growth rate, so when the P/E rises to average or above average—compared with the stock's earnings growth rate and compared with its historical P/E and the P/Es of its peers—the stock is no longer a value stock. As the stock moves along the continuum from undervalued to overvalued, it is more likely that your risk will increase. When you're trying to minimize risk as a value investor, you obviously don't want to hold a stock that is overvalued or even one that is fully valued. A stock whose P/E ratio has risen to a point that it is equal to or greater than the stock's earnings growth rate is, by our definition, now fully valued, or perhaps overvalued. At that point, you should sell it and buy another that has the desired undervalued characteristics.

Keep in mind, however, *that if the earnings and the stock price improve at the same rate,* the stock still has the same value characteristics it had when you bought it. *This is an important point!* Take as an example a stock priced at $20 with annual earnings of $2.50 and hence a P/E ratio of 8. Let's say the stock's earnings improve 20 percent. *If* the stock price also goes up 20 percent, its standing as a value stock would stay the same. The price would be $24, with earnings of $3 and a P/E of 8. The P/E ratio would not have changed, and the growth potential would still be present, so the stock would still be considered a value stock. Remember GARP—you're looking for growth at a reasonable (bargain) price, and that is measured by a low P/E compared with the stock's earnings growth rate.

Value Trading: Finding Value in an Ordinary Stock

A stock does not necessarily have to be "beaten down" to be considered a value stock. An ordinary stock can be attractive to value investors through its normal price fluctuations. This is a somewhat different approach to value investing, but it can generate very good returns.

Let's look at an ordinary stock like Delta Airlines (DAL). As a buy-and-hold stock purchased 30 years ago, Delta would have returned 8 to 9 percent per year. Not terribly interesting. Now take a look at Figure 5–4, which shows trading channels overlaid on a 20-year Delta price chart. (Trading channels are somewhat arbitrarily defined boundaries of a stock's high and low price movements over time.)

On its climb from about $5 in the mid-1970s to $70 in 1998, Delta stock zigged and zagged all the way, rising rapidly, then retracing a large part of its gain repeatedly. What would have happened if you had bought the stock near the bottom of the trading channel, sold it when it neared the top of the trading channel, bought it back near the bottom of the channel, sold it again near the top, and so on over the next 20 years? You would have tripled or quadrupled your return, earning well over 25 percent per year. In effect, if you did this you would be playing the role of a value investor by buying the "dips."

Delta is obviously a major airline and a leader in an essential sector of our domestic economy. But fears about the economy and special factors such as interest rates and oil prices that influence airline profits cause the stock of Delta (and other airlines) to rise or fall on a somewhat regular basis. These fluctuations provide buying opportunities for value investors who recognize that Delta is not likely to fail altogether, and that the company will continue in its longer-term earnings and revenue trend despite short-term price swings.

FIGURE 5-4

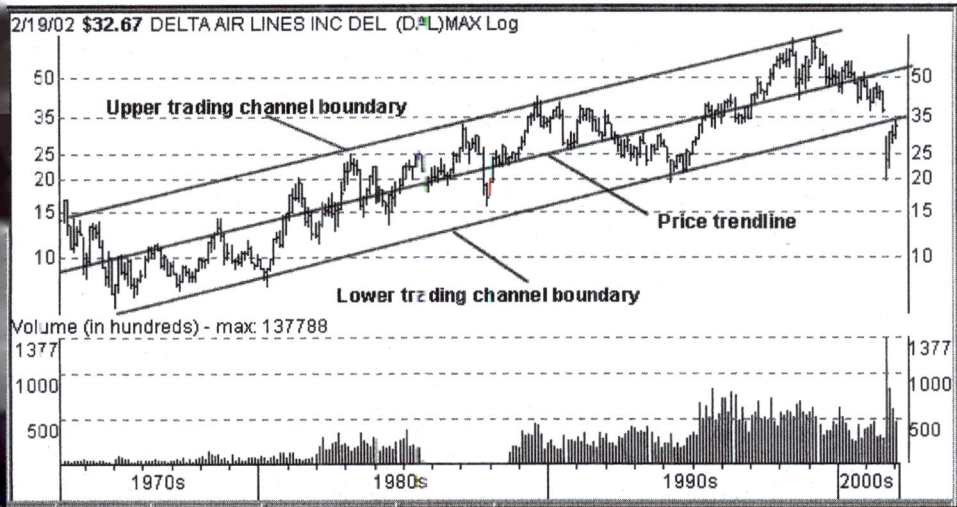

Delta Airlines (DAL) has moved within a consistent trading channel for nearly 30 years. The stock has exhibited a low P/E in the bottom channel, which provided opportunities for "value trading."

The attack on the World Trade Center hit all the airlines hard, including Delta, whose stock price dropped almost 50 percent. Nevertheless, it is unlikely that Delta's long-term prospects were really cut in half. In the short run, the lower prices were probably justified, but they also created long-term buying opportunities for the value investor. And, in fact, by October 1 shares of Delta had already recovered more than half its September losses.

Aside from the events of September 11, Delta's "trading" cycles are simply a result of the normal ebb and flow of the fortunes of an airline. Similar cycles can be found in other companies that react to the business cycle but are part of an industry that has good long-term growth, such as pharmaceuticals, housing, and petrochemicals.

Benjamin Graham, the father of value investing, attributes the continuous over-/undervaluation of an ordinary stock to the "miscalculation and excesses of optimism and pessimism [with which] the public has valued its shares." These cycles of optimism and pessimism create unique opportunities for those who like the concept of value investing but don't have the patience to wait for the truly long-term rewards. You might think of this kind of investing as "value trading," although, of course, it is trading only in the sense that you buy and sell a given company based on expected excursions of its price.

THE INVESTING PROCESS FOR VALUE INVESTORS

Stock selection is by far the most important step in the value investing process.

Stock Selection Strategies: The Search for Bargain Stocks

The bargain hunters who comb garage sales are looking for low prices, but not just for the sake of low prices. They're looking for items that have some intrinsic value, that can be useful in one way or another, and that are priced less than the same items would be priced in a department store. In selecting stocks, the goal of the value investor is similar. He or she is looking for low P/Es but *not* just for the sake of a low P/E. The P/E must be lower than the projected growth rate of earnings per share. The best value stocks have the greatest prospective growth for the smallest P/E. It is a plus if the P/E is also low in relationship to the stock's historical P/Es and to the P/Es of other stocks in the same industry group, but as we pointed out earlier, this point can be deceptive. The one unalterable rule is that the P/E must be lower than the prospective growth rate of earnings.

Screening for Value Stocks

Following are the key variables to use when creating a screen for value stocks. These variables are listed in order of importance.

- *Low P/E ratio.* Again, the P/E must be low relative to the stock's projected earnings growth rate. A low P/E ratio is half of the definition of a value stock.
- *High projected earnings growth rate.* This is the other half of the definition of a value stock. The stock's projected 3- to 5-

year growth rate of earnings per share should be higher
than its P/E.

+ *High historical earnings growth rate.* Future earnings are what
  we're buying, but past earnings give us confidence that future earnings will be realized. Historical earnings are the
  most dependable measure for assessing the ability of the
  company to produce earnings, since they are fact, but it is
  less important that historical earnings growth rates be
  higher than the P/E. Earnings equal to the P/E or even
  slightly lower (as long as they have been accelerating) are
  acceptable.

+ *Low P/E versus the P/Es of the company's industry group or major competitors.* P/Es tend to gravitate toward the average
  P/E of an industry. Stocks with P/Es lower than those of
  their peers have room to grow.

+ *Low relative P/E.* A low P/E compared to the stock's historical P/E range is nice but not essential. The P/E must be low
  compared with the earnings growth rate.

+ *Selling below its long-term price trend.* This is corroborating
  evidence that the stock is selling at a low P/E compared
  with its history. But, again, the P/E must be lower than the
  earnings growth rate.

+ *Selling below its long-term (200-day) moving average line.* This
  is more evidence that the stock is selling at a low P/E compared with its history.

+ *Insider buying.* A high level of insider buying gives us confidence that the people running the company see the same
  good value relative to growth potential that we see.

+ *Low price-to-book value* and *low price-to-revenues.* For a value
  stock, price-to-book value and price-to-revenues (or sales)
  would likely be low compared to the market. These criteria
  offer confirmation of a stock's relatively attractive valuation.

Evaluating a Short List of Value Stocks

Once you have a list of stocks from your search, you'll need to short-
en it to the four or five best value candidates. A good way to do this is
to eliminate the ones with the less desirable characteristics. Table 5–1

TABLE 5-1

Evaluating a Value Stock

Evaluation Question	Upgrade	Downgrade
Does the stock show the beginning signs of upward momentum?	Yes	No
How does the P/E ratio compare with the stock's EPS growth rate?	Well below	Same or marginally higher
How does the P/E ratio compare with the industry average and/or the S&P 500?	Same or below	Above
What is the stock's current price in relation to its long-term price trend?	Below	Above
Have analysts been revising estimates higher or lower?	Higher	Lower
How many analysts offer EPS projections?	More than 5	Less than 5
Have there been any positive or negative earnings surprises?	Positive	Negative
How many buy, hold, or sell recommendations does the stock have?	Mostly buys	More holds and sells than buys
Has there been any recent news on the company, good or bad?	Good news	Bad news
Has there been recent insider buying or selling?	Buyers outnumber sellers	Sellers outnumber buyers
How is the industry doing?	Above average	Below average

contains is a list of questions you might use to upgrade or downgrade the stocks on your list. Those stocks with the most upgrades are your potential buy candidates.

Through this evaluation you can eliminate the weakest of the stocks, but you may still end up with too many stocks to buy. At this juncture, concentrating on the best relationship of P/E to growth can serve you well. To find the candidates that show the greatest signs of upward potential, you may want to consider looking at a stock graph and some technical indicators.

Entry Strategies: Look for Signs of Recovery

Your entry strategy is particularly crucial if you are investing in value stocks because of the need to make sure that a value stock is not still in decline. By definition, value stocks have been in a long-term decline in price or they wouldn't have reached a point where they are attractive from a value perspective. The key is to buy a value stock when the long-term decline is over. Signs of some positive upward movement are the only way to confirm that the stock is more likely to move higher rather than lower.

Here are a few simple indicators that can help you assess the likelihood that a downward trend is ending: moving average crossovers, a long-term MACD breakout, or a breakthrough of long-term resistance.

Using moving average crossovers, you would plot a 50-day av-

FIGURE 5-5

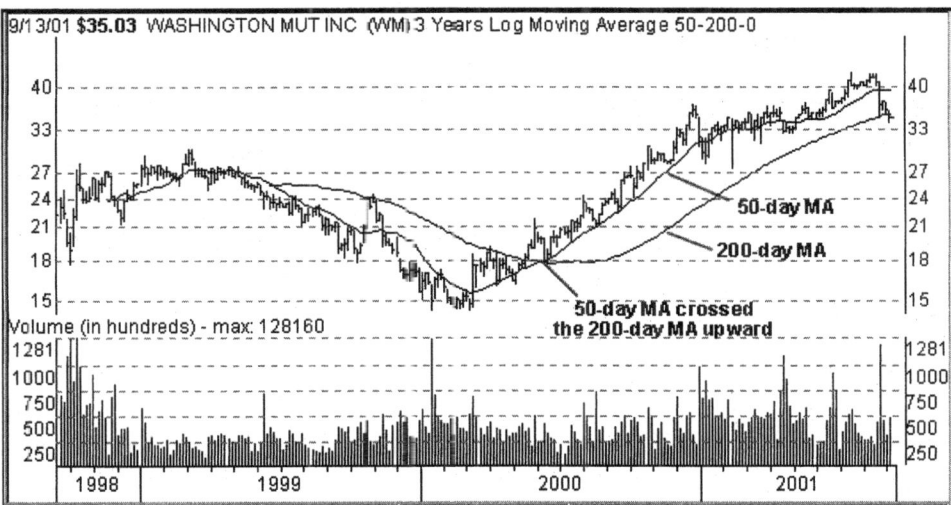

9/13/01 **$35.03** WASHINGTON MUT INC (WM) 3 Years Log Moving Average 50-200-0

Washington Mutual (WM) gave a buy signal in mid-2000 when the 50-day moving average crossed above the 200-day moving average. However, if you were looking for a value stock to enter today (9/10/01, in this example) you would probably wait on WM, as it has just broken through its 200-day moving average line to the downside.

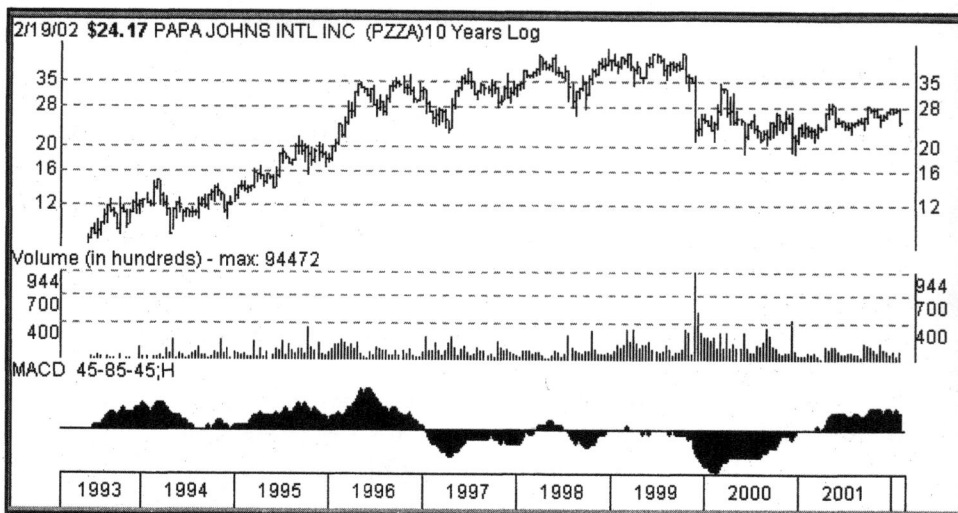

2/19/02 $24.17 PAPA JOHNS INTL INC (PZZA)10 Years Log

On this long-term graph for Papa John's (PZZA), note how the long-term MACD remained in positive territory from 1993 through 1996 as the stock moved up.

F I G U R E   5–7

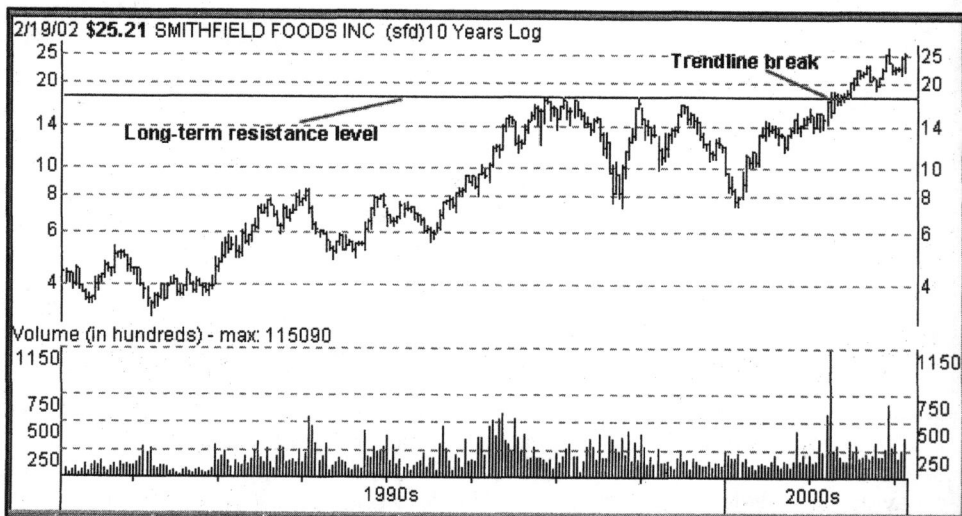

2/19/02 $25.21 SMITHFIELD FOODS INC (sfd)10 Years Log

Smithfield (SFD) shows a breakthrough of the long-term resistance line in mid-April 2001.

erage and a 200-day average on the stock graph and wait until the
50-day average crosses the 200-day average to the upside, as in Figure 5–5. This crossover implies a short-term trend change.

A long-term MACD is another good strategy for assessing an
entry point for a value stock. In Figure 5–6 a monthly MACD breakout is shown for Papa John's International (PZZA).

Another strategy is to enter the stock when it breaks through a
long-term resistance level, as shown in Figure 5–7.

Exit Strategies: Protecting against Mistakes and Successes

The exit strategies in value investing are important and somewhat
unique. You want a strategy to take you out of the stock quickly if
you've perhaps made a mistake or if the longer-term trend has taken another step lower. You also need a strategy to take you out when
you succeed—when a value stock ceases to be a value stock because
its P/E has outgrown its earnings growth rate.

When the P/E outgrows the stock's growth rate, it means you
were successful in your selection. You'll want to exit at this point because the relationship between the P/E ratio and growth rate no
longer matches your goals as a value investor. This doesn't mean the
stock is now a bad investment, but because you are a value investor
the stock no longer offers the same risk / reward profile you seek. So
the best thing to do is to exit this stock with a profit and look for another stock with better value characteristics. You will find, however, that you will make mistakes in your initial assessment. No matter how much work you've done or how carefully you've analyzed
a stock, you're going to be wrong some of the time, and the stock is
going to go down instead of up. What looked like a value stock may
turn out to be a stock that has declined in value because the company's product lines or business prospects are declining as well. In
such cases, the low P/E is warranted because the company is not going to grow as fast as implied by the P/E. Therefore, it is essential
that you have an exit strategy to take you out of bad trades.

The simplest exit strategy would be to use the opposite signal
from the same timing indicator you used to get into the stock. For
example, if you used a positive weekly MACD to enter a stock, you
would get out of the stock when the weekly MACD turned nega-

tive. If you bought a stock when the 50-day moving average crossed the 200-day moving average upward, you might sell it when the 50-day moving average crosses the 200-day average downward. If you used a breakthrough of long-term resistance, you might want to sell if the stock drops back through that resistance level.

Value Portfolio Strategies

Here are some portfolio management strategies to keep in mind when you are building and managing a portfolio of value stocks.

- *Diversify stocks and industries.* Because of the low time commitment, a value investor should be able to comfortably maintain a portfolio of 10 to 15 stocks spread over several industries.
- *Monitor your portfolio regularly.* Like a growth portfolio, a value portfolio requires a lot of time and attention during the building phase, but less daily monitoring once you are fully invested. The holding period for value stocks is generally lengthy—many months to several years—still it pays to monitor individual stocks on a weekly basis. If a value stock does what we hope it will do, it will move toward a point where it is no longer a value stock. So you should continue to monitor each stock's key value variables and weed out the ones that are no longer "value" stocks as determined by your system for evaluating value stocks.

  We recommend that you review your portfolio as a whole at least once a quarter, after earnings come out. Be alert for large moves in the stock price. If a large move takes place—let's say you bought a stock at $20 and 8 weeks later it is $40 (a nice problem to have)—the stock needs to be reviewed to make sure that it still fits the criteria for a value stock. If the price jump followed the company's announcement that it expects earnings to exceed current estimates, then the stock could well remain a value stock. Here's a good rule of thumb: If you would not have bought the stock at its current price compared to its current value characteristics, consider selling it.

- *Stay fully invested, if possible.* Value investors, in general, strive to stay fully invested. As a value investor, you're buying stocks that you believe have little market risk, so there is no point in maintaining a large cash position. This assumes, of course, that you can find good value candidates. In the spring of 2000, value investors who concentrated on large-cap stocks found a scarcity of attractively priced value stocks because large caps had become overvalued by the end of the bull market run. That would have been a good reason to increase your cash position—or to switch to small-cap stocks, which were out of favor at the time. (We'll talk more about market caps in Chapter 8.) Except for such rare times, there is likely to be an abundance of attractively priced value stocks in the major market caps.

CASE STUDY: WASHINGTON MUTUAL

The objective of this case study was to identify an undervalued large-cap candidate in order to demonstrate the selection process for value stocks.

Washington Mutual: A Large-Cap Value Stock

On November 2, 2001, Washington Mutual (WM) was one of the top stocks for undervalued companies within the large-cap universe. It had a market cap of $24 billion. Washington Mutual scored very well in terms of the basic characteristics of a value stock:

- A P/E ratio of 8, based on FY 2001 earnings
- A 3-year historical growth rate of 32 percent
- A 5-year historical earnings growth rate of 43 percent
- A 5-year projected EPS growth rate of 12.6 percent

Note that the 5-year projected EPS growth rate was based on the company's making no additional acquisitions because few analysts project earnings based on future acquisitions. If WM continues in its aggressive acquisition mode, earnings growth will likely be higher than projections.

Who Is Washington Mutual?

The first step in our evaluation process was to find out a little bit about the company. (Web sites that provide company profiles and related information are listed in Appendix A.) Washington Mutual, Inc., is one of the nation's largest thrift banks and second largest mortgage lender with nearly 2000 facilities nationwide. Its financial services affiliates provide consumer finance loans, annuities, selected insurance products, and mutual funds, as well as investment counseling and a full range of securities brokerage services.

The company was in an extensive expansion phase in the late 1990s, acquiring, among others, H. F. Ahmanson and Great Western Financial. In 2001 WM bought Bank United (of Texas), the mortgage business of PNC Financial, and Fleet Mortgage Corp.; WM had also announced the planned acquisition of Dime Bancorp (DME). These aggressive acquisitions have grown Washington Mutual into a national financial services company with operations in 42 states.

A Look at the Chart

Looking at WM's chart in Figure 5–8, one can see very steady price growth from $15 to $40 over the previous 2 years. The drop in late 2001 was owing to the eroding economy in the wake of September 11 and concerns about asset quality for lenders. In other words, lenders who make loans to marginal credit risks suffer more loan defaults during poor economic conditions.

The Value Stock Evaluation Checklist

After peaking in August 2001, Washington Mutual lost more than 33 percent of its value over the next 3 months, which made the stock an even more compelling value play. Based on studying the stock with the evaluation checklist in Table 5–1, WM was ripe for purchase in a typical value portfolio, with only a couple of minor negatives.

- *P/E to EPS growth rate.* Washington Mutual's 5-year EPS growth rate (43 percent) was five times its P/E ratio (8) for FY 2001.
- *P/E to industry and S&P 500.* Washington Mutual's P/E was

F I G U R E   5-8

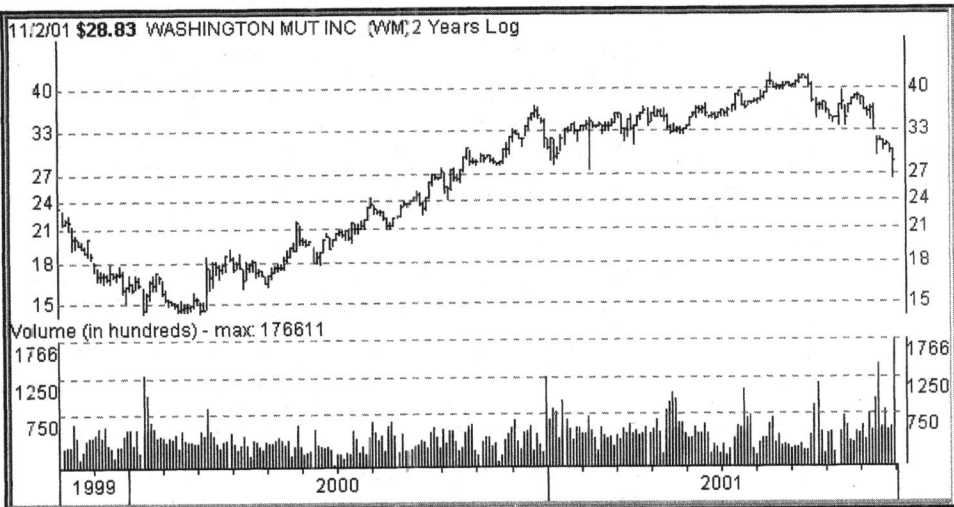

11/2/01 $28.83 WASHINGTON MUT INC (WM) 2 Years Log

This chart shows the price growth of Washington Mutual over the past 2 years.

lower than both its industry (12.30) and the S&P 500 (22.50).

- *Price to long-term trend.* Washington Mutual was trading 25 percent below its long-term trendline.
- *Earnings surprises.* Washington Mutual had positive earnings surprises in three out of the previous four quarters.
- *Analyst revisions.* In September 2001 analysts revised estimates higher for 2001 (to $3.57) and 2002 (to $3.96).
- *Number of analysts covering the stock.* There were 16 analysts offering 2001 estimates and 17 offering 2002 estimates.
- *Buy/hold/sell recommendations.* There were 12 buy recommendations (including 6 strong buys), 5 hold recommendations, and no sell recommendations.
- *News.* On November 1, 2001, Washington Mutual filed for a shelf registration with the SEC to sell up to $1 billion in debt securities. The company said it would use the pro-

ceeds for, among other things, acquisitions. This move was viewed positively since it implies a continuation of WM's aggressive acquisition activity.

♦ *Insider trading.* In July 2001 one officer sold 183,186 shares but still held almost 250,000 shares. Selling by just one insider is not considered significant.

♦ *Industry group.* The industry group performance was down owing to concern about lender asset quality, which was a negative.

♦ *Upward momentum.* At the time of evaluation, the stock was in a downtrend, so it would have been prudent to wait for a clear turnaround before entering a position.

Conclusion: WM's Acquisition Mode Adds to Value Rating

Considering the company's strong fundamentals and that it remained in acquisition mode, Washington Mutual appeared to be a superior value stock in November 2001. A P/E ratio of 8 was quite low compared to the company's historical earnings growth rate of 43 percent, and even compared with a 5-year projected earnings growth rate of 13 percent, the stock was attractive. Washington Mutual looked even better, though, when you considered that the projected 13 percent EPS growth rate was an internal growth rate that didn't take into account possible acquisitions. The aggressive acquisition policy of company management in the past and the new shelf offering increased the likelihood that earnings growth would be considerably higher.

FUNDS FOR VALUE STOCKS

Rather than build and manage a portfolio of stocks, many value investors opt for the convenience of investing in value-oriented mutual funds or exchange-traded funds (ETFs). (See the discussion on ETFs in Chapter 4.) A partial list of fund families appears in the online resources section of Appendix A, but perhaps the best way to find a value-oriented fund is to use one of the several free mutual fund search engines on the Web (also described in Appendix A).

There are several ETFs aimed at the value investor. In the fall of 2001 the following were available from iShares and street-TRACKS:

iShares S&P 500/BARRA Value Index (IVE)

iShares S&P MidCap 400/BARRA Value (IJJ)

iShares S&P SmallCap 600/BARRA Value (IJS)

iShares Russell 1000 Value Index Ticker (IWD)

iShares Russell 2000 Value Index (IWN)

iShares Russell 3000 Value Index (IWW)

streetTRACKS DJ US Large Cap Value (ELV)

streetTRACKS DJ US Small Cap Value (DSV)

Tips for Selecting a Value Fund

Here are some tips to consider when searching for value funds:

1. *What is the fund's objective and investment strategy?* Look for funds that seek attractively priced stocks or undervalued companies with strong profitability. If market cap is important to you, also note the market caps in which the fund invests.

2. *What are the risk factors?* The risk of a value fund will likely be moderate, but it is unlikely that a prospectus will say that.

3. *What is the past performance?* Note how the fund has performed during the most recent 1-, 3-, and 5-year periods. Past performance is no *guarantee* of future performance, but it can provide some clues. Of course, if the market has not favored value investing over the past few years, the results of a value fund might be below par, but those results shouldn't be held against the fund.

4. *Who is the portfolio manager?* Note his or her years of experience. If he or she manages other funds, look at the performance of those funds as well.

5. *Does the fund have a Morningstar rating?* Morningstar rates funds with one to five stars, to reflect the fund's historical risk-adjusted performance. A rating of four to five stars is considered excellent, but remember that Morningstar's star

ranking system is based on the past and is not necessarily indicative of the future, and not all funds are rated. (Morningstar ratings can be found at www.morningstar.com.)

6. *What are the top 10 holdings?* Most funds list their top 5 or 10 holdings, although these rankings can change without notice. Some funds also list the major sectors in which they are invested. Check to see if the companies (and the sectors) have the undervalued characteristics you're looking for.

7. *Does the fund represent diversity?* If all your investment capital is allocated to funds, make sure you diversify by seeking out funds in different sectors, different fund families, or different market caps. Or mix domestic funds with global funds.

Online Resources for Value Stocks

A list of Web sites that specialize in value stocks or offer features on value stocks appears in Appendix A. Such lists quickly become outdated, however, as new Web sites come on-line and current sites merge or disappear. So we are including a list of keywords that you can use with any of the major search engines to find a current list of Web sites related to value stocks, no matter when you might be reading this book.

VALUE INVESTING KEYWORDS

bargain stocks	low P/E stocks
Benjamin Graham	undervalued stocks
discounted growth	value investing
GARP (this could take you	value stocks
into growth stocks as well)	Warren Buffett

HINTS FOR SUCCESSFUL VALUE INVESTING

Value investing can produce great rewards but requires patience and perseverance. If you've picked a good value stock, you should be in it for the long term and not worry about day-to-day market fluctuations. Here are some hints on how to succeed as a value investor.

1. *Keep your emotions cut of the process.* This is the number one rule for any investor. Judge the stock on its merits. Period.

2. *Be alert for large price moves.* If one of your stocks has a big price move, check to see that it's still a value stock. A good rule of thumb: If you would *not* have bought the stock at its current price compared to its value characteristics, then you should consider selling it.

3. *Don't be afraid to take a loss.* All investors make mistakes, even the great ones, so don't be afraid to take a loss. Develop the discipline to use an appropriate entry/exit indicator to take you out of the stock based either on the largest loss you're willing to sustain (say, 20 percent) or an indicator that you have confidence in when it goes negative.

4. *Don't become obsessed with absolute valuation.* Don't buy a stock *just because it has a low P/E ratio.* Maybe a stock with a P/E of 5 has always had a P/E of 5. Maybe all its peers have a P/E of 5. What you're looking for is *relative* valuation in light of the stock's historical and projected earnings growth rates. If a stock with a P/E of 5 is not growing faster than 5 percent a year, it is not a value stock. Sometimes a stock with a P/E of 5 is appropriately priced.

5. *Look for value sectors.* Sometimes an entire sector can become undervalued, which renders good hunting ground for value stocks. To find undervalued sectors or industries, pay attention to financial news. If a basic industry is thought to be having problems, you can bet there will be opportunities for value players. Look at cyclical industries, such as airlines, health care, and oil and gas, that rotate into and out of favor due to economic factors.Check for best- and worst-performing sectors and industry groups by consulting the lists published by several Web sites (see Appendix A).

    Once you find an undervalued sector or group, look at a price chart of the sector to see where the sector is in the trend. Check the average P/Es of the group. Then search that group for undervalued stocks. Keep in mind that if the whole sector is down, a stock doesn't have to be low against the stocks in its group to be a value stock.

6. *Watch for expanding margins.* Expanding margins are an early

alert that a company is improving its operations, particularly
if the stock has declined in price owing to severe industry
competition. You'll find information on operating margins
in a company's 10K or 10Q.

7. *Look for value stocks in emerging industries.* Emerging industries are those that are on the cutting edge of technology,
   such as biotechnology or wireless communication. Companies in such industries can be undervalued if there has been
   some kind of disappointment or setback in a product. For example, if a pharmaceutical company has a drug that failed to
   receive FDA approval, the stock will no doubt take a hit and
   could be priced at a fraction of its former valuation. If there's
   a good chance for a rebound—upon the company's eventually obtaining FDA approval—the stock can be a value stock
   versus its group. To find such stocks in an emerging industry, look for companies that have the best current valuations
   relative to their own history.

CHAPTER 6

Strategies for
Momentum Investing

Most stocks make some kind of decisive move every year. This move, according to the philosophy behind momentum investing, follows the 80-20 adage: The stocks exhibit about 80 percent of their movement over 20 percent of the time. There are always those high flyers that seem to have 1 to 2 years of hyper-performance, but, generally speaking, most stocks have a "burst" of movement—or momentum—during a relatively short period. Fortunately for investors, different stocks seem to move at different times.

The key to momentum investing is to find the stocks that are moving now and be in on them while they are moving. Ideally, the momentum investor tries to catch the biggest waves, jump on at the "perfect" time, and get off at the "perfect" time—which would be just before the momentum reverses or, more likely, just after the momentum reverses. Perfect timing is impossible, of course, but getting in near the beginning of the upward momentum and getting out before it stops or shortly after it reverses is the goal of the momentum investor.

There is a fair amount of risk in attempting this kind of investment because stocks with momentum are typically the ones that have come the farthest the fastest. Often they will be at new highs and sometimes very pricey, and the inevitable correction can be swift and painful. But as a momentum investor you can't be afraid to buy a stock at a new high because, as William O'Neil, publisher of *Investor's Business Daily* and a leading momentum guru, says, a stock has to reach a new high to go higher. Just keep in mind that not every trade is going to be successful, and one of the important caveats for momentum investors is to take your losses quickly.

THE PQ CHART OF THE MOMENTUM INVESTOR

Those who are attracted to momentum investing expect big rewards and they expect them quickly. (Note the ratings of 9 for reward expectation and 2 for patience on the PQ chart in Figure 6–1.) There is no investing style that has the *potential* to earn as much—as quickly—as does momentum investing. Most of the extraordinary gains reported by momentum investors come from those who switch among many stocks over a period of a year, trying to capture gains from as many as possible. Those who do it well can see exceptional returns.

But with great reward usually goes great risk, so it should come as no surprise that momentum investing is one of the higher-risk strategies (rating a 9 for both risk tolerance and volatility tolerance on our PQ chart). Stocks that are on a momentum roll frequently have had extraordinary earnings announcements, and any hint that the earnings growth might not continue can stop them in their tracks on any given day. As a result, momentum stocks can take some pretty big drops.

Perhaps the most important characteristic of the momentum investor is the need for discipline, which we rated a 10 on the PQ chart. Because of the need to get in and out of a stock quickly, a momentum investor must have the discipline to act decisively on entry and exit signals, even when the exit signal is telling you to get out of a stock you've only recently entered and you know you'll suffer a loss. Learning to take quick losses can save you from suffering larger losses in the future. In the quick-moving, short-term world of the momentum investor, one who hesitates or second-guesses him- or herself will likely see lower returns.

Momentum investing requires a heavy time commitment, probably more so than any other major style of investing. When building a momentum portfolio, you have to survey dozens of stocks in order to identify those with the best momentum, and you must be prepared to act quickly in order to enjoy as much of the ride as you

FIGURE 6–1

PQ Chart for the Momentum Investor

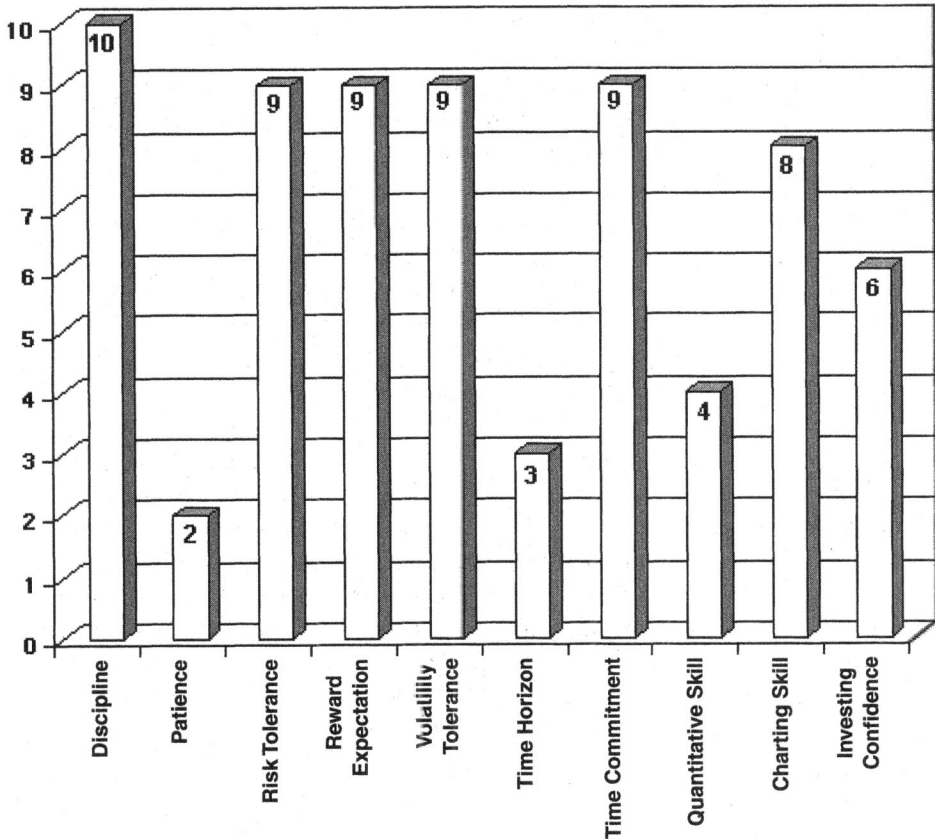

can. But with a portfolio of momentum stocks, you can't afford to rest on your laurels.. Once you have invested, you must look at daily charts of the stocks you own so you can get off when the ride is over. Also you should monitor a watch list of potential stocks, so that when you see one that has better momentum characteristics than a stock you currently own, you can make a quick switch. That means comparing a lot of stocks and industry groups on a daily basis.

While charting skills are important—rating an 8 on our PQ chart for the momentum investor—the best momentum runs normally follow good earnings reports, so you can't be just a chart person; you will also need to compare earnings reports, so your quantitative skills must be good.

Compared with value and growth investing, momentum investing scores somewhat lower in terms of the degree of confidence the investor should have. As a momentum investor, you must act quickly and decisively, but once you've learned to spot a momentum stock and learned your rules for entry and exit—in other words, once you've built a "mechanical trading system"—you don't have to make tough judgment calls on a daily basis. Your system will make those decisions for you. In that sense, momentum investing is basically a juggling act. You have to keep a lot of balls in the air at one time and know when to let a ball go and when to exchange a red ball for a green one.

Momentum investing is a style for investors who don't like agonizing over the kinds of questions that often stymie growth and value investors: Is this a reasonable price for this level of earnings growth? Has this undervalued stock truly begun a recovery? Momentum investors can just go by the numbers: Buy when the signal says buy; sell when the signal says sell. And that means when a stock gives a fake move or the group rotation is out of phase, you must respect your signal and exit the stock even if it means you have to take a loss. The ability to take small losses quickly can prevent small losses from becoming bigger losses.

ANATOMY OF A MOMENTUM STOCK

A momentum stock is one that is exhibiting a rapid and sustained price movement. The underlying cause for that price movement can vary, however, and the wise momentum investor will look for the source of the momentum. In a high-risk environment, what lies beneath can alleviate or aggravate the risk.

The least risky momentum play is a stock whose underlying cause for momentum is a significant "event," such as earnings growth. A stock whose strong price momentum is based on earnings momentum in recent quarters has a better chance of sustaining short-term momentum than do other stocks. Earnings growth could also turn an undervalued stock into a less risky momentum play as investors discover the stock and begin to bid up the price.

Another way to lessen the risk of investing in a momentum stock is to find one in a top-performing industry group or sector. A rising tide lifts all boats, and when a sector or industry group rises to the top, for whatever reason, the top stocks in that group are buoyed by the group momentum. The most recent case in point was the Internet sector during 1998 and 1999. A stock whose underlying cause for momentum is that it is part of a top-performing group is likely to retain its momentum as long as the group is on a roll. Therefore it is prudent to identify industry groups with the best positive momentum and then target stocks in those industry groups that have the best earnings momentum. This is a *top-down strategy*, and you can learn more about it in Chapter 9.

More risky are those stocks whose price momentum is based on rumors of mergers or takeovers or a new product release. If the event falls through, the stock will likely retrace most of its move. The least attractive and most risky are stocks whose underlying momentum is based on day trader activity, message board and chat rooms, or a mention in the media by some analyst or pundit. These stocks are the most vulnerable to setbacks and serious drops because the underlying causes are based solely on perception. When the perception changes—which it can in a flash—the stock can melt down so fast that no exit strategy in the world can get you out unscathed.

Typical Patterns of Momentum Stocks

Let's look at a few charts and observe the typical patterns of momentum stocks. Understand that we are not trying to teach you the details of how to be a momentum investor. We're simply trying to give you a flavor of this style and to emphasize that momentum investing can be either short-term or long-term. Our objective is to introduce you to the various styles of investing so that you can research at your leisure those styles that you find most appealing.

In this chapter we have drawn trendlines on the charts to show the moves that would have likely been captured by the typical momentum investor. We're not suggesting that these represent actual entry and exit points. Most momentum investors use a combination of trendlines and their favorite technical indicator to enter and exit from a stock.

Lennar Corporation (LEN) would have been attractive to both long-term and short-term momentum investors in 2001. The longer-term investor would probably hold Lennar throughout the move from $26 to $48, whereas the shorter-term investor would try to capture the best parts of each new upsurge, shown by trendlines on the chart in Figure 6–2.

Mim Corporation (MIMS) would have been of most interest to a longer-term momentum investor. By using rather loose stops, say 20 percent of profit gain, the long-term investor could have enjoyed the 8-month ride from $1 to $12 with trend support all the way, as shown by the trendline in Figure 6–3. But there were plenty of opportunities for short-term investors as well. During those 8 months the stock moved upward in short spurts—halting, sometimes retracing itself, then moving sideways within a narrow price range ("basing," as it is called), and finally resuming its upward movement. The retracements would have taken out the short-term in-

FIGURE   6–2

In 2001 Lennar Corporation (LEN) was a stock with both long-term and short-term momentum.

FIGURE 6-3

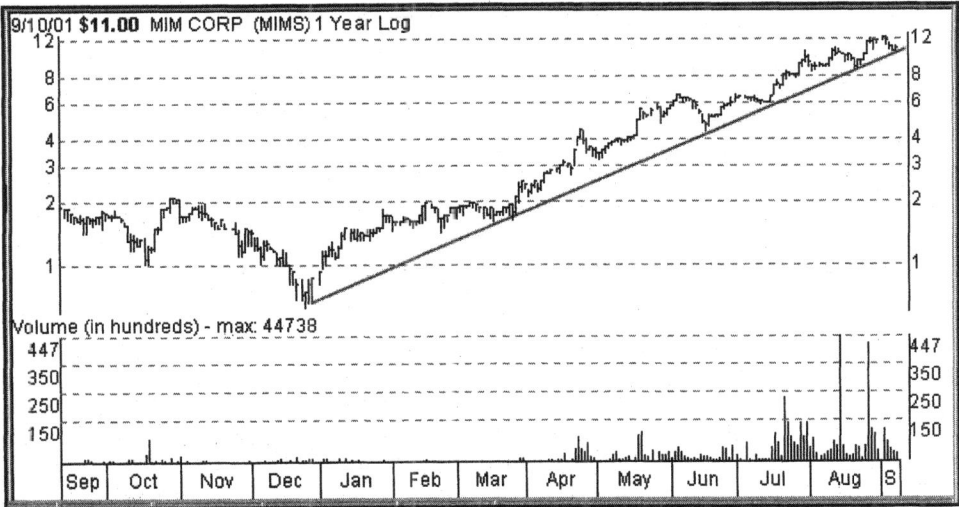

Mim Corporation (MIMS) had a long-term run from late December 2000 through early September 2001.

vestor who might have re-entered the stock when it broke out of the various basing periods, as happened in late March, mid-May, and mid-July. These short runs could have provided additional short-term profits.

Aggressive short-term momentum players look for volatile stocks like eBay (Figure 6–4). Basically, the stock went nowhere over the entire period, but nonetheless it presented opportunities for the momentum investor. There were two good runs in 2001: a short run in the first 2 weeks of January and then another one that started in April and peaked in early July. The aggressive momentum investor could have enjoyed approximately a 50 percent return on each of these runs. Incidentally, many momentum investors also take short positions, and the eBay chart shows several downtrends that could have increased the potential rewards for those willing to short the stock. (We'll talk about short-selling in Chapter 10.)

These charts demonstrate the opportunity for the momentum investor to capture highly profitable moves in a wide variety of stocks. Some of the momentum runs, like Mim's, are long and con-

FIGURE 6-4

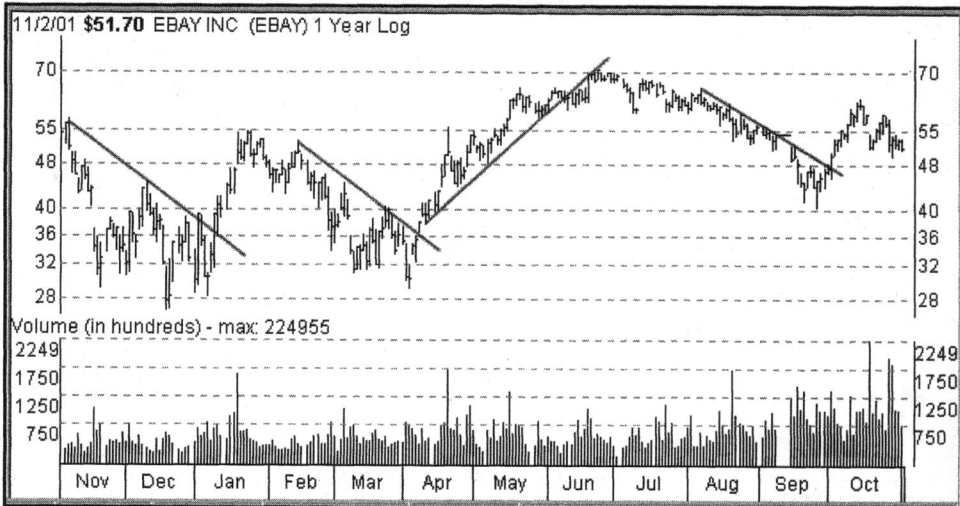

eBay, Inc. (EBAY) showed considerable volatility from November 2000 through March 2001, offering both uptrends and downtrends for the aggressive momentum investor.

sistent, while those like eBay's can be viewed as trading opportunities.

When Is a Momentum Stock Not a Momentum Stock?

A momentum stock ceases to be a momentum stock when it has lost its momentum. Obviously. The key is to determine when the real move is over, and doing so is not all that easy. If a stock has had a 15 percent run for 2 weeks and then stands still for 3 days in a row, is the momentum run over or is it pausing to refresh?

Consider Titan Corp. (Figure 6–5). From the beginning of January through February, Titan (TTN) was definitely a momentum stock, but the astute momentum investor would have exited sometime in late February or early March when the stock stalled between $23 and $24. After that, TTN retraced its entire 2-month gain, then based for a while in April and then became a momentum stock again, running all the way back up to $24. There was a 2- or 3-day period in which it stalled again (at the same resistance level) and

FIGURE 6-5

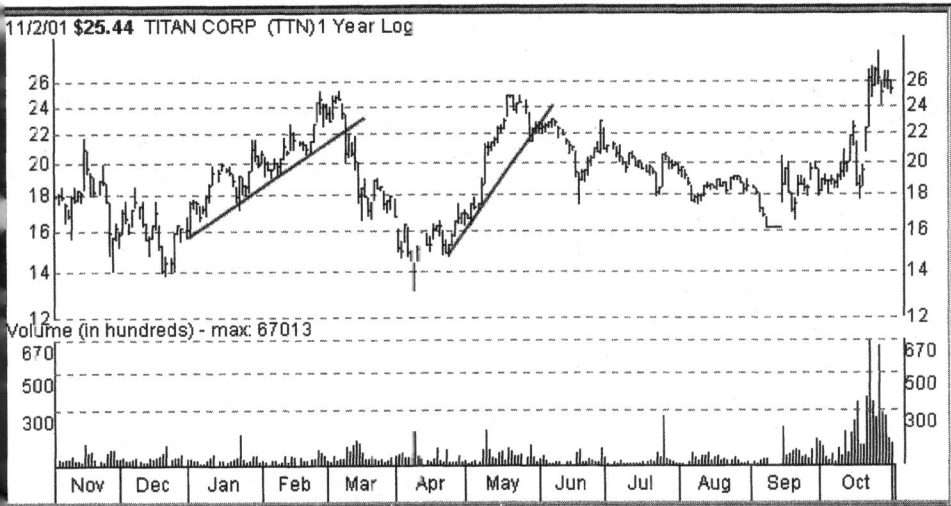

11/2/01 $25.44 TITAN CORP (TTN)1 Year Log

Titan Corp. (TTN) had three sharp momentum runs from December 2000 through October 2001. The two shown on the chart were well defined and would have been likely profitable moves for the momentum investor; the third run in mid-October 2001 would have been more difficult to trade because it was so fast.

then began another retreat. In mid-June, the stock had a burst of energy but didn't go very far, and then in mid-October TTN shot through the previous resistance at $24 and appears to be basing at $26 of this writing.

So you see, a momentum stock is a changling. It's a momentum stock, and then it's not. It changes sometimes slowly, sometimes rapidly. It may pause in the middle of a run and then pick up steam again, or it may falter and take back all it has given.

WebEx (Figure 6–6) shows an even more rapidly changing pattern of momentum and retracement. The four momentum runs in March, May, June, and October last from about 1 to 4 weeks and offer from 4 to about 12 points each (25 to 50 percent gains) for the nimble momentum investor.

AmeriCredit (ACF; Figure 6–7) is an excellent example of why the momentum investor should exit each time the upward trend is broken. From December 2000 through July 2001 ACF was

F I G U R E   6–6

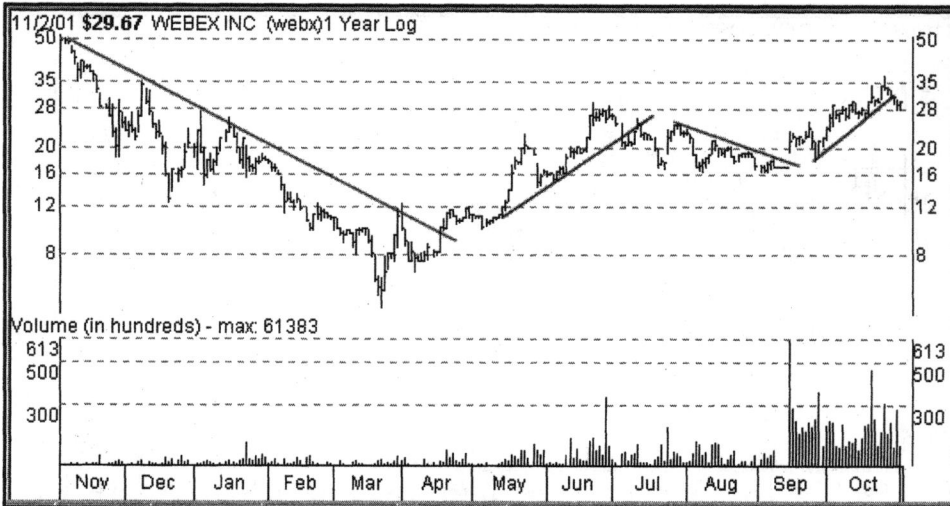

WebEx (WEBX) offered four handsome moves for the short-term investor: two opportunities to short the stock and two to go long, as shown by the trendlines on this chart.

in a long uptrend, moving from about $20 to $60 over this 8-month period. In retrospect, one might argue that if you got in around $20 why not hold on all the way to $60? The reason is, we can only see the long uptrend in retrospect. When the stock started basing and then broke trendline support in February and again in early June, you could not have known *at the time* that the trendbreak was short-lived. It could just as easily have signaled a major breakdown, as happened in August 2001. By the time you realized that the July trendbreak was a major reversal, you might well have given away some 50 percent of your profits! That's why you sell when the momentum runs out—you don't know what's going to happen next.

So how can you know? It takes a combination of quantitative skills and technical analysis skills to discern the end of a momentum run. No bell rings telling you the uptrend is over, so you have to have some method of getting out, which we'll discuss under "Exit Strategies" in the next section.

FIGURE 6-7

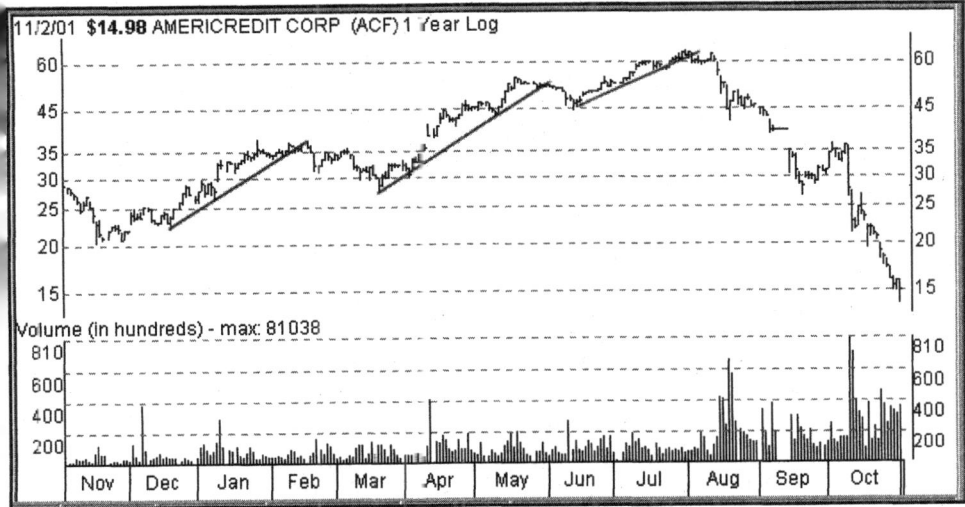

AmeriCredit exhibits three momentum runs in 2000, each of which paused, retraced a bit, then picked up steam again, but in July 2001 the momentum definitely ran out of gas.

THE INVESTING PROCESS FOR MOMENTUM INVESTORS

In momentum investing, all three steps in the investing process are very important, especially for short-term investors who want to make a lot of money quickly on a stock. Because of the fast-paced nature of momentum investing, it is critical to select the right stocks, to define clearly your entry and exit strategies, and to keep a very close eye on your portfolio.

Stock Selection Strategies:
Looking for the Next Big Wave

Momentum stocks are somewhat difficult to find, because once you identify a stock that is making a move (this part is not so hard) you should then ascertain the underlying cause for the move. As we discussed earlier, the least risky stocks are those whose momentum is based on earnings, basic value, or good industry group performance. The most undesirable stocks have momentum based on rumors, day trading activity, message boards, or chat rooms.

Investor's Business Daily (IBD) has developed two indicators that can help you identify stocks with price and earnings momentum, as well as industry groups with momentum. *Investor's Business Daily's price rank* indicator identifies the top stocks and industry groups that have exhibited rapid price movement over fairly short time periods, and *IBD's earnings rank* indicator identifies stocks that have been exhibiting a period of earnings momentum in recent quarters. *Investor's Business Daily* publishes daily lists of top price rankings (for stocks and groups) and top earnings rankings (for stocks). These lists are available to subscribers to the *Investor's Business Daily*, who also have access to the *IBD* Web site at www.investors.com.

Perhaps the best way to identify momentum stocks is with a good screening program. If you're a top-down investor, you will first want to find the industry groups with the best momentum and then screen those groups for the best momentum stocks. Keep in mind that industry groups can only become top-performing groups if most of the stocks in the group have already exhibited significant momentum, so you have to be careful when using this method to select momentum stocks. You can either look for groups that are just beginning to rotate upward—those that may have been out of favor and are just now moving into favor. Then look for the top momentum stocks in those groups, which are the stocks that are pushing the group upward. Alternatively, you can look at the current top-performing groups and search for stocks within those groups that haven't yet rotated upward—and that deserve to do so. We'll talk more about top-down investing in Chapter 9.

Screening for Momentum Stocks

Following are several specific variables to use when you are creating a screen or filter for momentum stocks.

- ◆ *Highest price change as a percentage over the last day, last week, last month.* This is the percentage change of the stock price over a specified period of time. It is irrelevant that a stock is up $2 or $28. It is the *percentage change* we're looking for.
- ◆ *Basing period breakouts.* When a stock trades within a nar-

row range for an extended period, it is called a *basing peri-od*. When it moves out of that range upward, it has a posi-tive *basing period breakout*. Particularly good momentum candidates are those stocks that have broken out of a bas-ing pattern on an earnings event. There are a number of stock filters that enable you to screen for basing period breakouts.

♦ *Highest short-term earnings growth, quarter over quarter.* An increase in this quarter's earnings compared to the same quarter last year can be a basis for a strong momentum move. (The increase should be expressed as a percentage to be meaningful.) For example, if stock A had a 75-cent or 20 percent gain over last quarter, and stock B had a 22-cent or 80 percent gain over last quarter, stock B obviously has the greatest momentum. Stock B is moving up the fastest, which is what you're looking for as a momentum investor. You're seeking the *best* percentage gainers in earnings growth.

♦ *Upward one-month change in earnings estimates by analysts.* Past research by us and others has showed that an upward revision in analysts' estimates is one of the best leading in-dicators of strong price movement. When analysts who closely follow a stock revise their previously published es-timates to a higher level, the announcement is usually very well received by the investing public.

♦ *Highest money flow.* Use either an accumulation/distribu-tion or the Chaiken money flow indicator to assess the flow of money into a stock. High scores on these indicators show that money is flowing into the stocks. (Simplistically speaking, these indicators measure the volume on up days as compared to the volume on down days. The stocks that show the highest money flow are probably owing to insti-tutional investments in the respective stocks.)

If you are doing top-down investing you would use the fol-lowing industry group criteria:

♦ *Highest industry group price change over the last day, last week, and last month.* These criteria will give you the top-performing industry groups. In some search programs, you may have to run a filter on industry groups first, and then limit your stock search to those groups.

Evaluating a Short List of Momentum Stocks

Once you have a list of top momentum stocks, you'll need to shorten it to the four or five best candidates to buy right now. A good way to do this is to downgrade stocks for which you can find no strong underlying cause of the momentum, or stocks that don't have a

TABLE 6–1

Evaluating a Momentum Stock

Evaluation Question	Upgrade	Downgrade
Does the stock have a pattern of well-defined momentum runs on the stock chart?	Yes	No
Is there recent quarter-over-quarter earnings momentum?	Yes	No
Does the stock have a high—25 percent or more—earnings growth rate over the past 1 to 2 years?	Yes	No
Have analysts been revising estimates higher or lower?	Higher	Lower
What is the stock's current price in relation to its 30-day average?	Above	Below
Is there money flowing into the stock?	Yes	No
How many buy, hold, or sell recommendations does the stock have?	Mostly buys	More holds and sells than buys
Has the stock recently broken through a resistance level?	Yes	No
Where is the stock in relation to its short-term support level?	Bounced off	Fallen through
What is the stock's technical pattern, using your favorite indicator. (For example, if using MACD, is the stock in positive or negative territory?)	Robust	Not robust
Has there been any recent news on the company, good or bad?	Good news	Bad news
How is the industry group doing?	Above average	Below average

good historical pattern of momentum runs. Table 6–1 contains a list of questions you might use to upgrade or downgrade the stock picks on your list. You might consider those stocks with the highest number of upgrade indications as potential buy candidates.

Using this evaluation process, you can eliminate the weakest of the stocks, but you may still end up with too many stocks to buy at one time. To find the ones with the best momentum right now, you'll need a good entry strategy.

Entry Strategies: Is the Momentum for Real?

A good entry strategy is half the ball game for the momentum investor (the other half, of course, is a good exit strategy). You must enter the stock at a point where you're confident the momentum is for real. So you'll want to use an indicator that has a good record of indicating trend reversals. Figures 6–8, 6–9, and 6–10 show three of the more popular trend-reversal indicators—the MACD, the Stochastics index, and the Wilder Relative Strength Indicator (RSI).

FIGURE 6–8

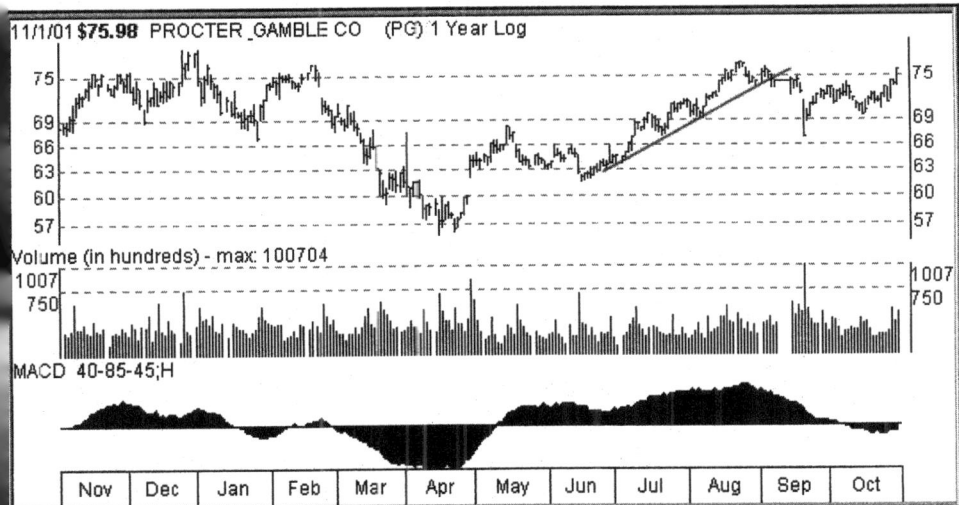

This weekly MACD graph indicates a good entry for Procter & Gamble (PG) in early May at about $63. The typical momentum investor might have exited with the trendline break in late August at about $75 a share.

F I G U R E   6–9

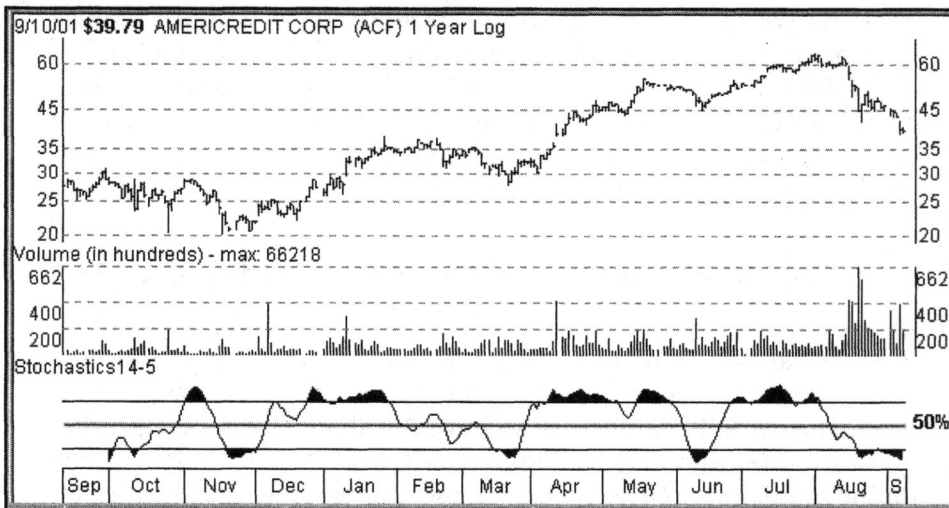

```
9/10/01 $39.79 AMERICREDIT CORP (ACF) 1 Year Log
```

A momentum investor could have used 14/5 Stochastics to take advantage of AmeriCredit's three short-term momentum runs, entering when the Stochastics crossed upward above the 50 percent line and exiting when it crossed below that line. (This 50 percent rule is an interpretation by Luiz V. Alvim of the classic Stochastics index. A description of the 50 percent rule appears in our 1994 book *CyberInvesting: Cracking Wall Street with Your Personal Computer.*)

These indicators are used by many momentum investors as both entry and exit signals.

Exit Strategies: Forget the Peaks

Exit strategies are the other half of the momentum investing ball game. Most technical indicators don't indicate that a trend is going to *end*—they signal when a trend has run its course and has started to reverse. Granted, there are some indicators that tell you when a trend may be losing steam, such as those that show decreasing volume on price increases. These indicators can give you a hint of the reversal of money flow, but most momentum investors rely on indicators that suggest the trend has ended, and they get out after the peak. (The MACD, Wilder RSI, and Stochastics indicators discussed

FIGURE 6-10

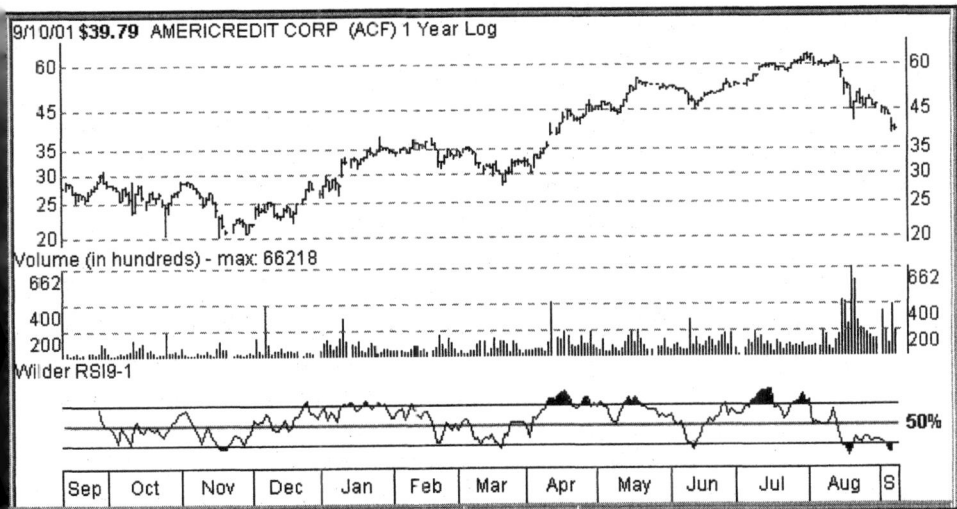

9/10/01 $39.79 AMERICREDIT CORP (ACF) 1 Year Log

A 9-bar Wilder RSI gives similar signals to the Stochastics index, with a buy signal when the RSI crosses above the 50 percent line and a sell signal when it crosses below that line. (This is an adaptation of Luiz V. Alvim's 50 percent Stochastics rule, described previously, applied to the standard RSI technique.)

earlier are trend-reversal indicators.) Most momentum investors use the reverse of their entry signal or a breakdown of the upward trendline. Keep in mind that if the stock breaks down shortly after you purchase it, you may get an exit signal after you've bought the stock, which could easily generate a loss. Our advice is to take the quick loss because sometimes things just don't work out. So listen to your exit signals.

There are other ways momentum investors can determine that the momentum of a stock has slowed or stopped. One way is to compare the stock to the appropriate index. (Tech stocks can be compared to the Nasdaq Composite Index, and large-cap stocks to the S&P 500.) What you're looking for is a divergence between the index and the stock. If the stock has fallen back along with the index, there's not as much need for concern, but if the stock has fallen back and index has not, this is a much better indication that the stock has run out of gas.

Another way to determine that the momentum run is over is to look at the underlying cause of the momentum and see if that cause has changed. If group momentum was the driving force behind a stock's momentum, a good time to exit is at the first sign of a slowdown in the group momentum (if the stock has not already given you an exit signal). If exploding earnings were the underlying cause of the momentum, a warning that next quarter's earnings will not be as great as expected will reverse the momentum. Even just a hint that earnings may not come in as planned can change perception or confidence about the stock to the point that the P/E craters and any change in perception can be lethal to a momentum stock.

Trend reversals aren't the only reason to exit a momentum stock, however. Sometimes you may want to trade a perfectly good momentum stock for an even better momentum stock. Momentum investing is unique in this way. If you have a limited amount of investment funds, for example, and you find a stock with better momentum characteristics than any you own, you may want to sell Stock A to buy Stock B, even though Stock A still appears to have some momentum left.

It is less important which exit strategy you use than that you use one. An exit strategy will increase the odds that you will cut your losses quickly and keep most of the profits from a momentum run. Whether it is a simple technical indicator or a complex mechanical system, choose one in which you have the most confidence, which is easy to use, and to which you have easy access. And monitor your portfolio closely.

Momentum Portfolio Strategies

Portfolio management is crucial to the momentum investor. Here are some strategies to keep in mind when building and managing a portfolio of momentum stocks.

- ◆ *Diversification.* Momentum investors usually have smaller portfolios than do value and growth investors, typically holding 5 to 10 stocks at any given time. They justify the lack of diversification because of the short-term nature of the portfolios, and the heavy time commitment required for monitoring the stocks. Nevertheless, you would be better off to have as many stocks as possible spread through two or three industries. Keep in mind that if you have only five stocks at any given time, each one represents about 20 percent of your portfolio. A 50 percent drop in just one stock would mean a 10 percent drop in your entire portfolio.

- *Monitoring your portfolio.* Momentum investing is a short-term game because the momentum can be very short-lived as the market ebbs and flows. That's why momentum investors tend to monitor their portfolios on a daily basis. Not only do you need to keep an eye on your own stocks for signs of a trend reversal, you need to be aware of earnings announcements and industry group performance and other events that might affect your portfolio or present new and better opportunities. You need to monitor the industry groups of the stocks you own and be aware of the performance of comparable indexes. You need to review the stocks on your watch list continuously and be ready to act when an opportunity presents itself. Momentum investing is a never-ending quest for the next best thing, and it requires constant vigilance and the ability to act quickly and decisively.

- *Cash position.* Cash management varies among momentum investors. During lean times, some may hold as much as 50 percent cash; others stay fully invested at all times. The best momentum investors (with whom we are familiar) go to a larger cash position when they are having a difficult time finding momentum stocks or if they are encountering a string of losses. In such cases, they frequently step aside for a time or cut back their holdings until the market behavior is more conducive to their investing style.

CASE STUDY: DISCOUNT AUTO PARTS (DAP)

The objective of this case study was to identify a small-cap company for investment in order to demonstrate the selection process for momentum stocks.

DAP: A Small-Cap Momentum Stock

On October 17, 2001, Discount Auto Parts (DAP) appeared as one of the top momentum stocks within the small-cap universe. It had a market cap of $259 million and a P/E ratio of 14.60 based on FY 2002

EPS estimates (FY ends 5/02). Discount Auto Parts scored exceptionally well for the basic characteristics of a momentum stock:

- A percentage price change of 18 percent over the past month
- Ranked in the top 94th percentile of all stocks for price momentum
- Ranked in the 99th percentile of all stocks for earnings momentum
- Ranked in the 88th percentile in accumulation/distribution, which measures money flow

What Is DAP?

The first step in our evaluation process was to find out a little bit about the company. Discount Auto Parts is a leading seller of auto replacement parts, maintenance items, and car accessories to professional mechanics and do-it-yourselfers. As of August 28, 2001, DAP had 668 stores in operation in Alabama, Florida, Georgia, Louisiana, Mississippi, and South Carolina. The company, which is 25 percent family-owned, had agreed to a merger with Advance Auto Parts, a private company that is the second largest auto parts store operator in the United States.

Typically, a stock that is going to be bought out at a specific price for cash would not be a candidate for momentum investing, once it has moved near the acquisition price. But DAP's situation was a merger, which would create a new company made up of the merging companies, which would trade on the New York Stock Exchange (NYSE). Investors could continue to follow the stock as an individual stock. Therefore the impending merger could be treated as another bullish event in an already bullish stock.

A Look at the Chart

From a low of $5 in late December, DAP had a short momentum run to $7 in early January (see Figure 6–11). Then the stock based for several months and finally broke out in mid-April for a nice run to almost $14 in early June. After retracing part of those gains, the stock surged again only to find major resistance at $14.

Despite excellent earnings figures reported by the company in

F I G U R E   6–11

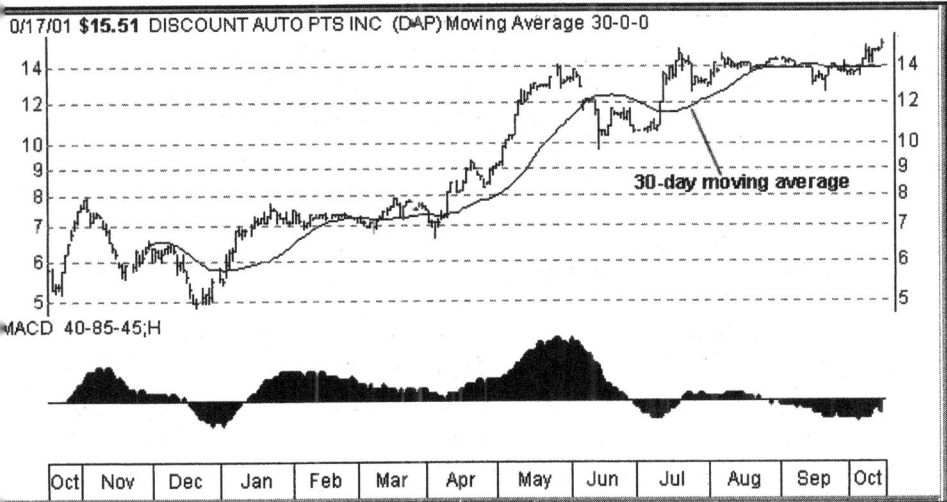

0/17/01 **$15.51** DISCOUNT AUTO PTS INC (DAP) Moving Average 30-0-0

30-day moving average

MACD 40-85-45;H

Oct | Nov | Dec | Jan | Feb | Mar | Apr | May | Jun | Jul | Aug | Sep | Oct

DAP had several good momentum runs over the past year and in mid-October appeared to be poised for another because it had broken the 30-day moving average and the MACD appeared to be ready to go positive.

September and the pending merger, the stock held constant in the $14 range, basing for a good 2 months, until a breakout in early October. That long basing period may well have occurred while Wall Street was digesting the economics of the merger, but, as we have pointed out, the economics were excellent to outstanding, and the breakout of that basing pattern was the main reason DAP was accepted as a momentum pick in mid-October. That breakout was on high upside volume, and the stock closed above that major resistance with a 52-week high on October 17.

The Momentum Stock Evaluation Checklist

At the time of this study, DAP was still one of the high-ranking stocks on momentum characteristics, and an evaluation using the evaluation checklist in Table 6–1 indicated it was ripe for purchase in a typical momentum portfolio.

- *Momentum patterns.* Over the past 2 years, DAP exhibited several short-term momentum runs, and the stock was on a long-term uptrend in 2001, starting in January, with a couple of basing periods and a retracement.
- *Recent quarter-over-quarter earnings momentum.* Reported earnings were $0.35 for the first quarter 2002 (ending August 31, 2001) as compared with $0.21 per share for the first quarter of fiscal 2001 (FY 2002 ends 5/3/02).
- *High earnings growth rate over the past 1 to 2 years.* Discount Auto Parts' historical earnings growth over the past year was about 70 percent.
- *Analyst revisions.* There were no upward revisions by analysts. In fact, coverage of this stock was very sparse—only one analyst was following the stock—but that was not surprising given the size of the company.
- *Earnings surprises.* In the only previous quarter for which there was an estimate, DAP beat the estimate by almost 30 percent (estimate: $0.44; actual $0.57).
- *Buy/hold/sell recommendations.* There was one moderate buy recommendation.
- *Stock price in relation to 30-day average.* Discount Auto Parts was above its 30-day moving average (Figure 6–11).
- *Money flow.* There was money flowing into the stock, as witnessed by the fact that DAP ranked in the 88th percentile for accumulation/distribution.
- *Resistance breakthrough.* The stock recently broke through a major resistance level at $14.
- *Price in relation to short-term support.* The stock is above strong short-term support at $14.
- *MACD technical pattern.* Discount Auto Parts was in positive MACD territory at the time of analysis, having had a positive breakout a couple of weeks earlier (Figure 6–11). This is a very positive pattern.
- *Recent news.* Discount Auto Parts had agreed to merge with the nation's second largest auto parts dealer, Advance Auto Parts. (Note: The merger was completed on November 29, 2001, and the new company now trades on the

NYSE as Advance Auto Parts, Inc., under the symbol
AAP.)

◆ *Industry group performance.* The Retail Stores / Specialty industry group was above average in October 2001, ranking
in the top 80th percentile for group momentum.

Conclusion: A Stock with Earnings and Price Momentum

Discount Auto Parts had earnings momentum behind its price momentum, so it was a good candidate for a momentum investor in
mid-October. The projected earnings growth rate for FY 2002 was
27.4 percent and for FY 2003, 24.4 percent, which was well above its
industry and the S&P 500. Clearly the stock's performance met the
quantitative goals of momentum stocks. Because of its positive
scores on most of the items in the evaluation checklist, DAP would
have been accepted as an excellent momentum stock on October 17.

FUNDS FOR MOMENTUM INVESTORS—NOT!

Mutual funds are contrary to the whole idea of momentum investing. Those who are attracted to the momentum style of investing
like a lot of action and want quick, substantial rewards, neither of
which is likely to happen with mutual funds. The sheer size of most
mutual funds makes momentum investing impractical. Most fund
managers need to be able to invest millions of dollars in each position, which prevents them from moving in and out of stocks quickly. And, of course, moving quickly is the essence of momentum investing.

Of course, you can look for funds with short-term performance
as their most important goal or look for a money manager who has
a momentum style. That kind of fund may give you the flavor of
momentum investing, but it's a bit like riding Amtrak cross-coun-
try when you've got your heart set on riding a roller coaster at
Coney Island.

An exchange-traded fund (ETF) provides a bit more action,
even though it is made up of a specific basket of stocks that never
changes. A momentum-oriented investor might identify a sector
that has momentum and buy an ETF that represents that sector.

If you're an accredited investor—that is, have a net worth of at least $1 million or an annual income of $200,000 or more—hedge funds are a possibility. Hedge funds have fewer regulations than do mutual funds, which means hedge fund managers have more freedom to use aggressive portfolio techniques, such as shorting, margin, or outright borrowing, and hedge funds need not diversify as much as the typical mutual fund has to. If you're interested, check online resources (listed in Appendix A) for a hedge fund with momentum investing as its goal.

Online Resources for Momentum Stocks

A list of momentum-related Web sites appears in Appendix A. Such lists quickly become outdated, however, as new Web sites come online and current sites merge or disappear. Here is a list of keywords that you can use with the major search engines to find momentum-related Web sites—no matter when you might be reading this book.

MOMENTUM STOCK KEYWORDS

CANSLIM*	sector rotation
earnings momentum	top stocks
high growth stock investing	top-down investing
industry group rotation	top-performing industries
momentum gurus	William O'Neil
momentum portfolios	winning stocks
momentum stocks	

*This is an acronym for William O'Neil's popular stock selection process for momentum stocks

---

HINTS FOR SUCCESSFUL MOMENTUM INVESTING

1. *Keep your emotions out of the process.* This is the number one rule for any investor, but it is especially important for the momentum player.
2. *Be disciplined.* Discipline is probably more important in momentum investing than in any other style of investing. If you're seeking dramatic moves in stocks—which is the

essence of momentum investing—you must know when to get out, and you must have the discipline to follow your system. You must exit when your timing indicators say the momentum move is likely over. You aren't a momentum investor if you sit there and watch the stock melt down.

3. *Develop a system for entering and exiting stocks.* It is absolutely critical for a momentum investor to have a system for entering and exiting stocks efficiently. Most likely, the system will be based on technical analysis. Select an indicator that works well for you, such as MACD, RSI, Stochastics, or if you're an advanced investor, a mechanical trading system—and *follow it*

4. *Be nimble.* Get in quickly, and get out quickly.

5. *Don't fall in love with your stock.* This is good advice for any investor, but it is especially crucial for the momentum investor.

6. *Be prepared to spend time every day on your stocks.* A move in a momentum stock can begin or end in a day. You have to spend time every day looking at the charts of the stock you own, and be prepared to exit quickly when the signal comes. You also have to spend time looking at charts and ranking indicators of stocks on your watch list and be prepared to enter quickly when the entry signal comes.

7. *Apply top-down investing.* Top-down investing means finding the top-performing industry groups first, then searching for the hottest stocks in those groups (see Chapter 9). This means keeping a steady eye on the performance of the groups represented by your stocks. If the industry group turns down, there's a good chance your momentum stock may fall as well, and you'll need to be quick on the trigger.

8. *Watch for changes in analysts' forecasts.* Pay attention to downgrades or lowered estimates. These can be predictive of a short-term decline in a momentum stock.

9. *Watch for press releases from the company.* Hints of future events that could negatively impact the stock can often be found in company press releases. Although you are not in a momentum stock for very long, it behooves you to watch for company announcements just in case there is a precursor of bad news. Unlike with other styles of investing, the

typical momentum investor exits first and asks questions later.

10. *Take your losses quickly.* If your indicator gives an exit signal that will result in your taking a loss, take it! Unfortunately, far too many investors are unwilling to admit they were wrong, and they resist taking a loss. But if you don't take that small loss when the signal comes, you may find yourself up the proverbial creek without a paddle because the indicator has already given an exit signal and you no longer have a signal to rely on. So what would have been a small loss becomes bigger and bigger. This is one of the most serious problems for all investors, but it is especially acute for the momentum investor, who needs to act quickly. When you get an exit signal from whatever indicator you're following, take it, even if you have to admit you made a mistake in selecting the stock in the first place.

CHAPTER 7

Strategies for Technical Investing

Pure technicians are investors who believe that everything about a company is likely factored into the stock price. They believe that company fundamentals, earnings reports, earnings estimates, industry group performance, the latest news, even whisper numbers or rumors of impending mergers or acquisitions, are *already* reflected in the stock price. Technicians are concerned only with the patterns on the stock chart, specifically the uptrends and the downtrends.

Technicians have at their disposal hundreds of technical indicators to help them determine when an upward trend is beginning and when it is over. Most use just a few indicators or systems, and the ones they choose depend on whether they are short-term or long-term technicians. Short-term technicians use indicators that give them short-term buy and sell signals within a given period. Longer-term players ignore the short-term ups and downs and look for a definitive change in the longer-term trend.

Technicians are similar to momentum investors in that they use charting to find stocks that are about to have a positive or negative trend reversal. But unlike momentum investors, who generally base their chart analysis on underlying earnings momentum, technicians rarely look for the underlying cause of a trend. They believe that by interpreting classic chart patterns they can capture the larger part of any move, whatever its source. Technicians may hold a stock less than a week in an attempt to simply capture the biggest portion of a new trend—and they exit when their indicators tell them the current trend is likely at an end.

THE ART OF TECHNICAL INVESTING

Despite the use of technical systems for entry and exit signals, technical investing is not a strictly mechanical style. There is an art to interpreting a chart, and some technicians are better at it than others.

The art of reading charts is the art of pattern recognition. Stock charts, of course, do not all look exactly the same. There is no "ping" that sounds when a chart formation matches a particular pattern. You have to be able to recognize the different formations and realize which formations have formed a pattern that has led to an uptrend or downtrend in the past. For example, if patterns A, B, and C appear in a stock chart, the stock is more likely to start a new uptrend because that is what has happened over and over in the past. The pattern is not telling you to enter but to get ready to enter. It is like the hunter who is carrying his rifle through the forest. When he hears a rustle of the leaves or sees a movement that might be a deer, he aims the gun and gets ready to fire. But he waits until he has a clear shot before he pulls the trigger. When the technician sees a certain chart pattern, she knows to start watching the stock very closely and *if* X happens—if the deer appears in the clearing—that is the time to pull the trigger.

The technician is looking for patterns that normally result in a buy or sell signal. Martin Pring, author of *Technical Analysis Explained*[1] calls this a "preponderance of evidence." When there is a preponderance of evidence that a new uptrend or downtrend is near or has begun, that is the trigger to act. The more evidence you gather, the more inclined you might be to act on a specific signal. The exact patterns and the exact triggers depend on the technical indicator or system you are using. For example, you might watch for certain patterns, such as cups and handles or double bottoms, but if the MACD is the indicator you rely on, you wouldn't buy until you get a clear MACD breakout. If you favor Bollinger Bands, you would get ready to act once the bands start to squeeze together

---

[1] Martin Pring, *Technical Analysis Explained: The Successful Investor's Guide to Spotting Investment Trends and Turning Points*, 3d ed. (McGraw-Hill Professional Publishing, 1991).

(which usually indicates that the next move will be a major one), but you'd wait for the actual move before you pull the trigger.

This is the art of technical analysis, and it is only after you learn to read the patterns of your particular indicator that you can then rely on the entry and exit signals of that indicator.

THE PQ CHART OF THE TECHNICIAN

The two indispensable traits a technician needs are discipline and, of course, excellent charting skills. We gave both a 10 on the PQ chart (Figure 7–1). Charting is the name of the technical game, so you need to know how to read stock charts and how to detect the particular patterns in which you're interested. You'll need discipline equal to that of a momentum investor. The technician, like the momentum investor, must be able to act quickly and decisively on entry and exit signals when they are given. Technical investing is an investing style that requires that you act expeditiously.

With regard to time commitment, we need to differentiate between the time it takes to learn technical analysis—which is considerable—and the time it takes an experienced chartist to browse through numerous charts seeking good candidates—which is not very much time. In the time it takes to analyze one financial statement, a chartist can examine 50 stock charts and find the two or three that merit consideration. So the learning curve is high, but once you are good with charts, the stock selection phase is rapid. Because of the learning curve and the need to monitor holdings for changes in trends, the time commitment required for technical investing is above average. We gave it an 8 on the PQ chart.

The time an investor needs to wait to see rewards from technical investing is relatively short compared with other major investing styles. A short-term technician might hold a position for less than a day to a week or so; a longer-term technician might hold a position for a month or longer. So we gave time horizon a 3 on the PQ chart.

Patience is typically measured relative to time horizon—the length of time your money is tied up in your investment—but for technicians, patience is rated a little differently. Your time horizon may be relatively short compared with, say, growth or value investing, but you will need patience to wait for technical patterns to develop and give the signal to enter or exit. You'll also need patience

FIGURE 7-1

PQ Chart for the Technician

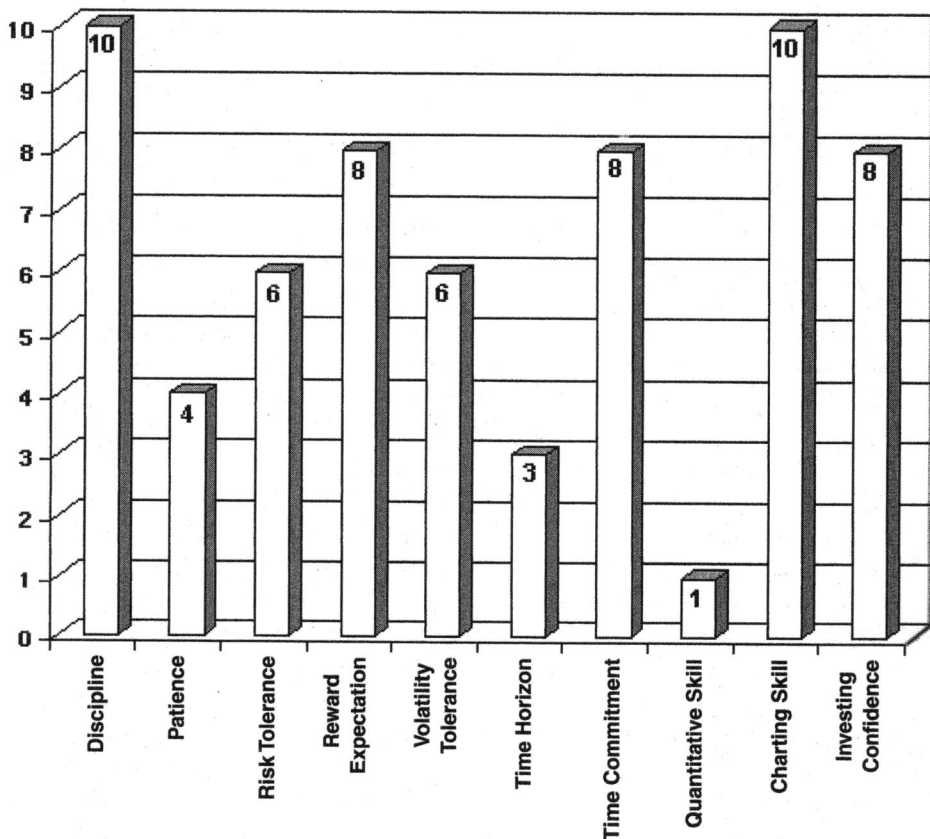

during the learning process to study charts patterns and back-test indicators to determine which systems or indicators to put your faith in. Once you've mastered your system, though, technical investing can be quite rote, but you'll still need the patience to wait for the pattern to develop.

Because pure technicians care only about chart patterns, they need little or no quantitative skills. They usually don't read financial statements or compare various numbers and ratios to see which stock is the better value. Most technicians never even look at financial statements, and they are technicians for precisely that reason. They *like* the fact that they don't have to make judgment calls. If their technical indicator says *Enter*, they buy the stock; if it says *Exit*, they sell the stock. Or at least that is what they claim and in fact are taught.

Not having to make judgment calls on the merits of an investment would normally mean a low PQ chart score for investing confidence. But technicians must have a great deal of confidence in the technical tools they use and in their ability to recognize the best and worst chart patterns. To practice any art you must have great confidence in your skills and talent, so we gave investing confidence an 8 on the PQ chart.

Risk and reward, interestingly, are not necessarily in lockstep for technicians. Technicians expect high rewards (otherwise they wouldn't commit the time required for learning this style of investing), but they usually believe they are taking very little risk because they usually employ trend-following indicators. This may or may not be the case in reality. Investors who buy into the stock of a company they are not familiar with increase their risk, in our opinion, whether or not they will acknowledge it. All things considered, technical investing entails average tolerance for risk and volatility because technicians depend on their indicators to get them out of a stock before it drops significantly.

ANATOMY OF A TECHNICAL STOCK

Dozens of technical theories have been developed to try to explain the movement of stock prices, and hundreds of indicators have been derived from those theories in an attempt to predict that movement. As a result, it is impossible to use a single technical theory to try to deconstruct the "anatomy" of a typical technical stock; there *is* no typical technical stock. Instead, we will talk about the psychology behind the price and volume movements of a stock and how that psychology creates the different patterns that appear on a stock chart. Through their technical theories, technicians try to understand this psychology and obtain signals based on price and volume behaviors to guide them in and out of a stock.

The Psychology Behind Chart Patterns

We will use a very simplistic scenario to illustrate the psychology behind chart patterns and give you a hint of how a technician can "read" it by interpreting chart patterns.

Imagine a stock that is more or less at equilibrium—let's call it ABC Company. ABC has been trading between $19 and $20 for a number of weeks with an average daily volume of 100,000 shares. If a stock is trading in such a narrow range, there are more or less as many investors who want to own it as there are those who want to sell it, so anytime a buy order comes in for 100 or 500 or 1000 shares, there is someone ready to sell that many shares. Obviously, when there is as much supply as there is demand, the stock doesn't go anywhere. It moves within a narrow price range, which is called *basing*.

Now let's say that the word on the Street emerges that ABC Company is having a good quarter. Upon hearing this rumor, at least a few new buyers will want to purchase shares, and current owners might want to add to their position. This activity would likely show up as increased buying volume. The average daily volume of 100,000 shares might increase to 125,000 shares for a few days, but even though the volume increases, in this scenario the price may not go anywhere until the normal selling is absorbed. Still, there is more emphasis on buying than there was when the stock was basing, and eventually the increased buying volume will throw the buying and selling out of balance.

At this point, those who previously wanted to sell might take another look. The increased buying activity might pique their interest to the point that they decide to hold the stock instead of selling it. As a result, the selling might dry up at the same time that the buying increases. Then it becomes an issue of supply and demand. As supply decreases and demand increases, the price per share goes up. As buyers keep buying, they push the price per share higher and higher until the stock breaks out of its basing pattern on increased volume. This is a classic pattern that technicians look for: a breakout on increased volume.

The point of this little scenario is to illustrate that volume often leads price. There was increased volume at the beginning of our scenario, but the price of ABC didn't jump immediately. It was only when the supply dried up that the stock broke out of its basing pattern, and when this happens, momentum investors who see the stock starting to move may jump in. In addition, investors who base their decision on a company's fundamentals will be likely to buy the stock because of the perception that something positive is going on with the earnings. Here's how that might work.

Let's say that after the basing pattern breakout, ABC Company makes an announcement affirming that the company is having an excellent quarter and will meet expectations and may even beat them by as much as, say, 20 percent. Momentum investors who keep an eye out for a stock that is "moving" see the breakout and the momentum that is starting to build, so they may jump on. And investors who base their decisions on a company's future earnings prospects are likely to sit up and take notice. Perhaps they saw the stock break out of its basing pattern but now that earnings reports substantiate the move, they may be able to justify a price of, say, $24. As a result, more earnings-based buying comes into the stock, inching it up to, say, $22. So now you have increased buying *and* increased volume, driven by both momentum investors and earnings-based buyers.

What happens next is that some investors who were happy to sell at $19 or $20 stop selling. Whether or not they've heard the rumors, they can see the stock moving up on increasing volume, so they may think, "Wait a minute, maybe I should hold on to this stock," and they do. So buyers continue to outnumber sellers, and the price continues to climb on increasing volume.

These are patterns that technicians can see on a stock chart. They don't need to know anything about the underlying fundamentals or who's buying the stock or why. The fact that the stock moved out of a basing pattern on increasing volume signals a buy to a technician. Keep in mind that for the purpose of this simple example, nothing unusual is happening in the market; the behavior of the imaginary ABC Company appears to be unrelated to any activity in the underlying market and is unique to ABC.

Now, as the price continues to move up on increasing volume, momentum investors and technicians see this activity on their charts and they continue to buy. So you have the price moving up on increasing volume. But when the stock reaches, say, $25, the scenario shifts. Earnings-based buyers who bought on the earnings news and are delighted that the stock is moving ahead now step aside because the stock price now fully reflects that earnings enhancement. They continue to hold on to their positions, waiting to see what happens, but they stop buying. With a cessation of earnings-based buying, the volume may start to slow, but because momentum investors and technicians are still buying, the stock price continues to go up. At this point, some technicians might see this pattern—the stock continuing to go up on decreasing volume—and become concerned because that pattern is not a good one. In the past such a pattern often has resulted in a topping pattern followed by some retracement of the move. The technicians who see this pattern may step aside, which decreases the volume further.

On the other hand, when the stock moves past $25, the volume could continue to increase and the stock price could start basing— not going anywhere. There is no way to know what is really happening and where the increase in volume is coming from. It could be from momentum players who are still excited about the stock and keep buying, or it could be from earnings-based investors who believe the stock is overvalued and start selling. Volume is volume, and, in general, buying volume is indistinguishable from selling volume. For either reason, the fact is that volume picks up and the stock doesn't go anywhere. It has run out of gas. So what the technician sees when she looks at ABC Company is a stock that is basing, say, between $25 and $26 on heavy volume.

Buying Volume versus Selling Volume

A number of services offer indicators that attempt to distinguish the percentage of buying volume from selling volume on any given day. In general, these indicators label buying volume as that which is transacted on higher prices and selling volume as that which is transacted on lower prices. (TradeStation, described in Appendix A, is one of the services offering this feature.)

This pattern—of increasing volume and stalled stock price— is a classic sell signal for technicians. So the technical investors start to get out of the stock. But ABC may not start to decline immediately, because there are still buyers. Momentum investors, who almost always overshoot the trend, continue to buy, and the uninformed public—those who maybe have heard from a friend or a television pundit that ABC Company is up 20 percent—now get excited and jump in.

So guess what happens as ABC continues upward beyond the $25 to $26 range, reaching, say, $28? Volume finally starts to slow.

Most earnings-based buying dries up at about $28 because the stock is now overpriced for those investors; they thought it was a good buy at $24 but at $28 they're going to wait and see what happens. By the time the stock reaches $28 or so, most if not all technicians have exited because they have seen the price pause on increasing volume. And at this point, some momentum investors might decide to take their profits. As a result, the stock falls back, and now that the buying has dried up, the volume begins to decrease as well.

As the trend reverses, the momentum players and technicians who have not already jumped out now do so, and the stock heads back down to $24 or slightly below.

Ah . . . but remember who liked the stock at $24? Earnings-based buyers. As they start buying again, the price is likely to stabilize near $24. Eventually, however, earnings-based buying will move the stock all the way up to $26 or higher, and the same scenario starts all over again.

The point of this overly simplistic exercise was to show what can cause the patterns and trends the technicians see on a stock chart. (It also illustrates why you don't want to be the last one in or the last one out!) All of this activity is visible to the chartist: increasing volume on a stock that is basing, a breakout on increasing volume, a stock moving up on increasing volume, a stock moving up on lessening volume. These movements all form patterns that can be (because they have been in the past) interpreted by technicians to predict the next move of the stock. A good chart reader can make $4 to $5 a share in just a few weeks without knowing anything about the company behind the stock.

We're not trying to recruit you as a technician—we ourselves are not pure technicians—but we are trying to demonstrate that chart patterns are simply visible representations of the psychology behind the buying and selling of stocks. Because they can "read" the psychology of patterns, technicians believe they can see the beginning of a run and the beginning of the end of the run before other types of investors can.

Just keep in mind, our scenario was based on good underlying fundamentals. Not all stocks work that way. Sometimes the reason for an uptrend or run is based on an unfounded rumor, an analyst's error, chat board activity, or an overly zealous television pundit. There's a great deal more risk if you buy a stock without solid underlying fundamentals, but pure technicians would swear that fundamentals don't matter because they will watch the charts for the "telltale" signs of a reversal.

If the concept of technical investing appeals to you, you'll need to spend a lot of time learning about the subject. There are hundreds of tools to help the technician interpret stock patterns. For an overview, we recommend *The Encyclopedia of Technical Market Indicators* by Robert W. Colby and Thomas A. Meyers (McGraw-Hill Professional Publishing, 1988). For books on specific technical theories—and there are dozens of them—we suggest that you browse through Traders Library at www.traderslibrary.com. If you want to understand more about the psychology of investing, we particularly recommend the classic *Reminiscences of a Stock Operator* by Edwin LeFevre (John Wiley & Sons, 1994; originally published in 1923). It takes you into the mind of a fictionalized legendary trader and helps you understand the psychology of the market.

When Is a Stock Not a Technical Candidate?

Not all stocks are good candidates for technical investing. A stock chart needs to regularly exhibit patterns that can provide signals. If a stock's shareholder base is so diverse or fluid that the stock hasn't regularly exhibited definable trends, then it is not likely to develop them and so would not be a good stock to trade based on technical investing. The questions you need to ask yourself are: Has this stock shown a predictable pattern in the past? Would the signals (from whatever system you use) have worked in the past? If so, the stock could develop similar patterns in the future, and your signals would be likely to work similarly in the future.

Figure 7–2 shows a stock that is a good candidate for technical investing. Figure 7–3 shows a stock that is not a good candidate for technical investing.

AmeriCredit (ACF) in Figure 7–2 is a good technical stock because it has had four very nice, definable uptrends within the past

F I G U R E   7–2

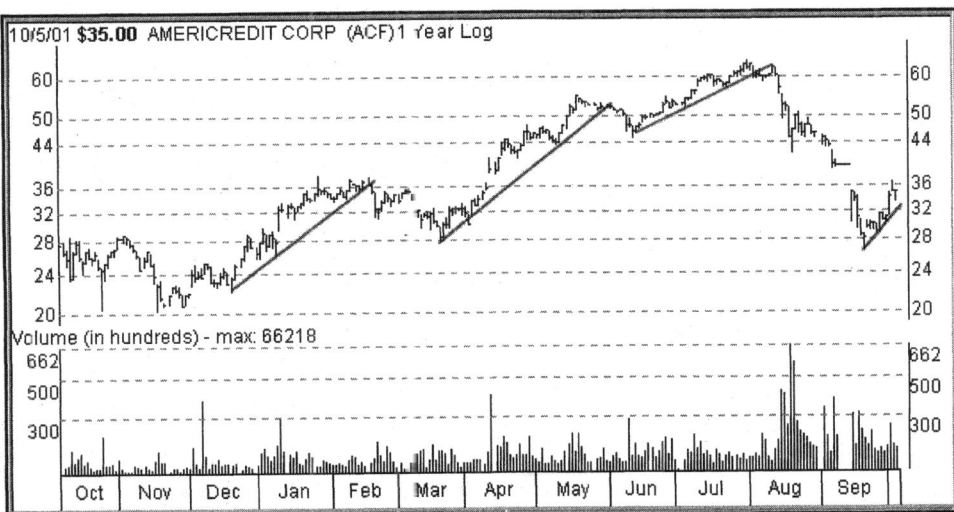

ACF shows three well-defined uptrends since December 2000 and the beginning of a new one in September 2001. It is an excellent stock for the technical investor and, in fact, was a favorite selection of an online technical stock picking service.

year, so it is safe to assume that it will continue to exhibit similar patterns. From December through July the stock moved 36 points, but it did so by going into an uptrend, pulling back, rallying, and pulling back, rallying again, and pulling back again, which presented several trading opportunities for the momentum investor. In August ACF went into a fairly major downtrend but appears to be headed up again.

Now look at Kellogg Company (K) in Figure 7–3. During the period shown, October 2000 through September 2001, Kellogg would have been challenging for the technician since there were few if any well-defined trends or trend breaks. You might have made four points if you'd bought the stock and held it through August, but technicians usually expect better returns over shorter periods. They know there are just too many stocks with good technical patterns to waste their time trying to make technical trades on buy-and-hold type stocks.

FIGURE   7–3

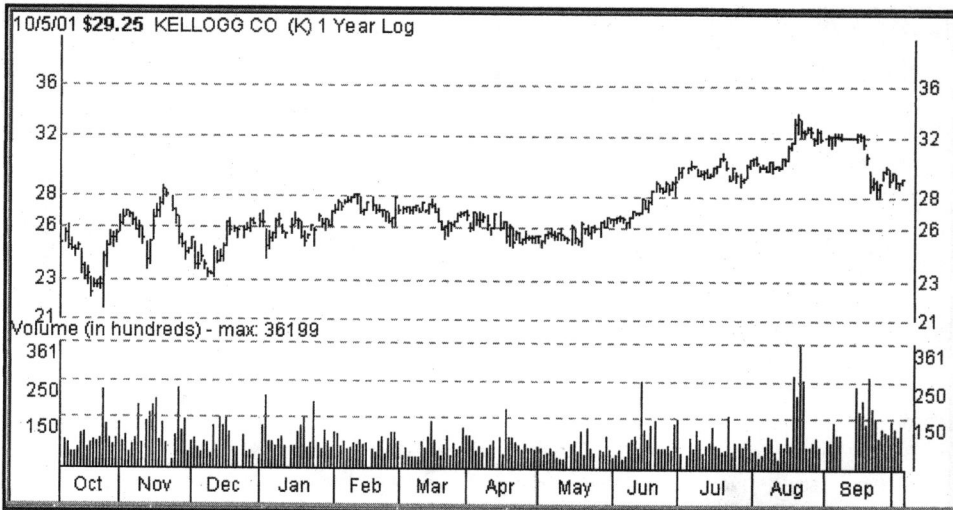

10/5/01 $29.25 KELLOGG CO (K) 1 Year Log

In 2000/2001 Kellogg would have been challenging for the technician since there were few if any well-defined trends or trend breaks.

THE INVESTING PROCESS FOR TECHNICIANS

The three steps of the investing process apply to technical investing just as they do with other styles of investing.

Stock Selection Strategies:
Using Technical Filters

Pure technicians use technical filters to find stocks with the patterns they believe are successful. Typically, they look for some kind of breakout on increasing volume. The break might be out of a basing pattern or off of support. It might be an MACD breakout or a bounce off the 50-day moving average. The point is to study technical analysis until you find the indicators you like, then develop your filter around those indicators.

Some technicians find stocks that repeatedly exhibit the good patterns and trade them again and again. Others combine technical investing with, say, growth or top-down investing, selecting stocks first for their growth characteristics or industry group performance, then applying technical filters. We'll talk more about this when we discuss the hybrid investor in Chapter 9.

Key Variables to Use in Screening or Filters

For a technical screen, you're looking for an increase in volume combined with a move that triggered a breakout of some technical indicator. You'll need two primary criteria:

- *Technical breakout.* Use the breakout criteria based on the indicator of your choice, such as an MACD breakout or a basing period breakout.
- *Volume indicators.* The ratio of today's volume to the 30-day or 90-day average volume and the ratio of the most recent 5-day average volume to the 90-day average volume will find stocks with unusual increases in volume.

Entry/Exit Strategies: Leave the Dance with the One Who Brought You

Your entry and exit signals will depend on the patterns you look for in selecting a stock. For example, if you look for stocks with basing patterns, your entry signal would be a basing pattern breakout. If you screen for stocks with good MACD patterns, the buy signal would come with the actual MACD breakout. If you like to buy stocks that have tested and found support, you'll need to look for stocks that have reversed at a major support level.

To sell a stock, many technicians use the reverse signal of the same indicator they used to enter the stock. For example, if you bought on a positive MACD breakout, you might sell on a negative MACD breakout. If you used a reversal from a support level to buy the stock, you might sell if the stock falls through that support level. Many technical investors use a break in the trendline as a sell signal, which would require watching the stock with your chart. More complex systems give precise buy and sell signals.

Portfolio Management Strategies for Technicians

Generally speaking, technical investing requires a great deal of portfolio management. You have to look at a lot of charts to find those with the right technical patterns and then monitor the stocks for the proper entry signal. Once you've bought a stock, you must constantly be alert to changes in the technical trend, which means you have to monitor your portfolio closely.

As a result, technicians don't usually hold a great many stocks at any one time, which means their portfolios are not as diversified as those of growth or value investors, and maybe even less diversified than those of momentum investors. Five to eight stocks seem to be the norm, but it depends completely on the time you have to devote to your stocks and on your individual preferences. As we mentioned earlier, some technical investors find a few favorite stocks that repeatedly develop good patterns, and they trade the same stocks over and over.

With regard to the cash versus stocks issue, there is no rule of thumb for technicians. We'd just suggest that you don't force the issue. If you're having trouble finding stocks with good patterns, hold on to your cash and wait until you find stocks that meet your technical criteria. Technicians who go both long and short will rarely have a lack of good technical candidates.

CASE STUDY: VITESSE SEMICONDUCTOR (VTSS)

The objective of this case study was to identify a stock with good technical patterns for investment in order to demonstrate the selection process for technical investing.

Background

Since a technician cares little or nothing about the fundamentals of a company, there was no "evaluation" process involved in selecting VTSS, just an examination of the stock's chart patterns. A note on the stock's technical background seems appropriate, however. Vitesse Semiconductor made a split-adjusted low of 30 cents in November 1992 and an all-time high of $115.69 in March 2000. Then the stock crashed to a recent low of $6.75 on September 27. The long-term chart showed that the stock formed a triple bottom with lows in late 1997 and 1998, and that support, unless violated, presaged higher prices for VTSS in the future. On October 25, 2001, the date of the analysis, the stock rallied, closing 68 percent above its September 27 low.

FIGURE 7-4

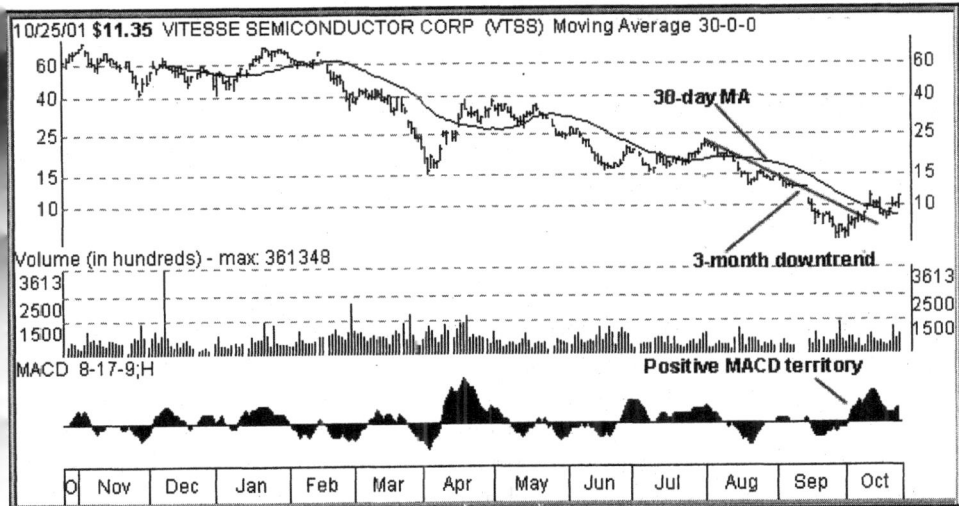

This chart showed VTSS in positive MACD territory in October after a positive breakout early in the month. By October 25 the stock had closed above its 30-day moving average and had also broken above a 3-month downtrend.

A Look at the Chart

In early October 2001, VTSS had a positive MACD breakout and was in positive territory on the date of the analysis (Figure 7–4). The weekly MACD (not shown) had just given a positive breakout. The stock had also closed above its 30-day moving average and had broken through a three-month downtrend. The stock showed a strong price-volume relationship and a positive relative strength. There was short-term resistance near the present level, which was anticipated to be temporary, as long as the overall market kept its then current momentum.

Conclusion: A Good Technical Buy

Vitesse met the basic requirements for a technical buy signal in late October 2001. The downtrend had been broken, the stock was above its 30-day moving average, there was a positive MACD breakout on the weekly histogram, and the daily MACD was in positive territory. Further, the earliest resistance was at $15, which was more than 30 percent above the then-current entry. If that resistance were to be broken, the stock could have yielded a large move to $40.

APPLYING TECHNICAL ANALYSIS TO FUNDS

There are no mutual funds that we know of whose portfolio is grounded in technical charting. Nevertheless, that doesn't mean you can't apply technical analysis to the mutual funds themselves. Although most technicians believe that it is not efficient to use charting with mutual funds, funds do exhibit the same sorts of trends as stocks, with the same kinds of beginnings and endings of those trends, and at least one newsletter service we know of is based on trading mutual funds using technical analysis.

A better way to apply technical analysis to funds, if that is what you want to do, is to concentrate on exchange-traded funds (ETFs). On an ETF, volume and price change are unrelated (as explained in "Why Volume Is Unrelated to Price on ETFs"), but a chart pattern is still a chart pattern. Both mutual funds and ETFs exhibit trends better than stocks do, because funds are the accumulation of all the stocks in the fund or ETF. Exchange-traded funds may trend better and over a longer period of time than do mutual funds, because mutual funds with their hundreds of stocks in many different industries are less likely to exhibit recognizable patterns.

Why Volume Is Unrelated to Price on ETFs

Because of the way ETFs are structured, volume and price are basically unrelated. The sponsors of the ETFs—Merrill Lynch, streetTRACK, Barclays, and others—agree to maintain the price of the ETF at the price of the underlying stocks. So unusually high volume doesn't necessarily drive up (or pull down) the stock price. For example, you could buy or sell 1,000,000 shares of, say, the semiconductor HOLDR without affecting the price of the underlying stocks because those million shares are spread across the total number of stocks in the ETF. Similarly, if the underlying stocks have a bad day, the price of the semiconductor HOLDR might drop 10 percent, but it might have zero volume.

Of course, this noncorrelation of volume to price could change if, say, billions of dollars from an institutional investor should pour into a specific ETF. In that event, the purchase of the underlying individual stocks by the ETF sponsor could drive up the price of the individual underlying stocks to the point that the price of the ETFs would have to go higher. To date, nothing like the required volume for that scenario has materialized. For more on ETFs, see "Exchange-Traded Funds" in Chapter 4.

Online Resources for Technical Investing

Appendix A contains a list of current Web sites for charting and technical analysis. To find the most current or newest sites that may not have existed at the time of this writing, here are some key words to use with online search engines.

TECHNICAL KEYWORDS

breakouts	mechanical trading systems
chart patterns	moving averages
charting	pattern recognition
Gerald Appel	technical analysis
John Ehlers	technical breakouts
MACD	technician
Martin Pring	

HINTS FOR SUCCESSFUL TECHNICAL INVESTING

1. *Back-test your system.* Develop a set of entry/exit rules that are based as much as possible on back-testing. Several charting Web sites that offer back-testing are described in Appendix A.

2. *Learn your system.* Study your system until you know it inside out. Study books and charts. Attend seminars. Make sure your system is reliable before you use it.

3. *Be disciplined.* The most important quality of a technician is the discipline to stick to a system. Buy when it says buy; sell when it says sell.

4. *Don't rationalize.* Sometimes a stock will move counter to what you *wish* would happen and when your system gives a

sell signal, you'll try to rationalize hanging onto the stock. Don't! Listen to your system!

5. *Stick to your rules.* More than any other style, technical analysis takes the emotion out of investing, which is why it has relatively low risk (*if* you have a proven, back-tested system). But you *must* stick to your rules.

6. *Make sure your system is appropriate for market conditions.* Some indicators work well in a bullish market but falter in a bear market; others shine in a bear market and give confusing signals in a bull market. Some MACD technicians use one type of MACD in bullish conditions and another type in a bear market. Be aware of whether your system is appropriate for the current market conditions.

7. *Don't force your system on a stock.* Technical signals work best on stocks that have well-defined trends. Don't try to force signals onto stocks that don't have appropriate patterns. Use technical screens and filters to find stocks with good patterns.

8. *Be on the lookout for new indicators and new systems.* Technicians develop new indicators and new systems all the time. To stay abreast of the latest developments read *Stocks & Commodities* magazine and become a regular visitor of Web sites that specialize in charting (some of which are listed in Appendix A).

9. *Take your losses quickly.* If your indicator gives an exit signal that will result in your taking a loss, take it—even if you just bought the stock. Your indicator is trying to tell you that you made a mistake! You must be willing to admit you were wrong and take your medicine. If you don't, the problem will be exacerbated by the fact that your indicator has already given an exit signal; it won't do you any good to sit around and wait for another. This is as important for the technician as for the momentum investor. Take the exit signal when it comes, and keep your losses small.

CHAPTER 8

Using Market Cap
as an Investing Strategy

Market capitalization is a term that represents the total value that the market places on a company. Market cap, as it is called, is determined by multiplying the number of outstanding shares by the stock price. For example, a company that is selling stock for $30 a share and has 10 million shares of stock outstanding has a market capitalization of $300 million.

Why should you care about market caps? For one thing, you may have a natural preference for one cap over another, whether you realize it or not. Some people prefer small-cap companies with their greater growth potential (more about this later). Others favor the very large companies for their well-known brand names and stability. If you find that you have a natural preference for one type of cap over another, being cognizant of that will be helpful in narrowing down your lists of stocks to analyze.

The other reason to care about market caps is that the market tends to favor one or sometimes two market caps at various points in time. As an investor, you can use this "favoritism" to get an edge in the market. So let's learn more about market caps.

The practice of grouping stocks into market-cap segments began more than 40 years ago. In the beginning, there were only two general divisions: large-cap stocks and small-cap stocks. In 1971 Nasdaq was formed by the National Association of Security Dealers as an automated quotation system, making it easier for new companies to go public. As a result, new companies proliferated during the next two decades, and as the economy grew, companies consolidated with many of the former large-cap companies, creating *very* large companies, indeed. Market valuations exceeding $100 billion, which had been rare in earlier years, became commonplace, with valuations stretching to more than $600 billion by 1999 for the two largest domestic companies, General Electric and Microsoft. Even today, after the market meltdown of 2000 and 2001, GE has a market cap of nearly $400 billion with Microsoft only a tad behind, and about 25 companies are currently valued over $100 billion.

With the smallest small-caps ranging between $100 to $200 million (depending on whose classifications you use), the disparity between the giants and the small caps was more than two-thousand-fold! This great disparity gave birth to a new middle tier that encompassed the larger small caps and the smaller large caps. The market capitalizations of stocks in this new tier—called, not surprisingly, mid caps—ranged from a few billion to as much as $15 billion. In general, a mid-cap stock has corporate stability, much like a large cap, but still has some of the growth potential of a small cap.

Many classifiers still use just three market-cap segments—large, mid, and small—but as the upper end of the small caps grew to over $1 billion in size, a new "baby" classification emerged for the lower end of the small caps. Dubbed "micro caps," these smallest public companies generally range in size up to about $150 million. These four market segments—large caps, mid caps, small caps, and micro caps—now comfortably encompass the approximately 10,000 public companies.

We should point out that market cap is a fluid concept. Various publishers in the field use different ranges for the different classifications (see Table 8–1), but, more significantly, companies routinely float between classifications as their stock price changes or as they issue more stock. Small caps grow into mid caps, mid caps into large caps, and frequently a company will lose ground and regress into a smaller market capitalization. Clearly, market-cap designations are not rigid walls but quite loose concepts that serve to help us focus our interest.

Most classifiers acknowledge this fluidity by making adjustments to their rankings or indexes on a regular basis. The Russell indexes are adjusted once a year to reflect current market capitalizations (as of May 31), and Morningstar.com adjusts its rankings at the

TABLE 8-1

Market-Cap Ranges

Market Cap	Our Preferred Classifications	Frank Russell Co. Classifications	Morningstar.com Classifications*
Large caps	$15 billion and over	$8 billion and over	$10.7 billion and over
Mid caps	$1.5–$15 billion	$3–$8 million	$1.7–$10.7
Small caps	$150 million–$1.5 billion	Less than $3 billion	Less than $1.7 billion
Micro caps	Less than $150 million	—	—
*As of December 2000.			

end of each month. Interestingly, Morningstar ranks the 250 largest companies as large caps, the next 750 as mid caps, and everything else as small caps.[1] With nearly 10,000 domestic stocks traded on the major exchanges, Morningstar's ranking of 1000 companies as large caps and mid caps leaves an enormous group of companies as small caps. We prefer the groupings shown in Table 8–1. (By the way, if you wish to use Internet search engines to screen for stocks in a certain market cap, use "market capitalization" as a criterion and enter the ranges shown in Table 8–1.)

Declining Market Caps

In the last couple of years many large-cap companies lost 50 to even 90 percent of their market capitalization, but that didn't mean they became significantly smaller companies in other aspects. While there may be layoffs, it is unlikely that a lowered market cap will cause a company to employ significantly fewer people or result in decreased revenues for a company. A decline in market cap simply means the market does not value a company as highly as it once did. One serious side effect of a lowered market cap is that the company may no longer be able to use its stock to make acquisitions because of the dilution of its stock value. Of course, when market caps decline across the board, as they did in the market meltdown of 2000–2001, most companies lose market value, which makes dilution not as serious an issue since most companies are impacted in a similar fashion.

---

[1] Peter Di Teresa, "The Meaning of Market Cap," June 18, 2001, at www.morningstar.com.

ROUND AND ROUND THEY GO

Historically, the market has favored different-sized companies at different times, which creates a "rotation" of market caps into and out of favor. Market cap rotation can either enhance or negatively impact your ability to get good returns on your investments (at least in the short run), so it might be a good idea to pay attention to which market cap is the current favorite.

What brings a market cap into favor is basically a large influx of money into that group of stocks at a particular time, impelled by varying market and economic conditions. Driving the flow of money into a specific market cap are the institutional investors—the hundreds of pension funds, mutual funds, and index funds that control trillions of dollars. This rotation is primarily among the large-cap, mid-cap, and small-cap sectors because they have a large institutional shareholder base. Many institutional investors are restricted to large-cap stocks, a significant number of institutions can also invest in mid-cap stocks, and a somewhat lesser number can invest in small-cap companies. As a result, institutional support is great enough to create periods in which these groups are in favor. Yet it is safe to say that the market will probably never favor microcaps, since few institutions can legally invest in such small companies.

Two examples of rotation among market caps occurred in the early 1960s and late 1990s. In the 1950s and 1960s, there was a large-cap mania in which people bid up values of the largest companies. You may recall the "Nifty Fifty," roughly the 50 largest companies in America at that time, many of which became household names (such as IBM, Xerox, and Polaroid). These 50 or so stocks reached extraordinarily high valuations, which led inevitably to a steady erosion in their prices. The collapse of the Nifty Fifty stock prices was followed by small caps moving into favor for many years owing to their reasonable valuation and exciting growth prospects.

The second example of a market rotation occurred in the bull market of the late 1990s, when index mania turned the spotlight back on large-cap stocks and drove them to greater and greater values. Index mania was essentially a self-fulfilling prophecy, in that large amounts of money flowed into index funds, which were forced to buy specific stocks in the various indexes, such as those in the S&P 500. As a result, the index fund was forced to pour more money into the individual stocks that made up the index, causing the stock prices to rise, which caused the index fund to rise, thereby enticing even more people to buy into the index fund.

These are just two examples of the market rotating dramatically from one market cap to another. Throughout recent market history there have been many such rotations, albeit of a less dramatic fashion.

Tracking Market-Cap Rotation

Market-cap rotation can be followed by viewing stock graphs of various indexes and exchange-traded funds (ETFs). Indexes and ETFs for tracking market-cap rotation are listed in Tables 9–1 and 9–2 in Chapter 9.

What happens is that the market cap in favor becomes over-valued and the ones that are out of favor become undervalued, so the pendulum swings. When the market meltdown in 2000 brought heavy selling pressure on large-cap stocks because of their high valuations, investors turned to mid caps, which came into favor during the second half of 2000 and the first quarter of 2001. In the months leading up to September 2001, small caps were in favor partly because they had been ignored for many years, creating excellent valuations, and partly because the United States seemed headed for a recession. (A poor economy often impacts large caps more than small caps because smaller companies may operate in small niches unaffected by economic doldrums.) But the attack on the World Trade Center caused a quick return to the safety of blue chip stocks (although this move is not entirely rational because most blue chips were greatly affected by the economic malaise in the aftermath of the attack). Aside from that unprecedented event, investors typically search for stocks that will provide the greatest gains, so the market rotates to whichever market cap offers the greatest opportunity.

Perhaps it is now clear why market caps are worth studying. By paying attention to which market cap is in favor, you may find it easier to find suitable stocks in one sector or another, depending on your investing style.

CHARACTERISTICS OF THE MARKET CAPS

Each market cap has its own distinguishing characteristics.

Large Caps

Large-cap companies are typically more stable than are small caps, with larger, more diversified revenues and steady, more predictable earnings. That is not to say that many a large cap has not melted down (a recent prime example is Polaroid, which declared bankruptcy). But the mainstay of large-cap stocks are the blue chips—household names such as AT&T, Coca-Cola, ExxonMobil, General Electric, General Motors, IBM, McDonald's, and Wal-Mart. In addition to providing more predictable, more stable earnings, blue chip stocks often pay dividends.

Not all large caps are blue chips, but large caps are generally considered a less risky investment partly because of their stability and because they have a larger float—more outstanding shares—which makes them more liquid than the smaller caps. Large caps also have a much broader shareholder base and more significant research coverage.

The concept of the stable, established large cap was challenged during the Internet fever of 1999. New dot-com companies emerged almost overnight with market valuations in the upper half of large-cap stocks (Yahoo! and Amazon.com, to name two). But there was a significant difference. These newly minted large caps had low revenues and, in many cases, no earnings. The dot-com fallout separated the wheat from the chaff, so to speak. While many traditional large caps lost a great deal of their market value, the dot-com biggies fell 90 percent and more.

There are several indexes that track the performance of large caps. The Dow Jones Industrial Average (DJI), which is the most common barometer of the market in general, is made up of 30 large-cap stocks from various industries. The broader S&P 500 (SPX) is virtually all large caps, and the S&P 100 (OEX) consists of the largest 100 companies of the S&P 500. The Russell Top 200® Index tracks large-cap stocks with an average market cap of $48 billion. The ETFs that track large-cap stocks are shown in Table 9–2 in Chapter 9.

Mid Caps

Mid cap is a relatively new classification, as we mentioned earlier. These stocks tend to have some of the stability of the large caps but also some of the high-growth prospects of the small caps. Mid caps also have institutional ownership but to a lesser extent than large caps do. Some familiar mid-cap names are AmeriCredit (ACF), $1.6 billion; Scientific Atlanta (SFA), $3.446 billion; and Bed, Bath & Beyond (BBBY), $8.5 billion. Two former high-profile large caps, eBay (EBAY) and Yahoo! (YHOO), had slipped into the mid-cap segment in the fall of 2001, demonstrating the fluidity of market-cap classifications. eBay was sitting on the cusp, with a market cap of $15.3 billion in early November, so by the time you read this, it may be back in large-cap territory. Yahoo! has farther to go, with a current cap of $7.4 billion. (This Internet giant once had a market cap of some $100 billion.)

The S&P MidCap 400 and the Russell Midcap® Index measure the performance of the mid caps. Mid-cap ETFs are shown in Table 9–2 in Chapter 9.

Small Caps

One of the most enduring characteristics of small-cap stocks is their potential for rapid growth. After all, it is easier to double your market value if it is $100 million rather than $100 *billion*. (Obviously, this is because it is generally easier to quadruple an earnings base of $5 million than an earnings base of $500 million.) Reward and risk, however, usually go hand in hand, so it is not surprising that small caps tend toward more volatility and higher risk than larger caps do. One obvious reason for this is that the typical small-cap company has a single product line in a single market and is therefore more vulnerable. But small-cap aficionados will argue that a company with a single well-positioned product line can generate explosive earnings growth much more easily than can a company with hundreds of product lines in dozens of markets.

The shareholder base of small caps is often heavily weighted toward individual investors. Although there are many small-cap mutual funds, many institutional investors stick to large caps and mid caps. Further, many small-cap companies have little or no research coverage.

The small-cap sector is where you'll find high-growth stocks such as Metro One Communications (MTON), $906.1 million; Ulticom (ULCM), $406.9 million; CheckPoint Systems (CKP), $319.7 million; Toll Brothers (TOL), $1.158 billion; Knight Trading Group (NITE), $1.476 billion; and Stein Mart (SMRT), $345.3 million (market caps as of November 26, 2001). A great majority of small caps are listed on Nasdaq simply because new and smaller companies find a more receptive environment on the Nasdaq than on the New York Stock Exchange. The New York Stock Exchange conducts its business through floor traders, and small companies can get lost without someone to support them and make a market in their stock, which is what the Nasdaq market makers do. Many small-cap stocks have four or five or even a dozen market makers who help them maintain visibility until they can make it on their own reputation. Nevertheless, there are small-cap stocks on the NYSE and AMEX, and large-cap stocks on Nasdaq. Many companies, such as Microsoft (MSFT) and Intel (INTC), have retained their Nasdaq listings despite their multibillion-dollar market capitalizations.

One of the best-known benchmarks of small-cap performance is the Russell 2000® Index (RUX.X). It is made up of 2000 stocks with an average market cap of around $530 million as of fall 2001. Another small-cap index is the S&P 600, made up of 600 stocks with a mean market cap of $551 million. Small-cap ETFs are listed in Table 9–2 in Chapter 9.

Micro Caps

Micro caps are the newest market-cap segment, although micro caps are not officially recognized as a separate cap by Russell, Morningstar, or S&P. This may be because micro caps have virtually no research coverage and little if any institutional shareholders. Institutional investors, who routinely invest millions of dollars in a single position, rarely invest in a company with a market valuation of less than $100 million. One reason is that an investment of just a few million dollars in such a company would entail an unacceptable level of ownership in the small company because it would imply control or influence. In addition, the lack of liquidity of a micro cap would be totally unacceptable since most micro caps trade fewer than 50,000 shares per day.

Nevertheless, it is likely that the micro-cap status will endure and eventually be commonly recognized. For one thing, a company with a market value of less than $100 million is very hard to compare to a company with a billion-dollar market cap—a twentyfold difference. So a separate category is needed to group these smaller stocks.

We should point out that the micro caps we're talking about are the smallest stocks listed on the New York Stock Exchange, the American Stock Exchange, and the Nasdaq—they are *not* the stocks that are "listed" on the so-called bulletin board or pink sheets. For example, NYSE micro caps include such companies as Zapata Corp. (ZAP), with a market cap of $48 million and a stock price of $20; Rex Stores (RSC), with a market cap of $110.9 million and a stock price of $14; and Morton's Restaurants (MRG), with a market cap of $52.6 million and a stock price of $12 (as of November 6, 2001).

Micro Caps versus Bulletin Board Stocks

Bulletin board and pink sheet stocks—sometimes referred to as penny stocks—used to be traded literally "over the counter" with the traders and brokers negotiating the price of the stock. The stocks are now quoted electronically over the Internet through the OTC Bulletin Board (www.otcbb.com), which is a division of Nasdaq, and Pink Sheets, LLC (www.pinksheets.com), a privately owned company. Bulletin board and pink sheet stocks are much riskier than the stocks that are listed on the exchanges and Nasdaq, mainly because of the dearth of timely information on the companies because of less well-defined reporting requirements and lack of liquidity. In the past 2 years Nasdaq has tightened the reporting requirements of OTCBB stocks. Nasdaq now requires that all companies whose stocks are quoted through the OTCBB file 10Ks and 10Qs regularly with the Securities and Exchange Commission in order to keep their quotes listed.

Because of their size, micro caps offer the greatest potential for reward and, not surprisingly, entail the greatest risk. Investors looking for huge returns may turn to micro caps for the next big winners, regardless of which market cap is currently in favor. Just keep in mind that patience is required to invest in micro caps. A micro-cap company needs to produce some solid growth to see its market valuation grow enough to place it in the small- or mid-cap sectors—and it can be years before such growth happens. Only then will the stock be likely to attract research coverage and, it is to be hoped, a steadily growing P/E multiple that can produce the tremendous price runs that excite any investor. In general, micro caps have not yet reached profitability, so their potential must often be measured in terms of revenue growth. Obviously, all these factors increase the risk.

As we said earlier, it is highly unlikely that micro caps will ever be the favored cap simply because of the lack of institutional ownership. The only index we know of for tracking micro caps is the Microcap 1000 Index ($MC1000). You can obtain a quote at Stockpoint (investor.stockpoint.com) or at any online broker whose quotes are powered by Stockpoint. As of this writing, there are no ETFs for tracking micro caps.

HOW USING MARKET CAPS RELATES TO INVESTING STYLES

Using market caps as a strategy for investing is completely separate from choosing an investing style, although some styles are more compatible with specific market caps. For example, the greatest gains for momentum investors are usually in the favored market cap because those stocks will have the greatest momentum. Technicians may also find it easier to "go with the flow" of the currently favored market cap, rather than against it, even though they probably care about as much for the market cap as they do for the name of the companies behind their charts. The only cap that momentum and technical investors avoid is probably micro caps, because of their thin float and lack of liquidity.

Value investors are more or less contrarians when it comes to market caps, because the most undervalued companies are likely to be found in the out-of-favor segments, so that is where the value investors are likely to look. A lack of positive earnings usually keeps value investors away from micro caps.

Growth investors are less affected by market-cap rotation because they normally favor small caps and micro caps (for aggressive growth investors), which have a greater potential for high-percentage growth.

What it really comes down to is personal preference. Keeping in mind the risk factors of large versus small companies, the question is, Which market cap are you most comfortable with? You will probably find that you are more interested and more comfortable with one or two of the caps over the others. Some investors simply like the comfort of large caps, with their well-known names. Others thrill to the search for exciting newer, smaller companies with bold new products and entrepreneurial, visionary management. In the long run, individual investors can do well in any cap, so you should spend most of your selection effort on the caps that you favor personally. Just keep in mind that the market caps that are in favor can impact or enhance the immediacy of your returns.

Funds That Focus on Market Caps

There are hundreds of mutual funds and exchange-traded funds (ETFs) that specialize in large-, small-, or mid-cap stocks. Virtually every mutual fund family has one or more such funds, usually paired with an investing style (small-cap growth fund, large-cap value fund). A listing of Web sites for mutual fund families and ETFs appears in Appendix A.

Being aware of which market cap a stock belongs to and which caps are currently in favor can assist you in achieving better performance in the market. But don't make too much of this. Market capitalization is not a style—you probably wouldn't want to just be a small-cap investor without reference to an investing style. Our purpose here is to make you aware of market caps and how they rotate in and out of favor. Knowing about market caps can enhance your performance, but only if you combine this knowledge with the investing style that fits you best.

Minor Investing Styles and Other Strategies

There are several investing styles that are offshoots or combinations of the four major styles and, in one case, a once-major style that has diminished in popularity. We'll examine five of these minor styles in this chapter: fundamental investing, income investing, active trading, hybrid investing, and style surfing. We'll also look at two important strategies that can enhance any investing style—top-down investing and insider trading—and a handful of miscellaneous strategies that are included simply in an attempt to be thorough.

FUNDAMENTAL INVESTING: AN EYE ON THE BALANCE SHEET

Fundamental investing is very similar to value investing, but whereas the value investor focuses on the relationship of P/E to the earnings growth ratio, the fundamental investor focuses on a company's balance sheet or assets. In other words, value investors emphasize growth at a reasonable price (GARP), and fundamental investors emphasize balance sheet items, such as cash, low debt, and significant or undervalued fixed assets.

So what does the balance sheet of a good fundamental stock look like? It has low debt, lots of cash, fairly valued (as opposed to overvalued) receivables and inventory, and it might or might not have assets that are worth more than what is carried on the books. This latter point is difficult for the average investor to find out, but it is what fundamental investors look for. Primarily, they look for a company whose stock is selling for less than the company's assets are worth. This happens when the market, for whatever reason, has devalued the stock, perhaps because the company isn't using its assets to generate the kind of earnings it should. The result is a low price-to-book-value ratio. Book value, as you probably know, is made up of cash, real estate, and other assets that the company owns.

For example, let's say a company owns an office building for which it paid $10 million 20 years ago. The building may be depreciated on the books for close to the value of the land—say, a million dollars—but owing to inflation or general real estate appreciation, the building and the land together may be worth close to $40 million. Another undervalued asset might be an investment in a subsidiary that is worth more than it appears on the books. The true value of these kinds of assets comes to light only with very close scrutiny of the balance sheet and very likely some sleuth work as well.

Uncovering these kinds of undervalued assets takes more time and effort than the average investor will probably want to devote to selecting an investment. There may be some clues in the footnotes and schedules to the financial statements, or you might find this type of information in detailed research reports such as those published by most major brokerage firms, but finding undervalued assets is usually the province of professional investors and institutions.

Easier to spot are a low price-to-book ratio (below 1) and/or cash on hand that is worth more per share than the stock price. If a company's stock is selling for, say, $5 a share and has a cash position of $6 a share—and is not still "going through" the cash—the risk of the investment is almost zero because the company could theoretically be liquidated for perhaps $6 a share or more. This was the case with many post-crash Internet companies, which had not yet gone through the cash they raised in their initial public offerings. Of course, if the company is rapidly spending cash in losing ventures, the cash on hand is much less meaningful. Fundamental investors look for companies whose market capitalization is represented by hard assets.

Most investors don't plan to exit their position by liquidating the company, so in addition to a balance sheet with undervalued assets, fundamental investors also look for stocks with earnings growth potential, just as value investors do. But fundamental investors focus on the balance sheet. A stock with good earnings growth potential *without* a good balance sheet would not be the main interest of the fundamental investor.

We want to point out that the Warren Buffett–type of investor is not what we're really talking about here, although Buffett is the quintessential fundamental investor. His investing philosophy— looking for companies with undervalued assets with the intention of maximizing the value of the company by redeploying the assets more efficiently or even doing a partial liquidation—requires that the investor acquire a very large amount of stock, enough to entitle him or her to a seat on the board and a voice in the management of the company. We assume that our readers are not yet at that stage. Our fundamental investor is basically a value investor with a twist, and that twist is the focus on the balance sheet and undervalued assets.

The PQ Chart of the Fundamental Investor

Fundamental investing is an offshoot of value investing, so the PQ chart (Figure 9–1) is going to look very much like that of the value investor. But there are differences. The fundamental investor must have a significant amount of time to spend on his or her portfolio because it takes a lot of time to pore over balance sheets looking for the strongest of them—and if he or she is lucky—perhaps finding undervalued assets. (This is not very likely to be the typical online investor.) The fundamental investor also has to have near CPA- level of accounting smarts (quantitative skills) to be able to judge the relative merits of a particular balance sheet, as well as confidence in his or her judgment. Unlike, say, technical investing, the whole fundamental game is one of judgment calls.

The fundamental investor needs a lot of patience, both to find companies with undervalued assets and to wait for the rewards to materialize. A fundamental stock can increase in value only when institutional investors "discover" the stock and begin to appreciate the relative value of the company, which is why fundamental in-

FIGURE 9-1

PQ Chart of a Fundamental Investor

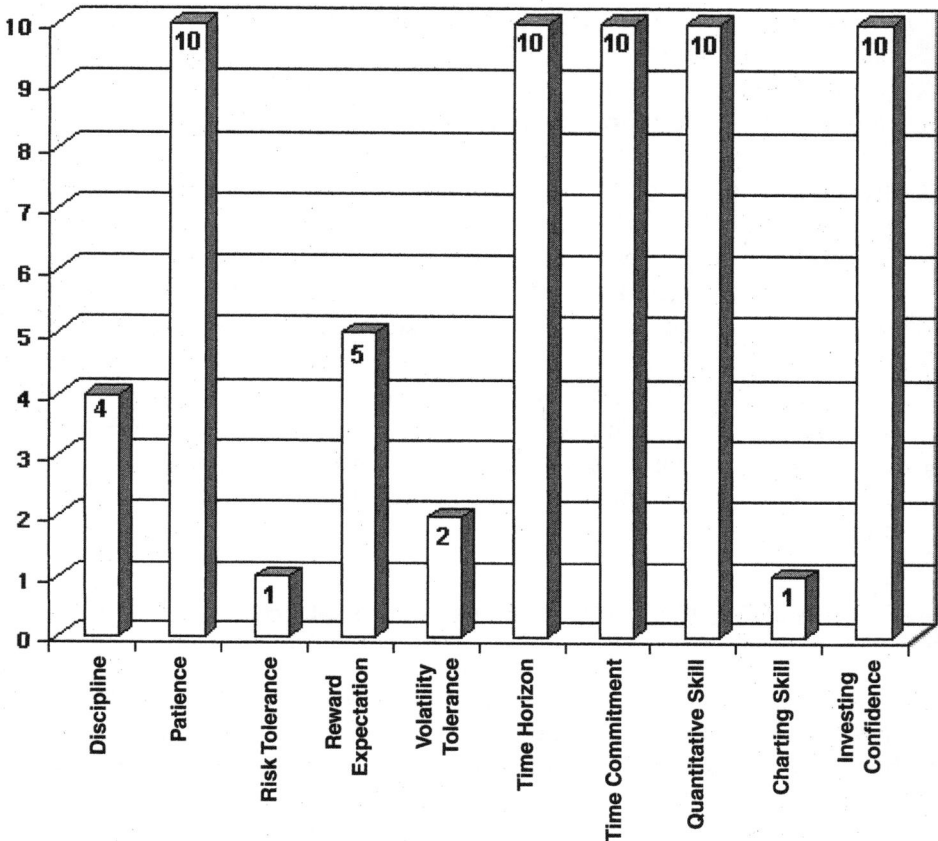

vestors also look for earnings growth potential. There has to be a reason for others to see the value in a stock.

The risk of fundamental investing is the least among all the investing styles, because, theoretically, the company's assets are worth more than the price of the stock. Consequently, reward expectations for this style of investing are probably lower than for other styles of investing and take longer to achieve. That is why fundamental investing appeals to the most conservative investors.

As you might expect, technical skills receive the lowest score on the fundamental PQ chart. No charting is required to find or enter the stocks, since this is essentially a buy-and-hold (for a long time) investing style.

How to Find a Fundamental Stock

Fundamental investors are looking for hard assets to back up the company, and they must comb balance sheets to find them. You can facilitate this process by using the same search described for value investing in Chapter 5, and adding criteria that screen for low price-to-book value or high cash-to-price ratio and other similar balance sheet criteria. You would also need to give the heaviest weight to the balance sheet criteria, assuming your search program offers a weighting feature. The fundamental investor also watches for overvalued items such as inventory when sales are slowing or receivables in a difficult economy. To judge the quality of receivables and inventory the fundamental investor looks at the ratio of sales growth to the change in receivables or change in inventory. If the days of outstanding receivables are increasing, that is a likely sign that there are potential credit problems with the receivables. Similarly, if the increase in inventory (inventory turns) is more than the increase in sales, it is possible that inventory write-downs may be near at hand. The key, of course, is the relative quality of the receivables and the relative salability of the inventory.

Fundamental investing is not a style for the beginning investor, unless you know your way around a balance sheet and have the patience to ferret out companies with undervalued assets.

Hints for Successful Fundamental Investing

1. *Analyze the balance sheet thoroughly.* Accountants will understand the need for proficiency in this skill. Others had better brush up on their accounting.
2. *Screen for balance sheet items.* A screening engine that allows you to screen for balance sheet items will be invaluable. See our reviews of screening programs in Appendix A.
3. *Don't overlook footnotes when reading financial statements.* That's where most of the important revelations are made by auditors.

4. *Be disciplined.* Discipline is needed primarily in the stock selection process, but it is as important to the fundamental investor as to any other type of investor.

INCOME INVESTING: SHOW ME THE MONEY

Equity income investors buy stocks that pay dividends; fixed income investors buy bonds, CDs, mortgages, and other fixed-income
vehicles. The point is, both types of investors are seeking income,
but since this is a book about investing in stocks, we will focus only
on the equity income investor here.

The greatest advantage of income investing, of course, is the income, and income stocks are, in general, usually fairly safe. Your annual return should be at least equal to the stock's annual dividend,
and an increase in stock price, if any, will be a bonus. So if the dividend is 3 percent, you'll make at least 3 percent a year on the stock
(minus, of course, any decrease in stock price). If the stock price rises, you'll get that return as well. If the stock price falls, the dividend
will stay the same, at least in the short run, so your dividend as a
percentage of stock price will actually increase. For example, if you
buy a $25 stock that pays an annual dividend of $1 per share, you
would make 4 percent on your investment. If the stock price falls to
$10 and the dividend remains at $1 per share, your dividend would
be 10 percent instead of 4 percent, but you would have suffered a 60
percent loss on your holdings. New purchasers of the stock might
be excited by the 10 percent dividend, but they would have to be
concerned that the dividend may not continue because companies
do cut dividends. Either the stock price will recover and the dividend percentage will return to a more normal level, or the company could decide that things are so bad they have to cut the dividend.

The Growth-and-Income Investor

An offshoot of income investing is growth-and-income investing.
While the pure equity income investor looks for stocks with the
largest dividends, the growth-and-income investor looks for growing companies that pay dividends and have a history of dividend
increases as has happened, for example, with Conagra Foods (CAG),
which has increased its dividends every quarter for the past 10

years. In a sense, growth-and-income investors have the best of both worlds, because they get a steadily growing income from the dividend as well as potential price appreciation.

Why Income Investing Went Out of Vogue

In past decades, income investing was one of the major styles. But then the era of high-tech companies with their extraordinary returns came along, and management rethought the tradition of paying dividends. If you're very good at making microchips, for example, and you are growing your company 18 percent or more per year, why pay out your earnings in cash dividends? Why not grow your company by reinvesting the earnings in research and development of new and better products? That is what the leading chipmaker Intel did, along with most other technology companies, and this move clearly accelerated their growth. But income investors insisted on stocks that paid dividends, so they didn't buy the sexy, high-flying tech stocks and consequently missed out on their phenomenal growth. Income investors also began to realize that over the years dividend-paying stocks have yielded an average annual return of only about 8 to 9 percent, compared with the 11 to 12 percent average return of all equities. For these reasons income investing has been relegated to a minor investing style.

The Role of Interest Rates in Income Investing

One nuance of income investing is the whole issue of interest rates. Income investing carries with it the risk that market interest rates will change. For example, if you bought a stock for, say, $25 with a 4 percent dividend in October 2000, you may have been pretty happy by the fall of 2001 because interest rates had fallen to below 3 percent. In all likelihood, the price of a stock that paid a 4 percent dividend probably increased as folks sold bonds and CDs to buy good dividend-paying stocks, so you got that price increase as a bonus. But if interest rates were to go back to, say, 10 percent, you wouldn't be such a happy camper. With higher interest rates, it is almost certain that the price of your 4 percent dividend stock would fall, as investors would expect high-yield stocks to have dividend rates well above 5 percent.

The point is, stocks that are bought primarily for their dividend yield carry the added risk that if interest rates go up, the price of the stocks will, in all likelihood, go down. If you're a long-term holder that really doesn't matter.

PQ Chart of the Income Investor

Income investors are, above all else, long-term investors, which is reflected in the PQ chart in Figure 9–2, with the only high scores being awarded for patience and time horizon. Not much discipline is

FIGURE 9–2

PQ Chart of an Income Investor

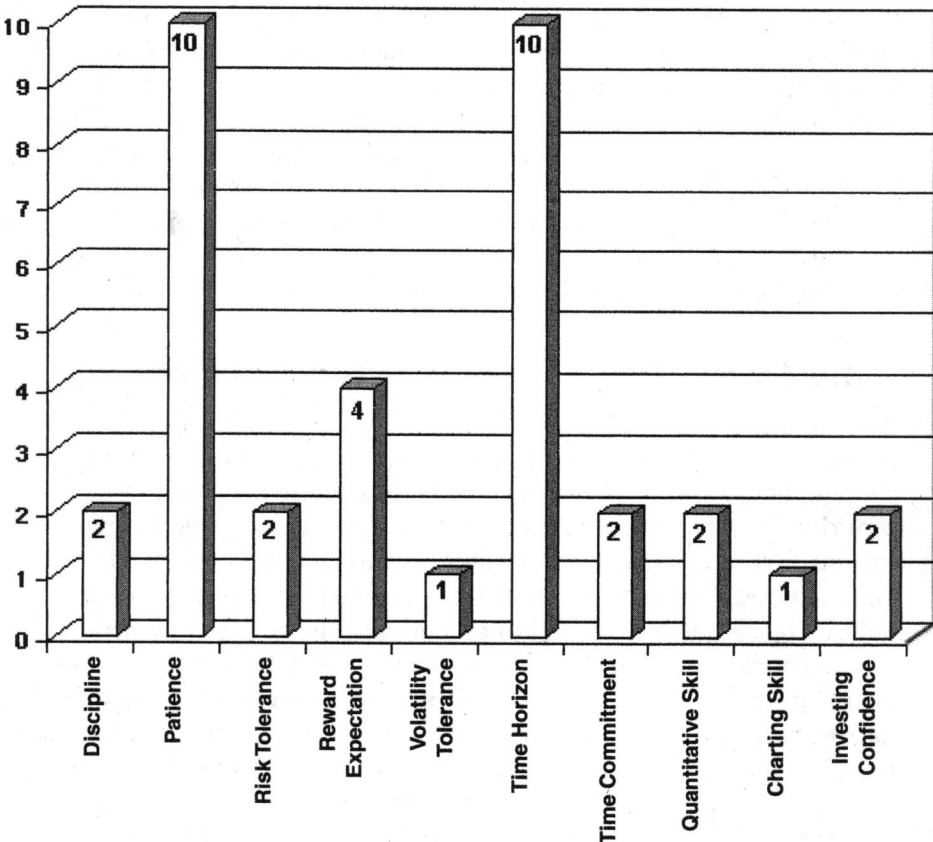

needed for this style of investing because an income investor rarely exits a good income stock. Income stocks, by their nature, are stable, well-established companies, so the risk that you'll lose your investment is lower, although there are occasional meltdowns of companies that pay dividends. One example was Pacific Gas & Electric in 2000/2001, owing to the utility crisis in California. Because of an energy crisis in the state, the company stopped paying dividends and the stock price fell precipitously; in fact, the company filed for bankruptcy protection. Another more recent and perhaps more painful example is Enron, which had been paying a dividend right up to the time of its demise. Nonetheless, the volatility risk for dividend-paying stocks is almost zero unless the dividend itself is at risk, as it was with PG&E and Enron.

It takes less time to build and maintain a portfolio of income stocks than any other style. It is easy to build an income portfolio—just look for stocks with the highest dividend yields—and even easier to maintain one, since income investors tend to hold on to their stocks as long as the dividend checks continue to arrive on time. Quantitative skills are not really necessary, nor are charting skills, unless you want to plot the growth of the annual dividend. Finally, it doesn't take much investing confidence to recognize large, stable, well-established companies that pay dividends!

The only difference on the PQ chart between the income investor and the growth-and-income investor would be a higher score for reward expectations on the latter.

Funds for the Income Investor

Virtually every fund family offers one or more income funds or growth-and-income funds. Just look for those words in the name or in the objective of the fund.

Screening for Income Stocks

To find income stocks, use the following screen:

- *High dividend yield.* Dividend yield is the annual dividend divided by the stock price. It may also be called percent yield or dividend rate, depending on who is providing the data.

♦ *Stability of dividends.* How long has the company paid dividends? Has it ever omitted them for a quarter or more?

The growth-and-income investor would add these criteria to the screen:

♦ *High historical dividend growth rate.* A high historical dividend growth rate will give you confidence that the company will continue to raise its dividends.

♦ *High dividend growth consistency.* Use your search engine to find the frequency with which the dividend has increased over the past 5 or 10 years. This information might be stated as the number or percentage of quarters in which a company increased dividends.

♦ *High projected earnings growth.* Dividends are usually paid from earnings; therefore it takes earnings growth to achieve dividend growth.

Hints for Successful Income Investing

1. *Look for companies with a history of dividend increases.* Such companies take pride in their record and will try very hard to keep the record going.

2. *Don't be taken in by high one-time dividends.* Companies sometimes pay a one-time dividend as a result of an unusual non-recurring event in the company. A one-time dividend could reflect an unusually high dividend yield, so be sure to check the history of dividend payments to avoid this problem.

3. *Beware of stocks with a very high yield.* Stocks that show a dividend yield well above market rates almost always carry the serious risk that the company will have to reduce or eliminate the dividend.

4. *Always consider the safety of the dividend.* One of the things you need to be aware of as an income investor is the strength of the company and the safety of the dividend. A good bond rating speaks to the strength and durability of the company. A dividend safety rating implies that the dividends will con-

tinue and perhaps may increase. VectorVest offers a free stock summary that includes a dividend safety rating, or you may want to subscribe to a rating service, such as S&P, Moody's, or Value Line. Value Line and VectorVest offer dividend rating as a screening criteria.

ACTIVE TRADING: FAST AND FREQUENTLY FURIOUS

Active trading might be thought of as momentum or technical investing carried to an extreme. Whereas the momentum or technical investor may make several trades a month, the active trader may make several trades a day or even several trades an hour. The objective of this investor is to make small (sometimes tiny) profits on dozens or hundreds of trades a week. Active traders may or may not be technicians. Some traders claim that they never look at a stock graph and depend instead on Nasdaq's Level 2 quotes to reveal the best trades based on market maker activity. Others swear by charting, using one or more technical indicators to trade intra-day or longer trends.

Active trading encompasses dozens of styles and strategies, which we will not go into here, but we will mention three somewhat distinct types of active trading, distinguished mainly by the frequency of the trades: day trading, swing trading, and position trading.

Day Trading

Day trading is the most active, active trading style. The definition of the classic day trader is someone who does not hold a position overnight. He or she may hold a position for a minute or less or for an hour or longer, but all positions are closed out before the end of the day.

Day trading began in the wake of the market crash of 1987, when the Securities and Exchange Commission ordered Nasdaq to change its order execution rules to protect small investors. The new system, the Small Order Execution System (SOES), made it mandatory for market makers to fill orders automatically from individual investors, rather than delaying or ignoring them as they had in the past. The original day traders were dubbed the "SOES bandits" because they "stole the spread"—the difference between the bid and the ask—from Nasdaq market makers. These new day traders were satisfied to make profits as low as one-sixteenth of a point (called *teenies*—about 6 cents a share) on each trade, but to make such tiny profits worth their while, they had to make very frequent and very large trades. Over the next decade, additional rulings by the SEC, as well as advances in technology and the Internet made day trading accessible to amateur traders, and day trading shops sprang up across the country.

Day trading entered its heyday during the dot-com boom. Day traders were credited with (or accused of) the extreme volatility that ruled the market in those days. The dot-com crash weeded out a large majority of the amateurs, but day trading is still very much on the scene. Because of the somewhat negative connotation associated with the term "day trader," most such traders now prefer to be called simply "active traders."

Swing Trading

The swing trader is a day trader with a little more patience and a longer time horizon. While the classic day trader may make 50 or 100 trades a day for teenies and closes his or her positions by the end of the day, the swing trader makes several trades a week and looks for profits of several points a share. The typical swing trader holds his or her positions for 1 to 5 days but not usually over a weekend.

Position Trading

A position trader is simply a swing trader with a longer time horizon, usually holding a position for 10 days or so. Position trading is virtually indistinguishable from short-term momentum or technical investing.

Using Direct Access Brokers

Because they need instantaneous executions, active traders, as a rule, make their trades through a direct-access broker. Such brokers offer special trading software that enables a trader to place trades directly through an electronic communications network (ECN), rather than routing trades through a favored market maker who pays for the order flow, as regular online brokers do. Paying for order flow is a legal practice, but it can raise the cost of a trade by 6 to 12 cents a share or more. When you're aiming for lots of tiny profits, the slippage of 6 or 12 cents a share can mean the difference between a profit and a loss.

The PQ Chart of the Active Trader

Active trading—particularly day trading—is highly intense and action-oriented. Day traders are glued to their computer screen for most of the market day, ready to pull the trigger when their system says to enter or exit.

Figure 9–3 shows the PQ chart for a classic day trader. It has among the highest scores for discipline, risk tolerance, volatility tolerance, reward expectation, and time commitment—and the lowest scores for patience and time horizon. Charting skill is necessary, in most cases, but quantitative skills are not really needed. A fair degree of investing confidence is needed to select a system and learn it well. Once you learn your system—and an active trader must have a system that he or she knows and can depend on—you must simply have confidence in your system and the discipline to follow the signals generated by the system. By far, the most important requirement of an active trader is the discipline to stick with a system.

A swing trader would need slightly less risk tolerance and time commitment than the day trader, and the PQ chart of the position trader would be virtually identical to that of the momentum investor.

Hints for Successful Active Trading

1. *Discipline, discipline, discipline.* Discipline is important in any investing style, but it is absolutely essential in active trading.
2. *Use a direct access broker.* You may have to go through a learning curve on the software, but using a direct access broker is the best way to get good executions.

FIGURE 9-3

PQ Chart of a Day Trader

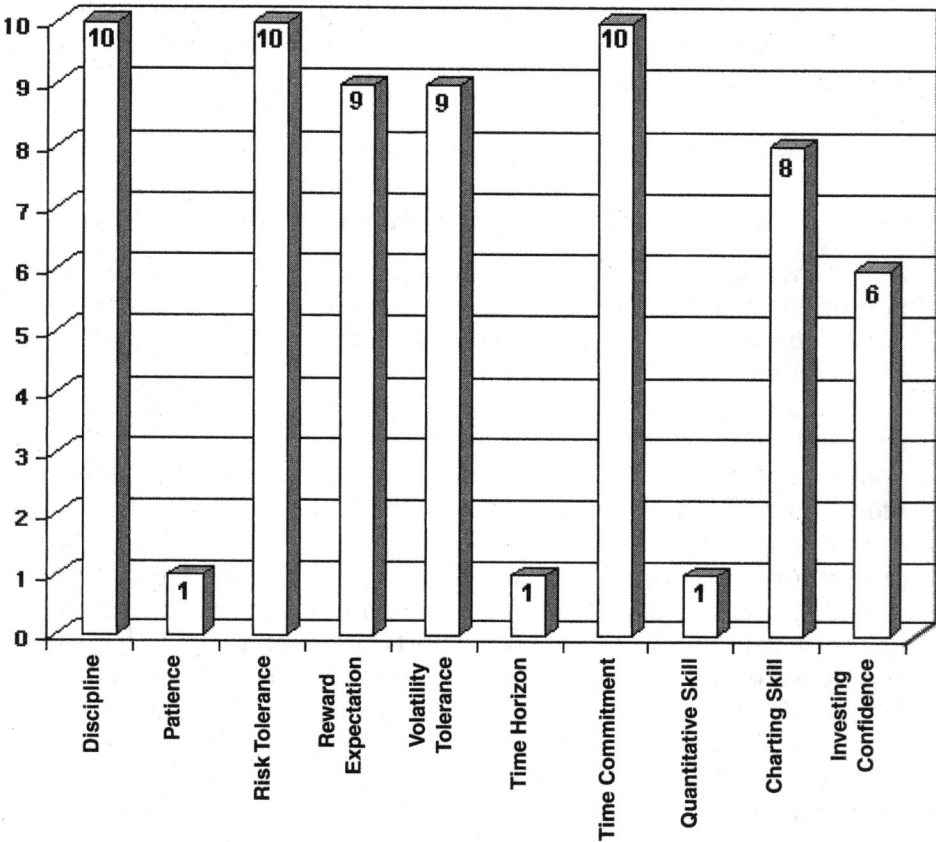

THE HYBRID INVESTOR: COMBINING STYLES

As you've been reading along, perhaps you've found yourself drawn to more than one investing style. Maybe high-growth stocks appeal to you, but you also like the idea of bargain hunting. Or maybe value investing appeals to your conservative side, but you lack the patience to wait years for your reward. If you are inclined to more than one investing style, you can in most cases combine investing styles into a hybrid style.

There are many hybrid styles that are simply a major style

cross-pollinated with a single aspect of a different style. Value investors who are short on patience might insist that a value stock has to be exhibiting some momentum before they're willing to purchase it. Of course, you would have to be willing to accept a higher P/E than a value investor would normally desire.

Two of the strategies mentioned at the end of this chapter—top-down investing and insider trading—can be combined with any style. You might be a top-down value investor or a top-down growth investor who uses insider buying as a primary condition for purchase.

Technical investing can also be combined with any style, and, in fact, we recommend that every style of investing use technical indicators or systems for entry and exit signals. But pure technicians might combine styles by applying their technical theories to a universe of high-growth stocks or even value stocks, or they may stick with the stocks that are exhibiting the greatest momentum. There is one drawback to combining other styles with technical investing: Technical investing by itself requires a heavy time commitment; if you add in the requirement to screen for growth or value or momentum stocks, that increases the time you'll have to spend on building and maintaining your portfolio.

Examples of two hybrid styles that are well defined and popular enough to have recognizable names are the undervalued growth investor and the growth-and-momentum or CANSLIM investor. There are many other hybrid styles as well.

The Undervalued Growth Hybrid

Growth investors who balk at the high prices of growth stocks tend to look for undervalued stocks with good growth potential. They are, essentially, GARP investors because they're looking for growth at a reasonable price. To find such stocks, the undervalued growth investor can create screens that eliminate high P/E stocks or stocks with high price-to-earnings-growth ratios.

PQ Chart of an Undervalued Growth Investor
A PQ chart for a hybrid investor will reflect the characteristics of the styles being combined. The PQ chart for the undervalued growth investor (Figure 9–4) retains three of the characteristics of the pure

FIGURE 9-4

PQ Chart of a Hybrid Investor: Undervalued Growth

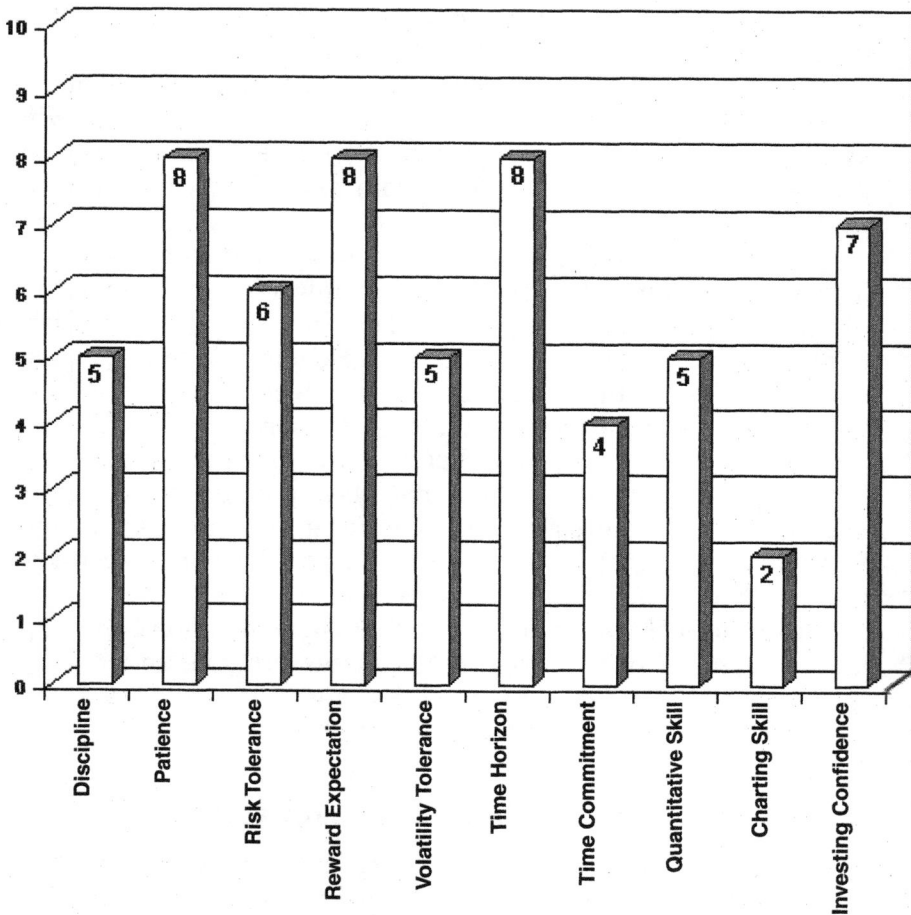

growth investor (discipline, reward expectation, and charting skill), but the other qualities are affected by traits the value investor needs to possess.

The Growth-and-Momentum Hybrid

One of the more popular hybrid styles of investing is growth-and-momentum investing, which looks for growth stocks that are fully discovered and exhibiting momentum. This style was popularized under the acronym CANSLIM by William J. O'Neil, publisher of *Investor's Business Daily*, in his book *How to Make Money in Stocks: A Winning System in Good Times or Bad*. Each letter in the acronym stands for a different characteristic of a winning stock, based on the CANSLIM strategy. The formula is outlined below; details can be found at www.canslim.net or in Mr. O'Neil's book.

- *Current earnings.* Current earnings must be up a minimum of 20 percent.
- *Annual earnings.* The average 5-year earnings growth should be between 15 and 50 percent.
- *New services, new products, or new highs.* New products or services are what drive stock prices high, and O'Neil advocates buying a stock at its all-time high.
- *Shares outstanding or supply.* O'Neil recommends buying stocks with less than 30 million shares outstanding and those with a large percentage owned by top management.
- *Leader or laggard?* Leopards rarely change their spots, and laggards rarely become leaders. A CANSLIM stock is a leader relative to the overall market.
- *Institutional ownership.* Stocks that move usually have an influx of institutional money. The CANSLIM strategy calls for at least a few institutional owners.
- *Market direction.* The market should be moving up or poised to move up. The CANSLIM strategy provides a lot of ways to judge the state of the market.

PQ Chart of the Growth-and-Momentum (CANSLIM) Investor

The PQ chart for the CANSLIM investor combines the traits of growth and momentum investors (Figure 9–5). The CANSLIM investor retains four qualities of the pure momentum investor (discipline, reward expectation, time commitment, and charting skill) and three of the pure growth investor (risk tolerance, volatility tolerance, and investing confidence). The other three qualities are a combination of growth and momentum traits.

FIGURE 9-5

FIGURE 9-5

PQ Chart of a Hybrid Investor: CANSLIM

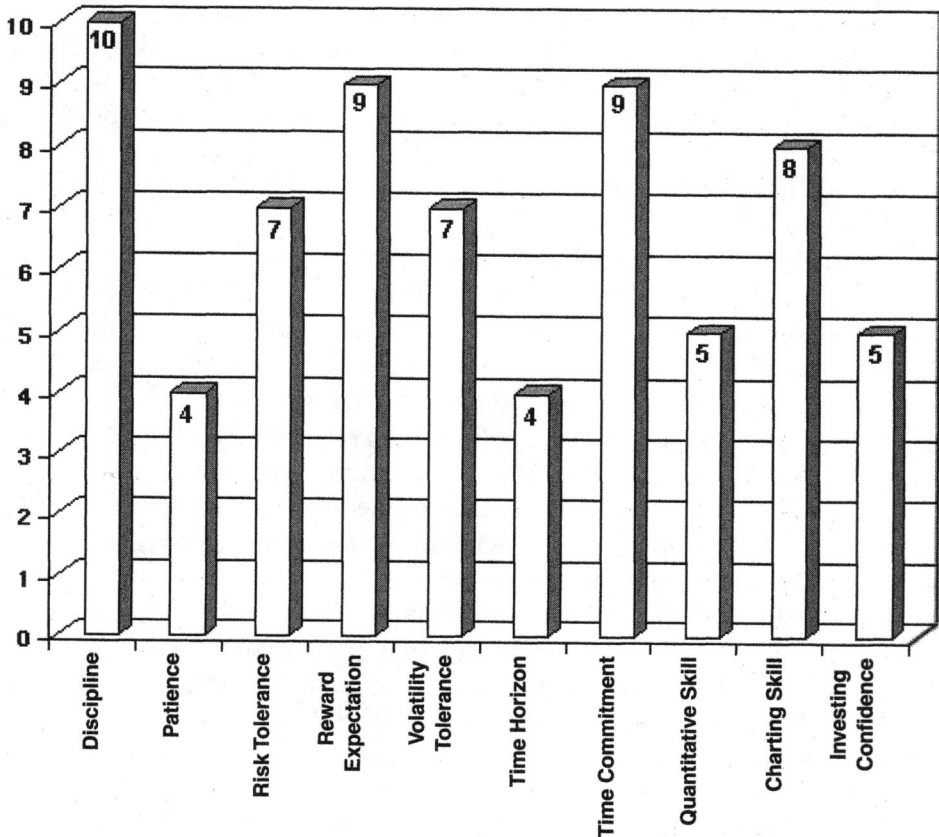

Hints for Successful Hybrid Investing

Hybrid investing is somewhat like wearing a custom-made suit: It enables you to create a style that fits every angle and curve of your investing personality. Just remember that the art of being a successful hybrid investor is in picking one style as your basic style and then overlaying it with compatible elements from other investing styles.

1. *Be disciplined.* As with any style, the key is to maintain your discipline and follow your rules.

2. *Don't try to force incompatible styles.* It is highly unlikely, for example, that you'll find extraordinary growth stocks with high momentum *and* value stock prices.

3. *Be aware of how the overlaid style affects the basic style of investing.* When combining styles, ask yourself whether overlaying certain features of another style enhances or detracts from the benefits of your basic investing style. For example, buying growth stocks with great momentum increases the risk of an already high-risk style. (Remember our discussion on the risk of falling P/Es in Chapter 1.) But requiring that value stocks show a little momentum before you enter probably will decrease the amount of time you must hold on to the stock before it offers up its reward.

THE STYLE SURFER: GOING WITH THE FLOW

Growth, value, and momentum investing styles perform differently in different markets and consequently rotate into and out of favor with investors. Momentum investing was the hot style during the dot-com boom in 1998 and 1999. After the bubble burst in the spring of 2000, valuations tumbled for stocks across the board, and as a result value investing came into the limelight. Market caps also rotate into and out of favor, as you'll recall from Chapter 8. Mid caps were hot in early 2001, followed by a focus on small caps in the month or two before September 11. In the wake of the terrorist attacks, there has been a flight to quality, to those large-cap stocks that were relatively unaffected by the attacks.

The biggest gains are usually to be made in the style or cap that is currently in favor simply because money is flowing into those stocks and demand is pushing the prices higher. It stands to reason that, assuming he or she does it well, an investor who can switch to the style and cap that is in favor will do better or at least make money faster than will an investor who sticks to one style and/or one market cap through thick and thin.

We have dubbed the investing style that goes along with the times *style surfing*. When value investing is in vogue, the style surfer is a value investor. When growth stocks dominate the market, he switches to growth investing. When momentum is the name of today's game, she becomes a momentum investor. When large caps lead the way, the style surfer builds a large-cap portfolio. When small caps are in, he switches to small-cap stocks. The style surfer switches styles and caps to be where the greatest action is, and by doing so increases her potential for rewards while decreasing the time it takes for the rewards to materialize.

It sounds like the best possible style, doesn't it? But we should point out that style surfing is probably the most demanding and sophisticated of all styles. First of all, you need to be psychologically inclined toward what is, in a sense, no style at all, and at the same time you need to be good at growth, value, and momentum investing—and have no real preference about market-cap size. You need an enormous amount of investing confidence because you have to be sure of your judgment in three different investing styles. This type of investing also takes an enormous amount of time. Not only do you have to spend time on the current style, building and maintaining your portfolio; you have to stay on top of the market and spend time learning which investing style and which market cap are in favor and watching all the indicators to make sure you can switch nimbly to the up-and-coming style or cap before the old one peaks.

The advantage to style surfing, if you have the time and smarts for it, is that your reward is likely to be higher because of the immediacy of the returns. Risk is also higher because you are unlikely to be equally good at all the styles *and* you need to be right about "where the action is."

Less patience is required for style surfing than for, say, pure growth or pure value investing, because if growth stocks or value stocks are the market favorites, the time horizon for reaping rewards should be greatly shortened. And for a style like momentum investing that normally has a short time span from buy to sell, the style surfer can make impressive gains. (Think dot-com boom!)

The PQ Chart of a Style Surfer

The PQ chart in Figure 9–6 says it all: Style surfing is heavy on discipline, reward expectation, time commitment, and investing confidence; medium-heavy on quantitative skills, charting skills, volatility tolerance, and risk tolerance, depending on which style you're focusing on; and light on patience and time horizon.

FIGURE 9-6

PQ Chart of a Style Surfer

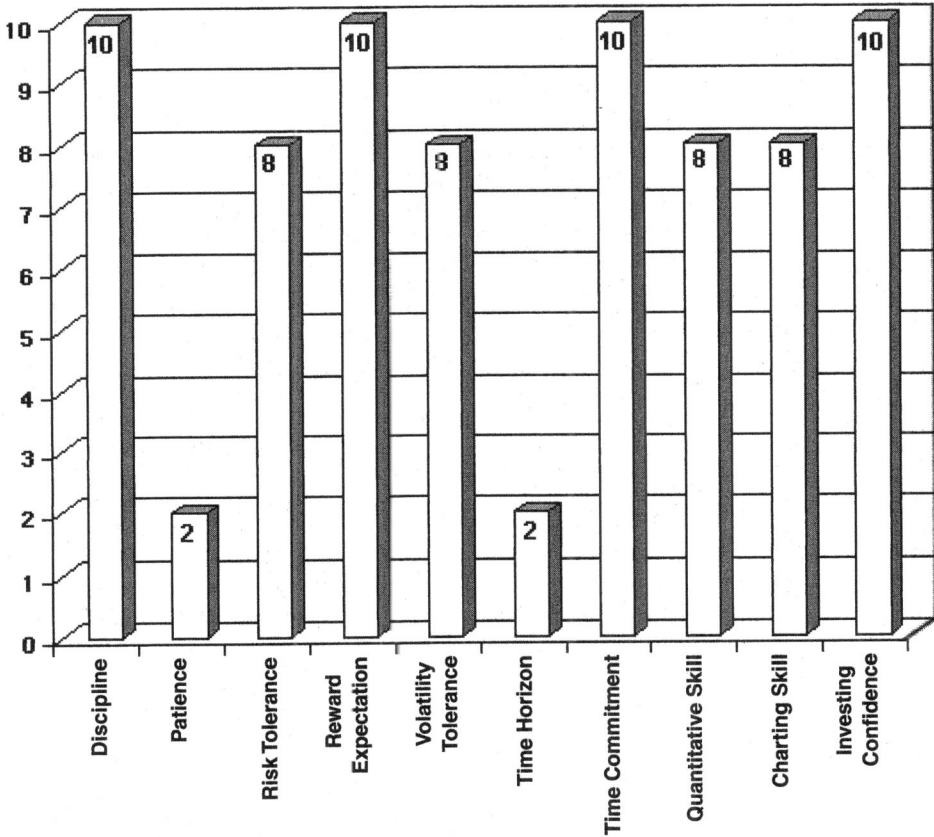

Strategies for Style Surfing

The strategies for style surfing are simple: Identify which style and which market cap are currently in favor—and then apply the rules for that style. Standard & Poor's and the Frank Russell Company offer a number of indexes that measure the performance of certain styles and market caps (Table 9–1), which can tell you which are hot and which are not. There are other Russell and S&P indexes, but most of them are too broad to track a specific market cap. In addition, you can use the exchange-traded funds (ETFs) shown in Table 9–2 as bell-

T A B L E   9–1

Indexes for Tracking Investing Styles and Market Caps

Investing Style or Market Cap	Index	Comments
Growth investing	Russell 1000® Growth Index Russell 2000® Growth Index Russell 2500™ Growth Index Russell 3000® Growth Index Russell Midcap® Growth Index Russell Top 200® Growth Index S&P/BARRA Growth Index	In general, growth indexes contain companies with *higher* price-to-book ratios. For a detailed description see the Frank Russell Co. and Standard & Poor's web sites, listed in the appendix.
Value investing	Russell 1000® Value Index Russell 2000® Value Index Russell 2500™ Value Index Russell 3000® Value Index Russell Midcap® Value Index Russell Top 200® Value Index S&P/BARRA Value Index	In general, value indexes contain companies with *lower* price-to-book ratios. For a detailed description see the Frank Russell Co. and Standard & Poor's web sites, listed in the appendix.
Large caps	Dow Jones Industrial Average (DJI)	30 large-cap blue chip stocks
	Russell Top 200® Index	Average market cap of $48 billion
	S&P 100 (OEX)	The largest 100 stocks in the S&P 500
	S&P 500 (OEX)	The standard for measuring the performance of large-cap U.S. stocks
Mid caps	Russell Midcap® Index	Average market cap of $4.0 billion
	S&P MidCap 400	Weighted average market cap of $2.9 billion
Small caps	Russell 2000® Index	Average market cap of $530 million
	S&P SmallCap 600	Weighted average market cap of $932 million
Micro caps	Microcap 1000 Index ($MC1000)	Average market cap not available

TABLE 9–2

Exchange-Traded Funds (EFTs) for Tracking Investing Styles and Market Caps

iShares Index Funds	Growth	Value	Large Caps	Mid Caps	Small Caps
Russell 1000 Index Fund (IWB)		✓	✓		
Russell 1000 Growth Index Fund (IWF)	✓		✓		
Russell 1000 Value Index Fund (IWD)		✓	✓		
Russell 2000 Growth Index Fund (IWO)	✓				✓
Russell 2000 Value Index Fund (IWN)		✓			✓
Russell 3000 Growth Index Fund (IWZ)	✓				
Russell 3000 Value Index Fund (IWW)		✓			
Russell Midcap Index Fund (IWR)				✓	
Russell Midcap Growth Index Fund (IWP)	✓			✓	
Russell Midcap Value Index Fund (IWS)		✓			
S&P 100 Index Fund (OEF)			✓		
S&P 500 Index Fund (IVV)			✓		
S&P 500/BARRA Growth Index Fund (IVW)	✓		✓		
S&P 500/BARRA Value Index Fund (IVE)		✓	✓		
S&P MidCap 400 Index Fund (IJH)					
S&P MidCap 400/BARRA Growth Index Fund (IJK)	✓			✓	
S&P MidCap 400/BARRA Value Index Fund (IJJ)		✓		✓	
S&P SmallCap 600/BARRA Growth Index Fund (IJT)	✓			✓	
S&P SmallCap 600/BARRA Value Index Fund (IJS)		✓		✓	
streetTRACKS Index Funds	**Growth**	**Value**	**Large Caps**	**Mid Caps**	**Small Caps**
U.S. Large Cap Growth Index Fund (DJUSGL)	✓		✓		
U.S. Large Cap Value Index Fund (DJUSVL)		✓	✓		
U.S. Small Cap Growth Index Fund (DJUSGS)	✓				✓
U.S. Small Cap Value Index Fund (DJUSVS)		✓			✓

wethers for growth and value investing styles, and for the three major market caps.

These indexes and ETFs can also reveal when a style or market cap is peaking and which style or cap is emerging into the spotlight. When value stocks start slowing down across the board, for instance, you know it's transition time. Transition to what is the question. You'll just have to keep an eye on the bellwether indexes and ETFs to find out.

With regard to momentum investing, you can safely assume that momentum stocks are in favor when the market is moving very briskly and a lot of money is coming into stocks. The most recent momentum markets were in 1997, 1998, and 1999, when stocks went up irrespective of their growth or value characteristics. And these were not just dot-com stocks. The mania for index investing fueled the momentum of an already hot market. The risk is high in such a market because P/E ratios become seriously inflated.

Surfing Funds

Although it is unlikely that you will find any mutual funds that admit in their investment objectives that they switch styles, you can assume that very aggressive funds that aim at the highest capital appreciation in the short run are essentially "style surfers." The management of such a fund would be very aggressive.

Another way to apply style surfing to mutual funds is to switch from one style to another within a fund family (it is less expensive if you stick to a family, although you could switch among families if you want to do the research). When value investing is in style, buy a value fund; when growth investing is in style, buy a growth fund. You can even combine the in-style with the in-cap: mid-cap value funds, for example, or small-cap growth funds. Style surfing can be applied to ETFs in the same way.

Hints for Successful Style Surfing

1. *Become knowledgeable in the three major investing styles.* If you're going to be a style surfer, you must become skilled at growth, value, and momentum investing.
2. *Know what's in and what's out.* Follow the trends by staying abreast of the ETFs and indexes in Tables 9–1 and 9–2. If an

investing style or a market cap shows losses several weeks or months in a row, it might be rotating out of favor. A more visual way to follow the trends is to use the SmartMoney Market Map at www.smartmoney.com. The map shows industry groups and stocks in color blocks of different sizes, the size representing roughly the market cap of the company, the color representing whether the stock is outperforming or underperforming the market. The map can be customized with the ETFs and market indexes in Tables 9–1 and 9–2 to provide you with an immediate visual representation of what's hot and what's not.

POPULAR STRATEGIES FOR MAJOR OR MINOR STYLES

Regardless of your style, there are two strategies that you can overlay on almost any style: Top-down investing and insider trading.

Top-Down Investing: Follow the Money

Top-down investing means looking first at the behavior of the broader market, for example, the country in which you're investing, and then drilling down through the stock exchanges to sectors to industry groups to stocks. What you're looking for is the best-performing areas at each level. The theory behind this strategy is that the performance of a stock depends to a large degree on the performance of its sector or industry group. In fact, a study cited by *Investor's Business Daily* states that 37 percent of a stock's movement is directly tied to the performance of the industry the stock is in, and another 12 percent of the movement is owing to strength in the stock's overall sector. It would seem like a good idea to make sure the stocks you buy are in the hottest industries and sectors, or at least not in the lackadaisical ones.

You might think of top-down investing as a series of descending levels:

1. The top level would be the country—for domestic investors, that would be the United States; for global investors, it would be whichever country has the best economy at the current time.

2. The next level is the exchanges. In the United States, for equity investors, there is a choice between the New York Stock Exchange or the Nasdaq. If they're doing about the same, you could just skip this step.
3. The third level is business sectors, those broad segments of the economy such as health care, energy, or technology. (There are 12 to 15 in all.) Sectors regularly rotate into and out of favor depending on the economy and other factors.
4. The fourth level is industry groups. There are from 100 to 200 industry groups within the broader sectors. Once you've found the best-performing sector, look for the best-performing industry group in that sector.
5. The fifth level is the stock itself. Once you've identified the best-performing country, exchange, sector, and industry group, you're ready to search for the best stocks in that group or groups that match your investing style. If you have no allegiance to market caps, you would at this point restrict your search to the market caps that are currently in favor.

Top-down investing is based primarily on the rotation of sectors and industry groups. The rotation of sectors and groups into and out of favor is tied to the flow of institutional money. As with market caps, money follows money into the different sectors and groups, creating waves of high performance that benefit the stocks in those sectors and groups, sometimes apart from the actual merits of the individual stocks. Underlying this herdlike rotation, though, is the ebb and flow of the economy. Typically, sectors rotate into favor because that segment of the general economy is doing well owing to specific events. For example, if interest rates are going down, that trend bodes well for the home construction sector, which in turn benefits related industries such as mortgage lenders, furniture sellers, lumber mills, and so on. If consumer confidence is high because of a booming economy, the retail sector is likely to be booming as well. Industry groups also rotate into favor simply because they've been out of favor. Out-of-favor groups are fertile ground for value stocks. Investors start to realize that there are particularly good values in a certain sector or group, and money starts flowing in, and then that sector or group rotates back into favor.

Industry groups are almost as fluid as market caps because the number and names of sectors and groups depend on who's doing the grouping. Smartmoney.com divides the economy into 11 sectors and 120 industry groups; *Investor's Business Daily* cuts the pie into approximately 11 sectors and 197 groups (see Table 9–3).

With more sectors and groups, *IBD* offers more precise groupings. A company like USA Networks, for example, belongs to *IBD's* Media-Radio/TV group, which is part of the Leisure and Entertainment sector. In the Smartmoney.com groupings, USA Networks is part of a much broader group, Media and Advertising, which is part of the much more general Consumer, Cyclical sector.

The idea behind top-down investing is that you can enhance your returns if you "follow the money." The downside is that if you're not careful, your timing could be too early and the wave may not peak (rotate positively) or you may jump on a wave that has already peaked (begun to rotate negatively) and miss the action altogether.

You can use top-down investing with any investing style by first determining the best performing sectors and industry groups, then searching within those sectors and groups for stocks that match your style. There are several Web sites that track the performance of industry groups (reviewed briefly in Appendix A). If you use these

TABLE 9–3

Sector Classifications

Smartmoney.com	Investor's Business Daily (IBD)*
Basic Materials	Banks
Consumer, Cyclical	Computers
Consumer, Noncyclical	Consumer
Financial	Chemicals
Energy	Defense
Health Care	Energy
Industrial	Gold
Internet	Internet
Technology	Leisure
Telecommunications	Retail
Utilities	Transportation

*IBD does not publish a list of sectors; these sectors were derived from an examination of the industry group listings.

sources, pay attention to the weekly and monthly performance, not daily performance. *Investor's Business Daily* publishes a group ranking, which is an amalgamation of several time periods weighted together to give a price movement rank.

Hints for Successful Top-Down Investing

1. *Be sure the group you've chosen is rotating up, not down.* A group whose performance is in, say, the 90th percentile of all groups, could be on its way down as well as up. Be sure you know which direction the group is going.
2. *Don't ignore out-of-favor groups.* Groups that are out of favor have stocks that are out of favor, which can be fertile ground for certain investing styles, such as value investing or short selling.

Insider Trading: Follow the Insiders

It is safe to say that corporate insiders rarely buy their company's stock if they think it is going down. With the exception of exercising company stock options, which occurs for a variety of reasons, insiders buy their own stock only when they foresee a rosy future for the company. It could be because they know of a specific not-yet-public event, or just because they think that things are going well for the company, or because they think the company isn't valued properly. That's why insider buying has proved to be a very positive predictor of stock price increases.

Insider buying is not a perfect indicator, of course. Sometimes unforeseen things happen that are outside management's control, such as unexpected competitive pressure, product failure, or a negative verdict in a major lawsuit. But all in all, heavy insider buying indicates good future performance for the stock price, and, in fact, one 1993 study showed that a group of stocks with heavy insider buying outperformed the market by 31 percentage points.[1]

Another 1976 study found that stocks with heavy insider buying outperformed the S&P 500 by almost 200 percent.[2] We're not talking about illegal insider activity, of course. Corporate insiders,

---

[1]Mark W. Arnold, *Trading on Tomorrow's Headlines* (Houston: Telescan, Inc., 1995).
[2]Martin Zweig, *Winning on Wall Street* (New York: Warner Books, 1994, 1986).

as you may know, are required to disclose their trading activity in their company's stock to the Securities and Exchange Commission (SEC) within 10 days after the first of the month following the trade. That information is available online as soon as it is published by the SEC.

Insider buying can be used with any investing style. On some search programs you may enter "insider trading" as one of the criteria (see Appendix A) and thus restrict your search to stocks with heavy insider buying. If your search program does not have this feature, you can get a list of the most recent insider trading activity for specific stocks at CNBC.com. or ThomsonFN.com. Incidentally, ThomsonFN offers a "buy score" and a "sell score" for individual insiders, which tells you which insiders at which companies are most predictive of an increase or decrease in stock price. A buy score of 60 or higher indicates that the stocks have typically gone up within a 6-month period following that insider's purchase; a sell score of 60 or higher indicates that the stocks have typically gone down within a 6-month period following that insider's sale.

Hints for Successful Trading with Insiders

1. *Follow those insiders whose buying tracks a rising stock price.* You can use the ThomsonFN buy score, if available, or use the charts at Wall Street City, which plot historical insider trading.

2. *Buy stocks where insider buying is increasing.* This activity is a sign of increasing confidence in the company's potential or its valuation.

3. *Pay particular attention to insider buying by CFOs.* The chief financial officer is one of the most financially astute insiders, and usually the most conservative, so when he or she buys the company's stock it should be a good sign that the stock is undervalued.

4. *Look for open market purchases.* Purchasing stock on the open market is much more significant than exercising stock options, even though both are technically insider buying. Most Web sites that deal with insider trading distinguish between an open market purchase and the exercise of an option.

5. *Don't rely on insider selling.* Insider selling is not as predictive

of a change in stock price as insider buying is, because insiders often sell for reasons that have nothing to do with their opinion of the company's future. This is particularly true of technology stocks, where stock options are used as part of an incentive package. Insiders often sell these stocks to supplement their income. Nonetheless, when important shareholders like the chairman or CEO sell most of their holdings, that is a very significant action and can be predictive of a decline in stock price.

In summary, following insider buying has proved to be one of the best strategies, regardless of investing style. At minimum, it should provide valuable insight as to the mind-set of management and its attitude toward the likely future performance of the stock.

MISCELLANEOUS "STRATEGIES"

There are a number of miscellaneous approaches to investing that we include here simply for the sake of completeness.

Buy-and-Hold Investing

A buy-and-hold strategy means that you build a portfolio of stocks and hold on to them for many years, ignoring short-term market fluctuations. Stocks have historically increased from 10 to 14 percent annually over the past 50 years, so the theory is if you buy good stocks and hold them, you'll probably make 10 to 14 percent annually over time. Which is probably true. You can, however, significantly increase your returns if you take a more active role in your investments and have the time and discipline to stick with your strategy or style.

If you adhere to the buy-and-hold theory, it will behoove you to spend some time and effort in the stock selection process to make sure that you have solid, stable stocks with good long-term growth prospects, and that you keep up with their progress. Contrary to the thought that there is no risk in buy-and-hold investing, there is a risk of a meltdown if you choose badly. Or sometimes even if you choose wisely. One of the blue chip stocks in the 1950's "Nifty Fifty" was Polaroid Corporation (PRD), but in October 2001 Polaroid filed for bankruptcy under Chapter 11, with its stock selling for $0.28.

Dow Investing and Dogs of the Dow

Dow investing is a somewhat simple-minded mechanical strategy; it is no longer as popular as it once was. Any Dow investing strategy starts with a list of the 30 stocks that make up the Dow Jones Industrial Average, which you can find several places online (see Appendix A). Using the Dogs of the Dow approach (also called the High Yield 10), you would buy the 10 stocks with the highest dividend yield (or percent yield) at the beginning of the year and hold on to them for 1 year. At the end of the year, you would adjust your portfolio to sell the stocks that are not on the new year's High Yield 10 list and replace them with the new stocks on the list. The theory behind this strategy is that the Dow stocks with the highest yield are somewhat beaten down and therefore are undervalued.

A variation on Dow investing is the high yield/low price "Beating the Dow 5" strategy described by Michael B. O'Higgins in *Beating the Dow* (New York: Harperbusiness, March 2000 revised and updated). According to this strategy, you buy the cheapest five stocks on the High Yield 10 list. (This strategy is also known as the Flying 5.) The Motley Fool popularized a variation on the Flying 5, called the Foolish Four, which used a ratio procedure to single out four turnaround stocks. The Fool no longer advocates any Dow strategy as a general-purpose strategy, but says, "It may have some value in a diversified retirement account where taxes are not an issue."[3] MSN/CNBC(www.moneycentral.msn.com/investor) has a prebuilt Dogs of the Dow search.

Contrarian Investing

A contrarian strategy is based on the observation that investors tend to overreact to both good news and bad news. Overreacting to good news creates an overly optimistic market, which, in the words of Alan Greenspan, is filled with "irrational exuberance." As a result, the market bids up stocks to the point where they are overvalued and the market is often overextended. Overreacting to bad news brings on a bout of pessimism, and investors retreat to the sidelines and wait for the bears to go back to their caves.

---

[3]Foolish Four Portfolio, Foolish Four Information Center, The Motley Fool (www.fool.com).

Because they believe that everyone else is overreacting, especially at market extremes, contrarian investors go against the prevailing mood. When everyone else is buying aggressively, the contrarian is quietly selling; when other investors are in a selling frenzy, the contrarian is picking up bargains. (In many ways, the value investor is a contrarian investor.) Contrarians believe that the best opportunities come during market extremes: at the top of a raging bull market and at the bottom of a bear market.

Contrarian investing takes a lot of investing confidence because you're going against the prevailing market sentiment. You have to be very sure of yourself and your judgment to be a successful contrarian.

Direct Investing (DSPs and DRIPs)

Direct investing is a way to buy stock directly from a company for relatively small transaction fees. It is not a style or a strategy but rather a way to build a portfolio through small monthly contributions. Direct investing is done through direct stock purchase plans (DSPs) and dividend reinvestment plans (DRIPs).

To buy stock directly from a company, the company must first have a direct stock purchase plan, which is usually administered by a bank. IBM, for example, has a plan that allows an initial investment of $500 and $50 a month (and the $500 minimum is waived if you allow a monthly debit of your bank account). For companies that pay dividends, the DSP usually includes a DRIP, the automatic reinvestment of any dividends into shares of the company. To search for companies that offer direct investing, go to Netstock Direct at www.netstockdirect.com.

Direct investing is a good way to build a portfolio without a lot of investment capital, and the regular contributions take advantage of dollar-cost averaging. (Dollar-cost averaging theoretically evens out the fluctuations in stock price through regular purchases at fixed intervals.) The disadvantage of direct investing is that you have to join a new plan for each company whose stock you want to own.

There is an alternative to joining numerous DSP plans. Netstock Direct's Sharebuilder™ allows you to choose from more than 4000 companies and index products. There is no account or investment minimum, and the cost per transaction is about $4 or a fixed fee of $12 per month.

The goal of this chapter has been to introduce you to some lesser-known investing styles for the sake of completeness. Keep in mind that these styles are called "minor" for a reason. Unlike the four major investing styles, the minor investing styles are not followed by millions and millions of investors. It stands to reason that if a style is not well followed, it may not provide the force of momentum behind your stock selections. Nonetheless, these minor styles have had at least a modest following for some time, and if any of them piques your curiosity, by all means, investigate it further.

CHAPTER 10

An Introduction to Advanced Investing Strategies

Experienced investors use dozens of advanced strategies to accomplish their investing goals, and new strategies surface regularly to meet the demands of the market. To give you a flavor of what's "out there," we will touch on four of the more popular advanced strategies:

- *Short-selling:* A very high-risk strategy that takes advantage of the downside of the market
- *Market-neutral investing:* A way to neutralize the ups and downs of the markets
- *Option trading:* A strategy that can be used for speculation, hedging, or to supplement income
- *Global investing:* A strategy for diversifying across world economies

These strategies are complex and fairly sophisticated, and each would require an entire book to treat it effectively. Our purpose in this chapter is simply to address each one briefly so that you will have a starting point if you choose to pursue any of them further.

SHORT-SELLING: BETTING ON THE DOWNSIDE

Short-selling is a strategy used by investors who believe a stock (or the entire market) is significantly overvalued. You sell the stock (which you borrow from your broker) at the current price, and wait (hope) for it to go down. When it does, you "cover your position" by buying the stock at the lower price, returning it to the broker, and pocketing the difference between the sales price and the price at which you buy it back, minus any charges the broker imposes for the loan of the stock.

There are professional short-sellers whose entire investing strategy is based on shorting stocks, rather than holding long positions. Used as a primary investing strategy, short-selling carries extreme risk since the potential for loss is unlimited. For example, if you buy a stock for $10 a share that you expect to go up and you are wrong, the most you can lose is $10 a share. But if you short a stock for $10 expecting it to go down, and you're wrong, your potential for loss is *unlimited*. You will have to buy the stock back at some price to deliver it to your broker. If you can buy it back at, say, $30, you'll have lost $20 a share. But if it goes to, say, $100, you will have lost $90 a share. If it goes to, say, $150, you will have lost $140 a share. The potential for loss is limitless because, theoretically, the upside for a stock is unlimited. You might think, well, if the stock starts to go up I'll cover my position quickly, but what exacerbates the problem is the amount of short-selling that has taken place, that is, the short interest. (Short interest is calculated as the number of days of normal trading it would take for shorts to buy back the total number of shares that have been shorted.) If the short interest is high and the stock turns around and heads up, the short-sellers themselves will drive the stock price higher and higher (and often very quickly) as they scramble to cover their positions. The problem is also exacerbated by the fact that if the short-sellers believed the stock was a good short at $10, many will think it is a better short at $15 and maybe even $20, and so the short position continues to grow even as the stock rebounds, until the trend becomes obvious, at which time the scramble to cover begins.

Short-selling can be applied to any investing style. You could build an antigrowth portfolio by looking for the flip side of high-growth stocks or an antimomentum portfolio by shorting stocks whose momentum has run its course. And you could certainly build an antivalue portfolio by shorting overvalued stocks (which is pretty much the definition of a good stock to short).

We would point out, however, that basing your entire investing strategy on shorting stocks is a very, very risky approach and best left to the professionals. A better strategy for the individual investor would be to incorporate short-selling in a market-neutral strategy, as described later in this chapter, or to buy an option (a put) on stocks that you expect will go down.

Hints for Successful Short-Selling

1. *Be careful.* Shorting stocks is not for the dilettante. Don't do it unless you're willing to bear the considerable risks involved.
2. *Protect yourself with stops.* Use stops to close out positions that go the wrong way.
3. *Be disciplined.* Discipline is even more important in short-selling because of the greater potential for loss.

MARKET-NEUTRAL INVESTING: PROTECTING YOUR DOWNSIDE

Market-neutral investing is a way of managing risk. It helps you protect against market volatility by simultaneously investing in both long and short positions, or by using options or index funds as a hedge.

A market-neutral portfolio would consist of long positions that would do well if the market does well and short positions that would do well if the market does poorly. The theory is that if the market does well, you'll make money on your long position; if it does poorly, you'll make money on your short position. In other words, you're saying to yourself: If the market is going up I want to own these stocks and if the market is going down I want to short these stocks. You don't know which way the market is going, of course, but if you believe it has, say, a 70 percent chance of going up, you'd invest 70 percent of your portfolio into long positions and 30 percent into short positions.

As an alternative, if short-selling isn't appealing, you could invest 30 percent of your portfolio in defensive stocks such as foods and pharmaceuticals that might do well in a poor economy. The point is to hedge to the opposite direction so that if your premise is wrong, you will have protection. In other words, you wish to be neutral to the market.

You must base your stock selections on the state of the current economy. For example, the fall of 2001 was a low interest rate environment in which construction stocks and housing stocks traditionally do well, and most investors would typically go long on those stocks. A market-neutral investor would then look for stocks that would likely do poorly if the market should go south, which might be brokerage stocks. So the market-neutral investor would short stocks like Merrill Lynch or Charles Schwab. It's conceivable that a market decline could result in further interest rate cuts, so it is possible that you'd make money on your short positions and that housing stocks would perhaps hold their own, but the purpose of market-neutral investing is to protect your downside.

Paired Trading

A slightly different market-neutral strategy is *paired trading*, buying one stock that you expect to go up and shorting another stock that is related inversely to your basic premise. The paired stocks can be competitive companies: Company A will do well at whose expense? For example, if you think that Dell Computer's success is detrimental to, say, Gateway, you'd buy Dell and short Gateway. If the stocks move the way you think they will—that is, Dell does well and Gateway does poorly—you'll make money on both. At the same time, if the market goes down, you would expect Gateway stock to fare particularly poorly so again you have protection.

Another way to find paired stocks is first to find a stock that you expect to go up and then look for companies to short that will not do well if things turn sour for the primary stock. For example, if Intel turns up as a great stock on one of your searches, you should pair it with a stock that depends on the success of Intel, so if things go badly for Intel the paired stock will do poorly as well. For example, if Intel is facing declining sales it probably won't be buying any more chip manufacturing equipment for a while, so if you buy Intel you might want to short a company that supplies Intel's chip manufacturing equipment, which is KLA-Tencor Corp (KLAC).

What you're looking for in pair trading are two stocks that are diametrically opposed—what makes one go up is likely to make the other go down (the Dell/Gateway example) or when one stock tanks, related stocks will also tank (the Intel/KLAC example). And if the whole market drops, you'll at least make money on your short position to cushion your losses on the long position.

Market-neutral investing can be applied to any style of investing. A value investor will buy undervalued stocks and short overvalued stocks. A growth investor will buy high-growth stocks and short stocks that have the opposite characteristics. A momentum investor will buy stocks just beginning their upward momentum and short stocks that have downward momentum. Technical investors will short stocks that have chart patterns opposite their basic strategy.

Keep in mind that a market-neutral strategy is not designed to speculate on the short side; it is a way to manage risk. The *primary* objective of your short or defensive positions is not to make money but to help protect you in the event of a market reversal.

Hints for Successful Market-Neutral Investing

1. *Study your short or defensive position carefully.* Think through each scenario to ensure that you have chosen the best possible combination of stocks.

2. *Commit the time to do it right.* Market-neutral investing almost doubles the amount of time you'd normally spend on the stock selection process because you're looking at both sides of the equation. How can I make money if the market goes up? How can I protect myself if the market goes down? If you don't have the time to study your positions carefully, you would be better off not to use a market-neutral strategy.

3. *Consider using options on index funds or options on stocks as hedges.* Using options on stocks for hedging can be less expensive than shorting stocks, and it certainly limits the risk. Further, as we will discuss in the next section, you can purchase a put option on an index fund as a means of hedging your entire portfolio.

OPTIONS: HEDGING YOUR BETS AND SUPPLEMENTING YOUR INCOME

Options can be used as a speculative investment, a protective hedge, or an additional income source. In this chapter we are talking about equity options, not options on futures or commodities.

Options derive their value from the value of the underlying security (which is why they're referred to as derivatives), but they also have value in and of themselves and can be traded just like stocks. Trading options falls under the subject of speculative trading, which is a complex strategy we will not go into in depth in this book. Instead we will limit our discussion to using options as a protective hedge or as an additional income source. But first, a brief overview of options.

A Brief Overview

An equity option is a contract to buy (a call) or sell (a put) 100 shares of stock at a specified future date. For this right to buy or sell the underlying stock, you have to pay only a fraction of the current stock price. Let's look at an example of two options for Microsoft (MSFT).

In early November 2001, Microsoft was priced at $65. If you thought Microsoft was going to go up, you could have paid $65 a share and waited to see what happened, or you could have bought a call option. At that time, a $65 call (an option to buy MSFT at $65) that would expire in January 2002 cost about $5 per share. If Microsoft did what you expected and exceeded $65 by January 2002, you could have exercised your option and bought it for $65 a share. (In reality, you probably wouldn't exercise the option and buy the stock, you would just sell the option, which would have increased in value.) If Microsoft doesn't exceed $65 a share by January—or if it should fall below $65—your option would have expired worthless, but you would have lost only your $5 a share.

On the other hand, if you thought Microsoft might go down, you could have shorted the stock for $65 and waited to see what happened. If you were wrong and the stock went to, say, $100, you would have lost $35 a share—and more if the stock kept rising. Instead of taking this risk, you could have bought a $65 December 2001 put (an option to sell MSFT at $65) for about $3 per share. If you were right and the stock went down, you could have exercised your option and sold MSFT for $65, pocketing the difference between that price and its current lower price. (Again, you would more likely have sold the option, which would have increased in value.) If you were wrong, if MSFT didn't go below $65 by December 2001, the option would have become worthless, but the most you could have lost was $3 a share, regardless of how high Microsoft went.

Let's consider the effect of the expiration date on the option's value. In the first Microsoft example, a $65 call option for January 2002 was priced at about $5. Compare that with a $65 call option for January 2004, which was priced at $17. Why the huge discrepancy in prices? Because the $5 option will expire worthless if Microsoft doesn't exceed $65 in 3 months. With a 2-year option, time is on our side. It is much more likely that Microsoft will exceed $65 in 2 years. Therefore, we'd pay more for the 2-year option than for the 3-month option. The other part of an option's value is related to the *strike price*—the price at which you can exercise the option to buy the underlying stock—and to the current price of the stock itself. This relationship is described as *in-the-money*, *at-the-money*, or *out-of-the-money*.

- *In-the-money* means the strike price is *less* for a call option and *greater* for a put option than the current stock price.
- *At-the-money* means the strike price is equal to the current stock price, regardless of whether it is a put or a call.
- *Out-of-the-money* means the strike price is *greater* for a call option and *less* for a put option than the current stock price.

Let us illustrate the difference with three-month call options for Microsoft. The stock was priced at $65 in early November; the following options all had expiration dates of January 2002:

$60 in-the-money call: $8.25

$65 at-the-money call: $5.00

$70 out-of-the-money call: $2.50

In other words, in-the-money or at-the-money means the option is worth money today; an out-of-the money option means it is worthless if exercised today but may be worth something in the future. Out-of-the-money options cost less but have more risk.

Because of the time component, an option goes down in value every single day assuming the underlying stock price is unchanged. It is like a time bomb ticking away, and on the final day—the expiration day—it doesn't "go off," it simply goes to worthless *unless* the strike price is less (a call option) or more (a put option) than the stock price at the expiration date.

Thus the risk with options is that the underlying stock has to go the direction you want *and* it has to do so within the time frame of the option.

The extra risk also means extra reward. You're able to invest a little bit of money with the potential of making a lot of money. If the stock doesn't perform the way you anticipate, all you lose is the price you paid for the option. Realize, however, that you must be right on both the direction and the time frame.

Using Options for Hedging

Remember the Intel/KLAC example we used for a market-neutral strategy? We suggested buying Intel and shorting its chip equipment supplier, KLAC, to create a market-neutral position. You could obtain the same market-neutral position with less cost and less risk by buying put options.

Instead of shorting KLAC and taking the chance that it will rise instead of fall, you could protect your downside by buying a put— a contract to sell 100 shares of KLAC at a specific future date. To illustrate, on November 8, 2001, KLAC closed at $49.55. On that day, an at-the-money put option to sell 100 shares of KLAC at $50 anytime before December 22 would have cost about $5 a share. (An out-of-the-money $45 put would have cost just $2.75.)

- If KLAC went to $40, for example, the day before your $50 option expired, it would have been selling for $10 so you'd sell the option. (Theoretically, you could have exercised the option, selling 100 shares of KLAC at $50, and immediately covering your position at whatever lower price KLAC had fallen to, pocketing the difference between the two.)
- If KLAC went up instead of down during that period, the option would have expired worthless, and you would have lost only the price of the option—$5 a share.

The limited risk of options makes them ideal for hedging individual stocks or your portfolio against a future downturn in the market. Short sales, as we have said, have infinite risk, but with options, the most you can lose is the cost of the option.

Hints for Successful Option Hedging

1. *Use a direct hedge on your own stocks.* The most direct hedge position you can take is to buy a put on the stocks you own.

For example, if you own Microsoft, an appropriate Microsoft put can provide some protection against a loss on Microsoft shares.

2. *Hedge your entire portfolio with an index put.* Options on indexes can be used to hedge your entire portfolio. To do this, you might buy an OEX put (on the S&P 100 index). If the whole market declines, the money you are likely to make on your put will help offset the losses in your regular portfolio.

3. *Minimize your costs.* Try to develop a hedge position at minimum cost. There are many sophisticated option strategies involving spreads that can reduce the cost of the hedge. They are beyond the scope of this book, but if you intend to pursue option hedging as a strategy, it would be wise to learn about these strategies.

Writing Covered Option Calls

Writing covered option calls is a popular strategy for those who want to supplement their income. The strategy is simply to sell (write) call options on stocks that you own. If you think one of your stocks isn't likely to change appreciably over the next 3 months, you can sell a call option for, say, $3 a share. If you're right and the stock doesn't go anywhere, you pocket the $3 *and* keep the stock, plus any dividends that it may pay. If the stock should go higher, it may be called away from you by the option holder, but you'll still get the strike price of the stock and the $3 a share for the option.

Covered option writing limits your upside, but it can add to your income and is an especially effective strategy in a flat market or for income-oriented investors.

Hints for Success in Writing Covered Calls

1. *Stick with stocks that pay dividends.* Covered call writing is best done with stocks that pay dividends.

2. *Avoid highly volatile stocks.* First, highly volatile stocks rarely pay dividends. Second, it is very difficult to make up in option premiums the large drop that can occur in a highly volatile stock.

3. *Study your stocks carefully to maximize your return.* To maximize your return, find stocks that have good option premiums, as well as paying dividends.

Option trading is very complex, and there are dozens of books on the subject if you care to pursue it. For a brief introduction to the basics, try the primer at the Learning Center of the Chicago Board Options Exchange at http://www.cboe.com.

GLOBAL INVESTING: INVESTING ACROSS BORDERS

The objective of global investing is to diversify your investments across global economies. By doing so you can take advantage of thriving economies around the globe, while lessening market risk on a broader scale. Global investing is not a zero-sum game, though. In a worldwide recession it may be impossible to find any economy that's doing well, but under normal circumstances there is usually the possibility that some economy in the world is doing better than other economies.

In a sense, global investing simply adds a level on top of top-down investing, which can then be combined with your regular investing style. Instead of starting with sectors, you first find the country with the best or fastest-growing economy, then you evaluate sectors or specific securities. The easiest way for an individual investor to play the global game is through American depository receipts (ADRs), closed-end country funds, or exchange-traded funds (ETFs). These vehicles are easier to trade, compared with investing directly in foreign stocks, and there is little or no currency risk. There are also hundreds of global mutual funds, if you prefer to leave the management to someone else.

The Internet has simplified the task of keeping up with global economies, and it has also facilitated access to global investment vehicles. All global securities are available through most on-line brokers; informational Web sites on ADRs, ETFs, and country and global funds are listed in Appendix A.

ADRs: Foreign Stocks in U.S. Clothing

American depository receipts (ADRs) are the easiest way to invest in a specific non-U.S. company, without all the hassle of cross-border

trading. An ADR represents ownership in a non-U.S. publicly traded company the same way that a stock certificate represents ownership in a U.S. public company. The ADR, which is sponsored by a
U.S. bank, is proof (in the form of a receipt) that the shares of the
non-U.S. company are actually held in trust in a bank in the country of the foreign company. Buying ADRs reduces but does not completely eliminate the risk of currency fluctuations.

The first ADR was created by J.P. Morgan in 1927 to allow Amer-
icans to invest in the British retailer Selfridge's. American depository receipts now include such names as Finland's Nokia Corporation, Japan's NEC, Germany's Deutsche Telekom, and the United
Kingdom's Vodafone. In all, there are more than 1600 ADRs from
more than 60 countries listed on the U.S. exchanges. The best place
to find them on the Web is at the Bank of New York, which has a
search engine for all ADRs listed on the NYSE, ASE, and Nasdaq
(see Appendix A for details).

Funds: Country, Global, and Exchange-Traded Funds

Buying a fund that invests in international securities is another way
to expand into global investing. There are three ways to do it: closed-
end funds, open-end funds, and exchange-traded funds (ETFs).

Closed-End Funds

Closed-end funds trade just like stocks with an initial public
offering and a finite number of shares. The price of shares trades
at a premium or discount to the fund's net asset value (NAV),
which rises and falls throughout the day based on the supply
and demand of buyers and sellers. Some investors trade closed-
end funds by buying a fund when the discount is the maximum
and selling it when the discount is at the minimum end of the
range.

Closed-end funds can be limited to a specific country or region,
or they may be global in nature, investing in the securities of different nations. Closed-end funds are traded primarily on the New
York Stock Exchange. For a tutorial on closed-end funds, go to
www.closed-endfunds.com.

Net Asset Value

Net Asset Value (NAV) is the value of a fund's underlying securities. It is arrived at by totaling the fund's assets, subtracting the liabilities, and dividing that figure by the number of outstanding shares.

Open-End Funds

Open-end funds, that is, what we normally think of as mutual funds, are traded once a day at their NAV by the funds themselves. Essentially, there is no limit to the amount of money that can be placed into an open-end fund, unless the fund itself places a restriction on the number of shares. Therein lies a dilemma. The successful mutual fund will attract very large amounts of money, perhaps making it difficult for the manager to continue his or her performance.

Generally speaking, open-end global funds invest in worldwide securities or concentrate on a specific region such as Europe or Latin America or Asia, although a few invest primarily in the securities of a specific country, such as Japan or Canada. Virtually every mutual fund family (listed in Appendix A) offers a variety of open-end global funds, as well as educational materials on mutual fund investing.

Exchange-Traded Funds

An exchange-traded fund (ETF) is a fixed basket of stocks that trades on an exchange just like a stock (see Chapter 4 for a complete description). A global ETF can represent stocks of a specific country or region or a specific industry in a country or a region. The value of an ETF is determined on a continuous basis by calculating the true NAV of the ETF (based on the changing value of the stocks that make up the ETF).

At this time there are a relatively small number of global ETFs, although this situation is likely to change in the future. Barclay's currently offers more than 28 country and regional ETFs through iShares (www.ishares.com); Merrill Lynch offers the Europe 2001 HOLDR (www.holdr.com); and streetTRACKS (www.streettracks.com) offers a Global Titan Index Fund (DJGT).

With global funds—whether they are closed-end, open-end, or ETFs—the stocks are selected to represent a cross-section of the economy of the country or to represent a sector or industry within the country or region. The differences among these global securities are important but often subtle. Table 10–1 might help you keep the differences straight.

TABLE 10–1

Closed-End Funds, Open-End Funds, and Exchange-Traded Funds

Fund Features	Closed-End Funds	Open-End Funds	Exchange-Traded Funds (ETFs)
Composition of fund	Stocks are not fixed	Stocks are not fixed	Fixed basket of stocks
Number of shares	Finite	Unlimited	Unlimited
How is it traded?	On an exchange (usually the NYSE), throughout the day at a premium or discount to the NAV	Through the fund itself, once a day, at the NAV	On an exchange, throughout the day at the approximate NAV of the ETF
How is the price of fund shares calculated?	Premium or discount to the NAV is based on supply and demand of buyers and sellers; NAV is continuously calculated throughout the day as stocks in the fund rise and fall	The NAV is calculated at the end of the day for transaction purposes.	The NAV of the ETF is continuously calculated based on the changing prices of the underlying stocks.
How is the fund managed?	Fund manager with management fees	Fund manager with management fees	Not managed
Where do I find these funds?	www.closed-endfunds.com	Any mutual fund family (see list in Appendix A)	www.ishares.com www.streetracks.com www.holdrs.com

Hints for Successful Global Investing

1. *Watch the trends.* Watch the charts on ETFs to see where the action is. (For a superior graphics representation, use the SmartMoney.com Market Map described in Appendix A.)

2. *Apply your investing style.* Whether you buy closed-end funds, open-end funds, or ETFs, invest in them as you would with domestic stocks using your particular investing style. For example, once you've decided on a country, select an ADR using the same investing style guidelines you would use for selecting domestic stocks. For country funds or ETFs, the growth investor would look for the fastest-growing economy; a value investor might look for bargain funds in a country that is perhaps having a difficult time. (One fund manager even says he shops for country fund bargains in countries hit by earthquakes, floods, political coups, or currency devaluations!) A momentum investor would be looking for the fastest-moving fund. A technician would simply compare the charts of the funds to see which had the best patterns.

Advanced strategies are the province of the advanced investor. The cursory overview in this chapter is intended simply to give you a hint of what's available. We are not suggesting that you proceed with any of them without further study. Nor are we suggesting that these are all of the advanced strategies available to the sophisticated investor. There are many more, and new ones continue to surface to meet the demands of investors and the changing marketplace. As with investing in general, considerable study and practice are needed to become adept at any advanced strategy. You might start with the free information that is available on the Internet, then progress to the many related books and seminars.

Throughout its 100-year history, the market has gone through sequential waves of "irrational exuberance," in Alan Greenspan's words, and equally irrational despondence. Predictably, investors always say "This time is different" or "This time the rules have changed." During the dot-com boom when stock valuations soared far above any former valuations, the pundits proclaimed a New Economy. Profits and revenues weren't that important, they chanted. Capturing market share or "eyeballs" was what the New Economy was all about.

As we found out in 2000, the pundits were wrong. The basics of the market are still important. The market's exuberance always corrects (and usually overcorrects) itself, just as its despondence always corrects (and often overcorrects) itself. The only certainty is that we never know what the newest bout of exuberance or despondency is going to look like or what it's going to be called. So it behooves us to adopt and execute an investing strategy and a process that shelters us to some extent from market uncertainties.

Our mission in writing this book has been to help you find an investing style or strategy that fits your basic personality to see you through the market's ups and downs. If, after having read this book, you realize that you need a strategy, if you recognize yourself in one or more of the strategies or styles we've discussed, if you understand the need for a systematic process for executing your strategy—a process for selecting stocks, a process for entering and exiting a stock, and a process for managing your portfolio—then we will consider our mission successful. Armed with an investing strategy that fits your personality, you won't have to worry as much about the gyrations of the market. While you will always have losses, a well-chosen strategy and an investing process should keep your losses smaller and your gains larger. In the end, if you have more winners than losers and your winners are bigger and your losers are smaller, you will succeed as an investor—and we will have succeeded in our mission.

Online Investing Resources
(By Category)

Below is a very abbreviated list of investing resources on the Web. This list is categorized by the topics discussed in this book. An alphabetical list of all Web sites mentioned here appears in Appendix B.

STOCKS

10Ks/10Qs

* **Securities & Exchange Commission** (SEC) (www.sec.gov) All 10K, 10Qs, and other filings available free at this site.
* **Edgar Online** (www.edgar-online.com) More user-friendly than the SEC site. Subscription-based.

ADRs

* **The Bank of New York** Depositary Receipts (www. adrbny.com) This Web site of The Bank of New York is devoted to depositary receipts and offers a search engine for all ADRs listed on the NYSE, AMEX, and Nasdaq.
* **Other ADR sites:** Citibank (www.citibank.com/ corpbank/adr) and J.P. Morgan (www.adr.com)

Company Profiles and News

Almost every online broker and financial Web site offers company profiles and news; here is one of our favorites:

* **MSN/CNBC** (http://moneycentral.msn.com/investor). Enter a stock symbol, click Print This Report, and you're given a choice of which items to print, including quote detail, options, intraday and 1-year chart, company report, earnings estimates and analyst ratings, various financial highlights and ratios, and insider trading transactions and planned sales. You can also get something called "Advisor FYI,"

which provides price and volume alerts, analyst alerts such as upgrades and downgrades, and news stories about the stock, including mention of the stock in any MSN article. You can also view the items separately online. Free.

Earnings Estimates and Announcements

- **Earnings calendar:** To check upcoming earnings announcements, try SmartMoney.com (www.smartmoney. com). The calendar (accessed from the Tools menu) displays the consensus estimate and once the announcement is made, it fills in the actual and positive or negative surprise. Registration required.

- **Earnings conference calls:** If you want to hear the CEO and/or CFO discuss the company's quarterly performance, listen in on an earnings conference call. A schedule of calls appears at Best Calls (www.bestcalls.com), or you can search for a particular company's scheduled call. A CallTracker allows you to receive advance e-mail notifications of specific conference calls. Free with registration.

- **Earnings estimates:** Zacks.com (www.zacks.com) is the place to go for earnings estimates. Zacks offers free overviews of estimates, and they also supply their reports to numerous financial Web sites.

Insider Trading

- **MSN/CNBC** (http://moneycentral.msn.com/investor). This site provides the insiders' names, number of shares sold, price, and current holdings. Free.

- **Sabrient Systems** (www.sabrient.com) offers a weekly stock pick based on insider trading. Subscription-based.

- **ThomsonFN.com** (www.thomsonfn.com) provides an "insider performance rating" that shows how well each insider did on his or her trades. Presumably, this will help you decide how much credence to put in that insider's trades. They also offer free e-mail alerts for insider trading. Registration required.

◆ **Wall Street City** (wallstreetcity.com) offers insider trading
as a screening indicator for its ProSearch searches, and it
plots insider trading on a stock graph so you can see
whether or not insider activity tracks the ups and downs
of the stock price. The site also provides insiders' names,
number of shares sold, price, and current holdings. These
insider trading features are free.

Investing Styles

◆ **Nasdaq** (www.nasdaq.com) Nasdaq's Guru Screener (under Investing Tools) lets you screen for stocks based on
growth, momentum, value, small cap, and others. Free.

◆ **Sabrient Systems** (www.sabrient.com) offers stock selections for four different investing styles: growth, value, momentum, and technical, along with proprietary entry and /
or exit signals. Subscription-based.

◆ **CANSLIM.Net** (www.canslim.net): "The source for
CANSLIM stocks on the Web." Basic services, free. Premium services with subscription.

◆ **Dogs of the Dow:** DogsoftheDow.com (dogsofthedow.
com) is devoted to this strategy. Also, MSN / CNBC
(http://moneycentral.msn.com /investor) has a prebuilt
Dogs of the Dow search. Both free.

Markets and Indexes

◆ **American Stock Exchange** (www.amex.com): Read about
exchange-traded funds (ETFs). Free.

◆ **Detachable market monitor:** Bloomberg.com (www.
bloomberg.com) offers a free market monitor that can be
detached so it remains on your screen after you leave the
Bloomberg site.

◆ **Dow stocks:** Stocks in the Dow Jones Industrial Average,
along with performance figures can be found at
Bloomberg.com. (www.bloomberg.com). (Click Markets,
then select Stocks in the Dow from left menu.) Free.

◆ **Global indexes:** One of the best places to track global in-

dices is the World Indices page at Bloomberg.com (www.
bloomberg.com). Free.

♦ **Nasdaq** (www.nasdaq.com): Nasdaq offers an Analyst Activity Table that displays the top 50 stocks with the most analyst activity during the past week. Free.

♦ **New York Stock Exchange** (www.nyse.com): Market information and everything you'd ever want to know about the NYSE.

♦ **Market indexes:** Learn about the different various market indexes: Russell indexes (www.russell.com); S&P indexes (www.standardandpoors.com); and The Wilshire 500 Index (www.wilshire.com).

Mechanical Trading Systems

Mechanical trading systems are for the advanced investor. This is only a sampling of the hundreds of available systems. For pricing and additional information, visit the respective Web sites.

♦ **The Alpha Trading System** (www.alphafin.com). Developed by Luiz V. Alvim for use in the futures market, the Alpha Trading System seeks to find trend reversals by identifying when an existing trend is losing strength and when a new one may be emerging. A recently completed manual called "The Alpha Trading System for Stocks—From Paper Profits to Real Profits" applies the system to stocks and can be used for daily or intraday chart analysis.

♦ **The Mesa2000 System** (www.mesasoftware.com). Developed by John Ehlers, the MESA2000 is a cycle-based trading program and is available for a variety of trading platforms, including TradeStation (4.0 and 2000i), SuperCharts, NeuroShell Trader, and Standalone. MESA also offers trading systems for commodities and bonds. The MESA software has received 25 Readers Choice awards over 7 years from *Stocks & Commodities* magazine.

♦ **TradeStation** (www.tradestation.com). The TradeStation software includes many mechanical systems from various developers.

Portfolios and Portfolio Alerts

Portfolios and portfolio alerts are available at every online broker and most financial sites. The advantage of using the portfolio at your online broker is that your trades are automatically entered into the portfolio. The disadvantage is that most brokerage portfolios do not offer some of the sexy features of other sites, such as these:

- **MSN/CNBC** (http://moneycentral.msn.com/investor). MSN Money Deluxe portfolio offers customization, column sorting, Advisor FYI alerts, plus news and message board alerts. You can import accounts from many online brokers. Free; requires download.
- **SmartMoney.com** (www.smartmoney.com). SmartMoney Select offers real-time portfolio updates, mapping of your portfolio with the SmartMoney Market Map (*see* Market Maps under Sector & Industry Group Resources), automatic updates on splits and dividends, access to stock screening, and importing data from Excel spreadsheets, Microsoft Money and others. Subscription-based.
- **Wall Street City** (www.wallstreetcity.com). The portfolio at Wall Street City offers tools that analyze your portfolio for short-term, intermediate-term, and long-term breakouts, insider trading, and a "ranking" view that shows with color-coded bars how the portfolio as a whole and the individual stocks rank on each of seven different criteria. Free with registration.

Research Reports from Third Parties

- **MultexInvestor** (www.multexinvestor.com) offers broker research reports at various prices.
- **Wall Street Research Net** (www.wsrn.com) offers ProVestor reports and others at various prices.

Rotation of Investing Styles and Market Caps

- **MSN/CNBC** (http://moneycentral.msn.com/investor). The Market Trends page at MSN/CNBC tracks value and growth investing styles and all four market caps. The tracking is rather simplistic, with only three ratings—In Favor, Neutral, and Out of Favor—and when we checked it in November 2001 and again in March 2002, both styles (growth and value) and all four market caps were in the Neutral zone. Free.

- **Nasdaq** (www.nasdaq.com) offers a free ETF Heatmap which color-codes ETFs based on their market activity and allows you to see trends that are developing. Nasdaq also has a Heatmap for the Nasdaq 100. At the Nasdaq Web site, click Market Activity, then Heatmaps.

- **SmartMoney Market Map** (www.smartmoney.com). Probably the very best way to track styles and caps is to use the Map Your Portfolio feature at Smart Money Select (subscription-based) and enter the appropriate ETFs. A list of ETFs that track market caps and investing styles appears in this book in Table 9–2, Chapter 9.

Sectors and Industry Groups

- **Industry group performance chart:** The Big Chart at Wall Street City (www.wallstreetcity.com) provides a weekly quantitative analysis of which industry groups are gaining momentum and which are losing momentum. This is part of the Wall Street City Pro package (subscription-based). Wall Street City also offers several free industry group tools, a color-coded bar chart of best and worst industries and best and worst stocks in each group, stock screening within groups, various rankings of stocks in groups, and industry group charts.

- **Market maps.** SmartMoney.com's (www.smartmoney.com) Market Maps provide a graphical view of the overall market in color-coded, multisized blocks that reveal at a glance the rotation of the market. The color indicates the performance (bright green—the best; bright red—the worst) and the size indicates the relative size of the sector. Eleven sector maps provide a close-up view of each sector. These are all free. If you want a more comprehensive market map with the ability to customize it (with ETFs, perhaps) and to map your own portfolio in real time, sign up for the subscription-based Smart Money Select.

Stock Screens and Filters

♦ **MSN/CNBC** (http://moneycentral.msn.com/investor). MSN/CNBC offers six preset searches, a custom screener, and a deluxe screener, all free. The preset searches include high momentum searches for large-cap, mid-cap, or small-cap stocks; a search for the cheapest stocks of large, growing companies; a search for highest-yielding stocks in the S&P 500; and a Dogs of the Dow search.

The custom screener offers seven criteria, including dividend yield, average daily volume, 12-month relative strength, revenue growth, P/E ratio, net profit margin, and debt/equity ratio. You may specify highest or lowest for the criteria, but you set minimum or maximum ranges. The screener allows you to limit your search to a specific industry and to large-, mid-, or small-cap companies, and you may specify whether or not the stock should be included in one of the Dow or S&P indexes.

You can download the free deluxe screener, which offers 500 criteria for creating custom searches and 11 preset deluxe searches, including a "great expectations" search that looks for small-cap value stocks, a momentum search, a growth stock search based on fund manager Jim O'Shaughnessy's quantitative backtesting, a search for stocks with recent upward revisions by analysts, a GARP search, and a contrarian search.

♦ **Wall Street City** (www.wallstreetcity.com). All the searches at Wall Street City are built using ProSearch, the professional stock search program from Telescan, which uses fuzzy logic. On the free site, you can build custom searches with more than 70 criteria, including all the standard criteria, plus insider trading, institutional holdings, market capitalization, projected EPS, 1-month change in projected EPS, percent of EPS surprises, inventory turnover, short interest ratio, and dividend consistency. You may customize criteria with minimum and maximum ranges and by specifying "high as possible" or "low as possible," and you can run both modes together. That means, for example, that you can search for stocks with highest projected EPS and eliminate all stocks that don't have, say, at least 20 percent projected EPS. You may also have the report display the value of a criteria without affecting the stock, which can be used for criteria like stock price. ProSearch engine allows you to limit your search to a specific exchange, a specific industry, or to optionable stocks.

Wall Street City also offers 22 category searches that preselect the criteria, but you must enter the values for each criteria. If you want to let someone else do all the work, try one of their featured searches that analyze the search and offer backtested results. On the day we checked out the site, the featured searches included Institutionally Held Stocks with Strong Revenue Growth, Large-cap Stocks Displaying Technical Strength, Searching for Companies with Strong Balance Sheets, and Stocks with Rising Earnings Estimates that May Top Expectations.

The full-blown version of ProSearch with over 300 search criteria is available with a subscription to Wall Street City Pro. ProSearch was named their Favorite Stock Screener by TheStreet.com. It includes the ability to backtest searches and access to the What's Working Now feature that spotlights the searches and the industries that are working best in the current market.

Strategy Testing

The following allow you to backtest your technical indicators and systems. See the respective Web sites for more information and pricing.

- **TradeStation Securities** (www.tradestation.com) offers the ability to test and automate your own trading strategies. This is for the more advanced technician. Strategy testing is free with the direct access software, but it requires a minimum of $30,000 in trading capital to open an account. TradeStation is also a direct access broker.

- **MetaStock** (www.metastock.com). The MetaStock Pro software allows you to test strategies.
- **TIP@WallStreet** (www.telescan.com). Telescan's charting program shows with every chart how well a technical indictor backtests by including the number of trades given by the signal in the time span of the chart, along with the profit or loss for that period.

Technical Analysis and Charting

Stocks and index charts, along with technical indicators, can be found at these sites:

- **ProphetFinance.com** (www.prophetfinance.com). Prophet's JavaCharts offer the most complete set of technical indicators on the Web for free. Among the dozens of popular and esoteric indicators are linear regression trendlines and channels (which are not available on most Web-based charting programs).
- **Other free charting sites** include Ask Research (www.askresearch.com) , Big Charts (http://bigcharts. marketwatch.com), ClearStation (www.clearstation.com), and Wall Street City (www.wallstreetcity.com).

Whisper Numbers

- **EarningsWhispers.com** (www.earningswhispers.com). This site claims to be the most accurate source of earnings whispers. A study by Bloomberg News is quoted as saying that EarningsWhispers.com's whisper numbers were twice as accurate as First Call's consensus estimates. They also gather their whisper numbers from analysts. Free and subscription-based services.
- **WhisperNumber.com** (www.whispernumber.com). This site allows registered users to input "whispers" but claims that their system of "checks and balances" spots those who are hyping a stock. They claim 50 to 58 percent accuracy in predicting stock movement. Free. Personal Watch List requires registration. Free and subscription-based services.

INVESTOR EDUCATION

All investor education Web sites are free, unless otherwise stated.

Investing Basics

- **IBD Learning Center** (www.investors.com). Investing lessons based on William O'Neil's research into stock performance, plus a guide to reading *Investor's Business Daily*.
- **Morningstar.com** (www.morningstar.com). In Morningstar's "university," you find an Investing Classroom with class series numbered from 100 to 500 to denote level of difficulty. Stocks, funds, portfolio management, and bonds are covered. Free with registration.
- **SmartMoney University** (www.university.smartmoney. com). A robust, comprehensive free learning site.

Technical Analysis Basics

- **ClearStation.com** (www.clearstation.com). The basics on reading price and indicator graphs, plus sections on trending, oscillators, and patterns. Registration required.
- **StockCharts.com** (www.stockcharts.com) Introduction to chart patterns, introduction to candlesticks, support and resistance, trendlines, and more.
- *Stocks & Commodities Magazine* (www.traders.com). Lots of articles, current and past. For the more advanced technician. Subscription-based but some articles are free.
- **Traders Library** (www.traderslibrary.com). Hundreds of books on specific technical indicators and theories. See Web site for pricing and availability of books.

Bond Basics

- **InvestingInBonds.com** (www.investinginbonds.com). This educational site of the Bond Market Association will tell you everything you want to know about bonds.

Options Basics

♦ **Chicago Board Options Exchange** (www.cboe.com). For a brief introduction to options, try the free primer at CBOE's Learning Center.

Active Trading Basics

♦ **TradeCourse** (www.tradecourse.com). Narrated and animated online courses and follow-up live virtual workshops allow the student to see the instructors' live trading screens and hear them talk as they discuss live market action, execute live trades, and so forth. Prices vary.

FUNDS

Closed-End Funds

♦ **Closed-End Fund Center** (www.closed-endfunds.com). News, research articles, lists of closed-end funds. Free.
♦ **New York Stock Exchange** (www.nyse.com). Closed-end funds are traded primarily on the NYSE. Free.

Exchange Traded Funds (ETFs)

♦ **American Stock Exchange** (www.amex.com). AMEX has information on broad-based index funds, such as DIAMONDS®, SPDRS™, and QQQ, the Nasdaq 100 tracking stock (also called Qubes), and the FFF, the Fortune 500® index tracking stock, as well as iShares, HOLDRs, streetTRACKs, ETFs, and VIPERs.
♦ **HOLDRs** (www.holdrs.com). HOLDRs are ETFs from Merrill Lynch that track primarily sectors.
♦ **Indexfunds** (www.indexfunds.com) is a hub for indexes, index funds, and ETFs. The site offers news; top 10 lists; a screening engine for indexes, index funds, and ETFs; articles; and a learning center for ETFs called ETFZone. Free.
♦ **iShares** (www.ishares.com). iShares are ETFs from Barclays Global Investors. iShares track indexes of the S&P,

Russell, Dow Jones, MSCI, Nasdaq, Cohen & Steers, and Goldman Sachs.

- **Morningstar.com** (www.morningstar.com) has a robust learning center for ETFs of all kinds.
- **streetTRACKS** (www.streettracks.com) is the Web site of State Street Global Advisors, which distributes ETFs that track indexes of Dow Jones, Fortune, Morgan Stanley, and Wilshire.

Open-End Funds

Open-end global funds can be found at most of the mutual funds families listed in this appendix.

Hedge Funds

- **Hedge Fund QA** (www.hedgefundqa.com) is a "knowledge base" for the hedge fund industry formatted in question-and-answer style, along with numerous articles on hedge funds.
- **Hedge Fund World** (www.hedgefundworld.com). Free information from the legal firm of Sadis & Goldberg on forming and maintaining a hedge fund.

Mutual Fund Families

Web sites of fund families offer not only information on domestic and global funds but are usually replete with excellent free learning materials for mutual fund investing. Here is a partial list.

AIM Funds (www.aimfunds.com)

Alliance Capital (www.alliancecapital.com)

American Century (www.americancentury.com)

Calvert Funds (www.calvertgroup.com/funds.html)

Columbia Funds (www.columbiafunds.com)

Dreyfus Funds (www.dreyfus.com)

Evergreen Funds (www.evergreen-funds.com)

Fidelity Funds (www100.fidelity.com)

INVESCO Funds (www.invesco.com)

Janus Funds (www.janus.com)

John Hancock Funds (www.jhancock.com)

Legg Mason Funds (www.leggmason.com/funds)

Oppenheimer Funds (www.oppenheimerfunds.com)

Prudential Funds (http://home.prudential.com/investments/mutualfunds)

Putnam Funds (www.putnaminvestments.com/individual/index.html)

Schwab Funds (www.schwab.com)

Scudder Funds (www.myscudder.com)

Stein Roe Funds (www.steinroe.com)

Strong Funds (www.estrong.com)

T Rowe Price (www.troweprice.com)

The Vanguard Group (www.personal.vanguard.com)

Mutual Fund Screening

- **Fidelity.com** (www.fidelity.com). The search engine at Fidelity screens both Fidelity and non-Fidelity funds to find those that match specific keywords, such as growth, value, income, and so forth. The results are categorized by fund family, investment objective, market cap, and by the actual fund names. Click on a fund name to see a profile that provides the objective of the fund, performance figures, management bios, Morningstar ratings, and other facts.
- **Charles Schwab & Co.** (www.schwab.com). Schwab's Mutual Fund Screener uses a database of more than 10,000 funds tracked by Morningstar, or you can search just Schwab funds. From pull-down menus or button-selections you may specify the investment objective, the fund size, the level of expense ratio, time span of return, and how many funds you want to see on the report. The report includes a handy risk icon that shows graphically whether the fund is low, medium, or high risk.
- **Morningstar.com** (www.morningstar.com). Morningstar.com's Fund Selector is easy to use, with pull-

down menus and boxes to check. To build a screen, you can customize 19 criteria, including fund type, cost and purchase criteria, Morningstar ratings and risk categories, performance, size of funds, and market cap of stocks. There are four different ways to review the results: Snapshot, performance, portfolio, and "nuts and bolts." You can click on any fund name for an overview of that fund. Or, if you don't want to go through building a screen, Morningstar offers six prebuilt screens, including Long-term Winners, Low-Cost U.S. Stock Funds, Solid Small-Growth Funds, Standout Foreign-Stock Funds, and Little Funds with Big Returns.

ONLINE BROKERS AND DIRECT STOCK PURCHASE

Direct Stock Purchase

- **NetStock Direct** (www.netstockdirect.com). Buy stock direct from the company through NetStock Direct.
- **ShareBuilder** (www.sharebuilder.com). ShareBuilder allows you to create a simple, recurring, dollar-based investment plan for the long run. It offers more than 4000 stocks and index products. There are no account minimums, no investment minimums, and no annual fees. There is a small cost per transaction or a set monthly fee for unlimited transactions. ShareBuilder also offers real-time trades for an average brokerage commission.

Online Brokers

A.B.Watley (www.abwatley.com)

Accutrade (www.accutrade.com)

American Express (www.americanexpress.com / trade)

Ameritrade (www.ameritrade.com)

Brown & Company (www.brownco.com)

Charles Schwab & Co. (www.schwab.com)

Cititrade.com (www.mycititrade.com)

CSFBdirect (www.csfbdirect.com)

Datek (www.datek.com)

E*Trade (www.etrade.com)

Fidelity Investments (personal100.fidelity.com)

J.B. Oxford & Co. (www.jboxford.com)

Merrill Lynch Direct (www.mldirect.ml.com)

Morgan Stanley Dean Witter (www.online.msdw.com)

My Discount Broker (www.mydiscountbroker.com)

Quick & Reilly (www.quick-reilly.com)

Scottrade Securities (www.scottrade.com)

SiebertNet.com (www.siebertnet.com)

TD Waterhouse Securities (www.waterhouse.com)

WellsTrade® (www.wellsfargo.com/per/online_brokerage/wt_overview.jhtml)

Direct Access Brokers

A.B. Watley (www.abwatley.com)

CyberTrader, a Charles Schwab Company (www.cybercorp.com)

EdgeTrade.com (www.edgetrade.com)

GRO Corporation (www.grotrader.com)

MBTrading.com (www.mbtrading.com)

TradeStation Securities (www.tradestation.com)

TrendTrader.com (www.trendtrader.com)

Online Investing Resources
(Alphabetical Listing)

A.B.Watley (www.abwatley.com)
Accutrade (www.accutrade.com)
AIM Funds (www.aimfunds.com)
Alliance Capital (www.alliancecapital.com)
The Alpha Trading System (www.alphafin.com)
American Century (www.americancentury.com)
American Express (www.americanexpress.com/trade)
American Stock Exchange (www.amex.com)
Ameritrade (www.ameritrade.com)
Ask Research (www.askresearch.com)
The Bank of New York Depositary Receipts (www.adrbny.com)
Best Calls (www.bestcalls.com)
Big Charts (www.bigcharts.marketwatch.com)
Bloomberg.com (www.bloomberg.com)
Brown & Company (www.brownco.com)
Calvert Funds (www.calvertgroup.com/funds.html)
CANSLIM.Net (www.canslim.net)
Charles Schwab & Co. (www.schwab.com)
Chicago Board Options Exchange (www.cboe.com)
Citibank (www.citibank.com/corpbank/adr)
Cititrade (www.mycititrade.com)
ClearStation (www.clearstation.com)
Closed-End Fund Center (www.closed-endfunds.com)
Columbia Funds (www.columbiafunds.com)
CSFBdirect (www.csfbdirect.com)
CyberTrader.com (www.cybercorp.com)
Datek (www.datek.com)
DogsoftheDow.com (www.dogsofthedow.com)
Dreyfus Funds (www.dreyfus.com)
E*Trade (www.etrade.com)

EarningsWhispers.com (www.earningswhispers.com)

Edgar Online (www.edgar-online.com)

EdgeTrade.com (www.edgetrade.com)

Evergreen Funds (www.evergreen-funds.com)

Fidelity Funds (www100.fidelity.com)

Fidelity Investments (personal100.fidelity.com)

GRO Corporation (www.grotrader.com)

Hedge Fund QA (www.hedgefundqa.com)

Hedge Fund World (www.hedgefundworld.com)

HOLDRs (www.holdrs.com)

IBD Learning Center (www.investors.com)

Indexfunds (www.indexfunds.com)

INVESCO Funds (www.invesco.com)

InvestingInBonds.com (www.investinginbonds.com)

INVESTools (www.investools.com)

iShares (www.ishares.com)

J.B. Oxford & Co. (www.jboxford.com)

J.P. Morgan (www.adr.com)

Janus Funds (www.janus.com)

John Hancock Funds (www.jhancock.com)

Legg Mason Funds (www.leggmason.com/funds)

MBTrading.com (www.mbtrading.com)

Merrill Lynch Direct (www.mldirect.ml.com)

MESA 2000 System (www.mesasoftware.com)

MetaStock Pro (www.metastock.com)

Morgan Stanley Dean Witter (www.online.msdw.com)

Morningstar.com (www.morningstar.com)

MSN/CNBC (http://moneycentral.msn.com/investor)

MultexInvestor (www.multexinvestor.com)

My Discount Broker (www.mydiscountbroker.com)

Nasdaq (www.nasdaq.com)

New York Stock Exchange (www.nyse.com)

Oppenheimer Funds (www.oppenheimerfunds.com)

ProphetFinance.com (www.prophetfinance.com)

Prudential Funds (http://home.prudential.com/investments/
   mutualfunds)

Putnam Funds (www.putnaminvestments.com/individual/ index.html)

Quick & Reilly (www.quick-reilly.com)

Russell Indices (www.russell.com)

S&P Indices (www.standardandpoors.com)

Sabrient Systems (www.sabrient.com)

Schwab Funds (www.schwab.com)

Scottrade Securities (www.scottrade.com)

Scudder Funds (www.myscudder.com)

Securities & Exchange Commission (SEC) (www.sec.gov)

ShareBuilder (www.sharebuilder.com)

SiebertNet.com (www.siebertnet.com)

SmartMoney Market Map (www.smartmoney.com)

SmartMoney University (www.university.smartmoney.com)

Stein Roe Funds (www.steinroe.com)

StockCharts.com (www.stockcharts.com)

Stocks & Commodities Magazine (www.traders.com)

streetTRACKS (www.streettracks.com)

Strong Funds (www.estrong.com)

T Rowe Price (www.troweprice.com)

TD Waterhouse Securities (www.waterhouse.com)

ThomsonFN.com (www.thomsonfn.com)

TIP@WallStreet (www.telescan.com)

TradeCourse (www.tradecourse.com)

Traders Library (www.traderslibrary.com)

TradeStation Securities (www.tradestation.com)

TrendTrader.com (www.trendtrader.com)

The Vanguard Group (www.personal.vanguard.com)

Wall Street City (www.wallstreetcity.com)

Wall Street Research Net (www.wsrn.com)

WellsTrade (www.wellsfargo.com/per/online_brokerage/ wt_overview.jhtml)

WhisperNumber.com (www.whispernumber.com)

Wilshire 500 Index (www.wilshire.com)

Zacks.com (www.zacks.com)

GLOSSARY

10K The annual report that public companies are required to file with the Securities and Exchange Commission (SEC). It contains an overview of operations and an audited financial statement (including balance sheet, income statement, and cash flow information) and is distributed to shareholders and filed within 90 days after the end of the company's fiscal year.

10Q A quarterly report filed by public companies with the SEC within 45 days after the close of the first, second, and third quarters of the company's fiscal year. It contains unaudited financial statements.

Absolute filter A type of screening mechanism used by search engines to eliminate all possibilities except those within minimum and maximum ranges.

Accumulation/distribution indicator A momentum indicator that measures the changes in price and volume by comparing volume on up days against the volume on down days, the premise being that volume precedes price. Similar to the Chaiken money flow indicator.

ADR (American Depository Receipt) A receipt issued by a U.S. bank that represents ownership in a non-U.S. publicly traded company. It verifies that shares of the non-U.S. company are held in trust in a bank in the country of the foreign company. ADRs are traded on a U.S. stock exchange.

Analyst An individual employed by a brokerage house or institutional investor to research a specific company and industry and write research reports on the condition and growth potential of both.

At-the-money An option whose strike price is equal to the market price of the underlying security.

Basing pattern A technical pattern that occurs when a stock trades within a relatively narrow price range for an extended period.

Basing period breakout A technical term used to describe the sharp move that occurs when a stock that has been in a basing pattern moves significantly higher or lower.

Bear market An extended period during which stock prices tend to fall across the market and popular market indexes are below their 200-day moving average.

Bollinger Bands A technical indicator created by John Bollinger in which a "trading envelope" is plotted at standard deviation levels above and below a (usually 20-day) moving average. This allows the bands to self-adjust to the volatility of the market, widening during periods of volatility and contracting during periods of calm. A stock is considered overbought when it touches the top band and oversold when it touches the bottom band.

Bull market   An extended period during which stock prices tend to rise across the board and popular market indexes are above their 200-day moving average.

Bulletin board stocks   Stocks formerly traded "over the counter" whose prices are quoted now by Nasdaq's OTC Bulletin Board (www.otcbb.com). Also called penny stocks.

Buy signal   A technical term that purportedly indicates the beginning of an uptrend on a stock chart.

Call   An option contract that gives the holder the right to buy the underlying security at a specified price for a certain fixed period of time.

CANSLIM   An investing style that combines growth and momentum characteristics, popularized by William J. O'Neil, publisher of *Investor's Business Daily*. Each letter stands for a different characteristic of a winning stock, based on this strategy. See Chapter 9 for details.

CD (Certificate of Deposit)   A time deposit at a bank or savings institution with a fixed rate of interest and a maturity date; CDs generally incur a penalty if withdrawn before the maturity date.

Chaiken money flow indicator   A technical indicator created by Mark Chaiken to measure the flow of money into and out of a security. Similar to the accumulation/distribution indicator.

Chartist   One who uses/studies stock charts and technical indicators; also called a *technician*.

Contrarian   An investor who goes against the prevailing mood of the market, selling in an extended bull market, and buying in a prolonged bear market.

Cup and handle   A technical pattern formed by a downward correction, a short basing pattern, and a recovery. It loosely resembles the shape of a coffee cup.

Defensive stocks   Stocks that traditionally perform well in an economic downturn, such as food and energy stocks.

DIAMONDS   One of the original exchange-traded funds (ETFs), which is based on the Dow Jones Industrial Average.

Direct access broker   A brokerage firm that provides direct access to the market via electronic communication networks (ECNs).

Dividend yield   The rate of return, stated as a percentage, paid on a stock in the form of dividends. Also called *stock yield* or simply *yield*.

Dogs of the Dow   A Dow investing strategy that is based on buying, at the beginning of the year, the ten stocks of the Dow 30 with the highest dividend yield (the High Yield 10) and holding them for 1 year. At the end of the year, stocks that are not on the new year's High Yield 10 are sold and replaced with the new stocks on the High Yield 10 list.

Dollar-cost averaging A method of investing a fixed sum at regular intervals, which presumably allows one to minimize market risk by acquiring more shares at lower prices and fewer shares at higher prices.

Double bottom A technical pattern that occurs when a stock price drops to the same or similar price level twice within a few weeks or months. The pattern resembles a "W" on a stock chart and is considered a bullish indicator.

DRIP (Dividend Reinvestment Plan) A plan that automatically buys shares of a company's stocks with a shareholder's dividends from that stock.

DSP (Direct Stock Purchase) A plan that allows an investor to buy shares directly from the company.

Earnings estimates Estimates made by industry analysts of a company's future quarterly and annual earnings per share.

Earnings rank An indicator used by *Investor's Business Daily* that ranks companies with respect to the degree of their earnings momentum.

Earnings surprise A situation in which a company exceeds the quarterly or annual earnings estimates projected by industry analysts.

ECN (electronic communications network) A computerized trading system that is sanctioned by Nasdaq and integrated into the Nasdaq quote system.

EPS (earnings per share) A company's quarterly or annual profits divided by the number of outstanding shares.

Equity investing Investing in stocks.

ETF (exchange-traded fund) A fixed basket of stocks linked to a specific stock index or category of companies. In essence, an ETF is a representation of the related index or the specific group of companies and trades on a stock exchange like a stock.

Extended market A description of the stock market at an extreme high.

FDA (Federal Drug Administration) The government agency responsible for approving the public distribution of drug-related products.

Federal Reserve Board The Board of Governors of the Federal Reserve System, currently headed by Alan Greenspan; commonly referred to as "the Fed."

Five-bagger A stock that has a fivefold increase in price.

Fixed income investments Investments such as bonds or CDs that offer a fixed rate of interest and can be redeemed at maturity for the amount for which they were originally issued.

Float The number of outstanding shares of a publicly owned company.

Fundamentals Aspects of a company that are evaluated to determine the company's basic health, such as balance sheet, income statement, products or services, markets, and management.

Fuzzy logic A type of screening mechanism used by search engines to "score" each possible "answer" and return a list of "answers" with the highest or lowest scores. Fuzzy logic does not require precise input or output. Also called *relevance searches*.

GARP (growth at a reasonable price)   A popular formula for judging the reasonableness of a stock's price-to-earnings ratio. For example, many GARP enthusiasts would resist paying more than 1.5 times growth in a low interest rate environment and not more than 1 times growth in a higher interest rate environment.

Global investing   Buying securities of a company that is domiciled outside one's own country.

Growth ratio   The growth rate of a stock's earnings per share (EPS) divided by its P/E ratio.

Hard stop   An order to your broker to sell a stock if it drops to a specific price level.

Hedging   An investing strategy that seeks to reduce the risk of a stock or portfolio.

HOLDRS   Exchange-traded funds (ETFs) sponsored by Merrill Lynch.

Index options   Options on indexes such as the OEX (the S&P 100) or the SPX (S&P 500).

Industry group   A grouping of stocks in similar businesses, such as computer software; a group of related industries make up a sector.

Industry group rotation   The movement of industry groups into and out of favor with investors based on economic or other reasons.

Institutional investors   Large organizations such as pension funds, mutual funds, hedge funds, and insurance companies that invest large amounts of money (often billions of dollars) in stocks and other securities.

In-the-money   An option whose strike price is greater than (if a put option) or less than (if a call option) the market price of the underlying security.

iShare   Exchange-traded funds (ETFs) sponsored by Barclay's Bank.

Large-cap stock   A stock whose market capitalization is among the very largest publicly held companies. In some classifications, large caps are those stocks with market caps over $15 billion; in the Frank Russell Co. classifications, large caps are $8 billion and over.

Liquidity   A measure of the ability to buy and sell with relative ease. In stocks, liquidity is measured by the volume of daily transactions in a stock. Frequently traded stocks with high daily volume would be considered highly liquid.

Long   The condition of owning a security; if you are long IBM, you own shares of IBM.

Loose stop   A reminder to yourself to reevaluate the merits of a stock if it drops to a specific price level; also called a *mental stop*.

MACD breakout   The moving of the MACD indicator from negative to positive territory (a positive breakout) or from positive to negative territory (a negative breakout).

MACD indicator   MACD stands for moving average convergence/divergence, a technical indicator, popularized by Gerald Appel, composed of three moving averages: a short average, a long average, and an average of the difference between the long and short averages. The convergence and divergence of the moving averages generate buy and sell signals.

Margin   (1) A company's profit margin; (2) The percentage of the market value of a stock that a broker will loan a customer on the stock.

Market cap rotation   The movement of different market caps (usually large caps, mid caps, and small caps) into and out of favor with the market.

Market capitalization   The number of outstanding shares of a company multiplied by the current stock price. Referred to as *market cap*, it is a way of measuring the market value of a company.

Market-neutral strategy   An investing strategy that seeks to protect the downside by shorting stocks (or buying puts on stocks or indexes) that would be expected to do poorly if the market turned down. The objective is to be neutral to the ups and downs of the market.

Mechanical trading system   A system that provides automatic buy and sell signals based on groups of specific technical indicators.

Micro-cap stock   A company that is among the smallest publicly held companies. Micro-cap stocks are those with market caps less than $150 million, according to some classifications.

Mid-cap stock   A company somewhat smaller than the largest publicly held companies but larger than small-cap companies. In some classifications, the mid-cap range is $1.5 to $15 billion; in the Frank Russell Co. classifications, the mid-cap range is $3 to $8 billion.

Morningstar rating   A one-to-five-star rating given by Morningstar, Inc., an investment research firm, to reflect a mutual funds' historical risk-adjusted performance.

Moving average   The average price of a security over a specified period of time, usually plotted on a price chart. A moving average is calculated by adding the security's daily closing prices over the period and dividing that sum by the number of days in the period. To make the average "move," the oldest variable in the average is deleted as you move forward in time.

Moving average crossover   (1) A stock price moving above or below its moving average; (2) A fast moving average crossing above or below a slower moving average, as in a 50-day moving average crossing over a 200-day moving average.

Nasdaq Composite Index (NASD)   An index consisting of more than 4000 Nasdaq stocks, which tracks the performance of the Nasdaq stock market.

NAV (net asset value)   The market price of one share of an open-end mutual fund. NAV is computed daily by subtracting liabilities from the value of the fund's investments, and dividing that number by the number of outstanding shares.

Option   A contract that gives the holder the right to buy or sell shares of the underlying security at a specified price within a specified time frame.

Option hedging   An investing strategy that uses options (puts and calls) in an attempt to protect the investor's downside.

Option premium   The price of the option contract.

Order flow   The buy and sell orders that brokerage firms send to market makers for execution; brokers often sell their order flow to specific market makers.

OTCBB (OTC Bulletin Board)   The electronic quotation system, owned by Nasdaq, which provides bid and asked prices of stocks that do not meet the requirements to be listed on the Nasdaq system.

Out-of-the-money   An option whose strike price is greater than (if a call option) or less than (if a put option) the market price of the underlying security.

Outstanding shares   The number of shares of stock issued and traded on the open market by a public company (as opposed to treasury stock that has not yet been issued).

Overvalued stock   A stock whose price is considered more than is justified by the company's economic worth. Some would suggest that if the P/E ratio is much greater than the expected future growth rate of earnings per share (EPS), the stock is overvalued.

Paired trading   An investing strategy that seeks to buy one stock that is expected to increase in price and shorting another stock that is expected to decrease in price, especially if the stocks are related in some economic way.

Penny stocks   Stocks traded "over-the-counter" and quoted on the OTC Bulletin Board and on pink sheets.

Pink sheets   A quotation system for penny stocks not quoted by the OTC Bulletin Board, so-called because the quotes were originally published on pink sheets of paper.

Price rank   A technical indicator used by *Investor's Business Daily* that ranks all stocks on the amount of price movement over fairly short periods. The ranking is from 99 to 1.

Price-to-book-value ratio A company's current stock price divided by its book value (total assets minus total liabilities); a comparison of the stock's market value to its book value.

Price-to-earnings ratio (P/E) Stock price divided by earnings per share. P/E can be viewed as a measure of how much the public is willing to pay for a company's earnings.

Projected earnings Projections of future earnings per share (on a quarterly and annual basis) by industry analysts

Protective stop A stop that is moved in the direction of the trend to protect profits; a trailing stop.

Put An option contract that gives the holder the right to sell the underlying security at a specified price for a certain fixed period of time.

QQQ An exchange-traded fund (ETF) based on the Nasdaq 100. Also called a *tracking stock* for the Nasdaq 100.

Quarter-over-quarter earnings The current quarter's earnings per share (EPS) compared with the same quarter of the previous year.

REIT (Real Estate Investment Trust) An entity that invests in real estate or loans secured by real estate and issues shares in such investments.

Relative P/E A stock's price-to-earnings ratio as compared with its own history.

Relative strength Movement of a stock price over a given period compared with a market index or another stock over the same period.

Research report A report on the condition and future prospects of a company and its industry, written by an analyst who follows the stock and industry closely and published usually by a independent third party (such as a brokerage house or institutional investor). Research reports usually contain future earnings estimates for the subject company.

Resistance level A price level at which a stock normally stops rising and either moves sideways or reverses direction. The more times a stock reaches a resistance level and backs off, the stronger the barrier to upward movement. Strong momentum is required to penetrate a strong resistance level.

Retracement A pattern on a stock chart made when a stock falls (or rises) in price and then recovers (retraces) most or all of its loss (or gain).

S&P 100 index The largest 100 stocks in the S&P 500 index.

S&P 500 index A market index composed of 500 major U.S. public companies, weighted for market capitalization. This index is frequently used to measure the performance of the entire U.S. domestic stock market.

Search engine (1) A *stock search engine* is a mechanism or program that uses stock filters or screens to sort through a universe of stocks and return a list of stocks that matches the criteria used in the filter or screen; (2) An *Internet search engine* is a mechanism for searching the entire Internet for Web sites or Web pages that have the greatest relevance to the keyword or keywords used.

SEC (Securities & Exchange Commission)   The U.S. agency that regulates the securities industry.

Sector   A broad segment of the economy comprised of related industries, such as health care, energy, or technology.

Sell signal   A technical term that purportedly indicates the beginning of a downtrend on a stock chart.

Shares outstanding   The number of shares of stock issued and traded on the open market by a public company (as opposed to treasury stock that has not yet been issued).

Short interest   Shares of a stock that have been sold short and not yet repurchased. Short interest is usually reported as the number of days it would take to cover the short position, assuming a continuation of the average volume of the past 30 days.

Short-selling   Selling shares of a borrowed security that you expect to decline in price with the intention of buying the shares at a lower price to replace those you borrowed. (The shares are borrowed from a broker.)

Slippage   The difference between the price of stock at the time you place a trade and the (often inferior) price at which it is executed.

Small-cap stock   Generally, a company that is among the smallest publicly held companies (other than micro caps). In some classifications, the small-cap range is $150 million to $1.5 billion; in the Frank Russell Co. classification, small caps are stocks with market caps of less than $3 billion.

SOES (Small Order Execution System)   An electronic order delivery system instituted by the SEC on behalf of individual investors that requires mandatory execution by Nasdaq market makers at the inside (best) quote.

SPDRS (pronounced "spider")   One of the original exchange-traded funds (ETFs), based on the S&P 500, which trades on the American Stock Exchange under the symbol (SPY). Stands for Standard & Poor's Depository Receipt.

Spread   The difference between the bid price and the asked price of a stock.

Stochastics index   A technical indicator that measures overbought and oversold conditions in a stock over a certain period.

Stock filter   One or more factors that create a specific definition of a stock to match an investor's special goals. A stock filter—or stock screen—is used by stock search engines to cull such stocks from a larger universe of stocks. A stock filter or screen might specify absolute ranges (such as a P/E between 5 and 30) or highest or lowest values (such as lowest P/Es or highest EPS), or it might specify both.

Stop   An order to your broker to sell a stock if it drops to a specific price (a hard stop) or a reminder to yourself to reevaluate the merits of a stock if it drops to a specific price (a "loose" or mental stop).

streetTRACKS   Exchange-traded funds sponsored by State Street Global Advisors based on indexes of Dow Jones, Wilshire, Morgan Stanley, and *Fortune* magazine.

Strike price   The price per share for which the underlying security may be purchased (if a call option) or sold (if a put option) by the option holder.

Support level   A price level at which a stock normally stops falling and either moves sideways or reverses direction. The more times a stock reaches a support level and backs off, the stronger the protection against continued downward movement. A penetration of a strong support level is very significant and usually indicative of a further price drop.

Technical analysis   A study of past trading patterns of a security in an attempt to predict future movements in that security.

Technical breakout   A signal of a trend reversal as given by a technical indicator.

Technical indicator   A computerized tool for determining trend reversals and other stock chart patterns.

Technical timing system   A system for timing the entry point for buying a stock and the exit point for selling a stock.

Technician   One who uses technical analysis as an investing style; also called a *chartist*.

Teenies   One-sixteenth of a point or $0.0625; used to describe the smallest unit of measure on a stock trade, prior to the current decimal system.

Ten-bagger   A stock that has a tenfold increase in price.

Top-down investing   An investing strategy that first considers the performance of an overall economy, then the exchange, then the sector, then the industry group, before the final selection of a stock.

Trading cycle   The continual undervaluation and overvaluation of a stock that occurs as a result of the normal ebb and flow of business cycles or investing cycles.

Trading range   The movement of a stock price above and below its moving average or a price trendline drawn to a specific formula. When extended beyond the current date, a trading range can provide a probable upper and lower range of future prices.

Trailing stop   A stop that is moved in the direction of the trend to protect profits; a protective stop.

Trend   The movement of a stock price (discernible on a stock graph) in a more or less continuous upward or downward fashion over an extended period of time.

Trend break   The sudden movement of a stock price above or below an existing trendline. In other words, the movement violates the recent trend either up or down from the expected move.

Trend reversal   A change of direction in a trend.

Undervalued stock   A stock whose price is considered less than is justified by the company's economic worth. Some would suggest that if the P/E ratio is much less than the expected future growth rate of earnings per share (EPS), the stock is undervalued.

Value trading   A term coined by the authors to describe the buying and selling of a stock which has value characteristics based on its trading cycles, rather than buying and holding the stock as in traditional value investing.

Volatility   A measure of a stock's price fluctuations. High volatility means large and frequent swings in stock price.

Volume   The number of shares traded in a security or an entire market during a given period, usually 1 day.

WEBS (World Equity Benchmark Shares)   Exchange-traded global funds sponsored by Morgan Stanley and Barclay's.

Whipsaws   Misleading signals given by a technical indicator when a stock moves rapidly between the buy and sell signals of that indicator; also called *chatter*.

Whisper number   An earnings number circulated in the investment community that is higher or lower than the published earnings estimates made by analysts. Whisper numbers are usually regarded as the earnings figure the company must meet or exceed in order to retain the market's favor.

Wilder relative strength index (RSI)   A momentum oscillator developed by J. Welles Wilder, Jr., that tracks price momentum by comparing a stock's highest highs and lowest lows over a period of time. Unlike other relative strength indicators, the Wilder RSI compares a stock's price performance to itself.

Yield   The rate of return, stated as a percentage, paid on a stock in the form of dividends. Also called *dividend yield* or stock yield.

INDEX

David Brown is the retired chairman and CEO of leading IT provider Telescan and a successful author on investing.

Kassandra Bentley is a writer specializing in technology and finance, and developer of the award-winning website CyberInvest.com.

www.ingramcontent.com/pod-product-compliance
Lightning Source LLC
Chambersburg PA
CBHW060331100426
42812CB00003B/951

* 9 7 8 0 0 7 1 8 3 1 6 3 5 *